Understanding Healthcare Economics

Managing Your Career in an Evolving Healthcare System

Understanding Healthcare Economics

Managing Your Career in an Evolving Healthcare System

Jeanne Wendel, PhD
William O'Donohue, PhD
Teresa D. Serratt, PhD, RN

Foreword by Mary A. Paterson, PhD, MSN

CRC Press
Taylor & Francis Group
Boca Raton   London   New York

CRC Press is an imprint of the
Taylor & Francis Group, an **informa** business

A PRODUCTIVITY PRESS BOOK

CRC Press
Taylor & Francis Group
6000 Broken Sound Parkway NW, Suite 300
Boca Raton, FL 33487-2742

Printed on acid-free paper
Version Date: 20130916

International Standard Book Number-13: 978-1-4822-0397-4 (Hardback)

Visit the Taylor & Francis Web site at
http://www.taylorandfrancis.com

and the CRC Press Web site at
http://www.crcpress.com

We'd like to dedicate this book to our families, Tom, Nathan, Jane, Katie, Anna, and Jim, for their support and encouragement.

Contents

Foreword

It is a privilege to introduce this important book to healthcare professionals. All of us in the provider community have been confounded by the complex problems we face in our healthcare system. Many of these problems arrive in our offices as we watch our patients present their insurance card. As providers we are the end of a long line of policy makers, payers, healthcare administrators, corporations, and interest groups. At the end of this line we stand along with our patients, the last stop on the journey through the health insurance, healthcare regulatory, and healthcare delivery maze. Despite whatever policies we confront such as necessary preauthorization, required second opinions, preferred provider lists, and authorized lengths of stay we are ethically and morally responsible to use our knowledge and skill to help and heal. It is the rare provider, facing a patient in need, who has not at times been so frustrated by the system that he or she wanted to do something to change it or just do something else. The question is what should be done? How can we be effective agents for change? What change should we be looking for? Although this book does not pretend to provide the final answers for any of these questions, it gives the committed reader much deeper insights into the economics of the system and the factors that need to be understood before the system can be improved.

The first section of the book presents economic evidence to support a more nuanced understanding of the three components of the system: access, cost and quality. Aaron Carroll (2012) referred to these three components as the iron triangle. According to Carroll the trade-offs among the three components of the iron triangle are an inescapable fact of health system change. For example, you can increase access to services for some or all of the population, but when you do this you will almost always increase cost. This is particularly true if you also define a minimum level of quality for the newly accessible services. If you want to control cost, you will likely constrain either access or quality. Most architects of health system change suggest that you can improve two, but not all three of these components with any given policy. This book provides a basic introduction to all three components and some insights into the nature of the trade-offs between them. It also provides excellent insights into why trade-offs are an essential part of any discussion about the healthcare system. This is critical knowledge for providers seeking to influence health system change.

"Wait a minute" I hear some of you saying. "Who said I wanted to try to influence health system change? As a provider let me tend to the job at hand—giving the best care possible to my patients. Let someone else worry about changing the system." Before you get too comfortable with that thought perhaps we should consider how that has worked out for us so far since the evidence suggests that we haven't been involved. The research on public involvement in healthcare policy is limited, but a recent Rand study (2010) reviews the available literature on this topic and concludes that not only is evidence scarce, but that the range and scope of involvement with policy are not well understood, measured, or defined. In fact, according to the study conclusions, there is a considerable lack of clarity about who the public is and what involvement of the public is intended to achieve. This lack of evidence suggests that healthcare providers, like other members of the public, have not assumed a commanding role in shaping health policy and have not been at all clear about what, if anything, we would like to happen. There is no doubt that providers and the organizations that represent them such as the American Medical Association, the American Nurses Association, and the American Public Health Association all engage in lobbying efforts and try to get a place at the table when major health policies are discussed, yet the individual professional is frequently silent on these important issues, preferring to let someone else do it. For example, one of the most fundamental indicators of involvement in policy is certainly voting participation. According to the joint voter turn-out study by the Bipartisan Policy Center and the Center for the Study of the American Electorate (2012), participation in the 2012 election was 57.5% of all eligible voters. This is a rate lower than the past two presidential elections. Since many commentators say the 2012 election was largely a referendum focused on the Patient Care Affordability Act, is it safe to assume that healthcare providers, along with many other members of the American electorate, just didn't show up at the polls? Thomas Jefferson once suggested that in a democracy you get the government you deserve. Perhaps we as healthcare providers have got the health system we deserve. In order to change this state of affairs, we need to decide to use the knowledge provided in this book and get involved.

So what should we do? Important options for changing the system are presented in Part II of the book as the authors review some major solution sets including adjusting incentives, managing care, promoting health, and using information more efficiently and effectively. The evidence for implementing these strategic solutions as well as some of the concerns inherent in implementing them is thoughtfully presented to us. Familiarity with these discussions provides not only an insight into the strategy under discussion, but also insight into the questions that need to be asked about any proposed solution. Since there are no magic bullets out there, the conclusions presented at the end of the section are worth much discussion and study. The authors suggest, for example, that if the drive for increased consumer choice and participation in the system has its intended result, we need to worry about what will become of those who lack fundamental skills in health literacy. Further questions occur to me. Will this deepen the already developing social divide between those who have and those who have not in U.S. society? How are providers going to cope with the increasing policy mandate to engage with the community and its health needs if the community lacks sufficient skill to define its needs? What if the needs it defines are unlikely to yield optimal or even beneficial results? How are we going to remedy deficiencies in basic health literacy or education? The basic economic models and analytic approaches provided in this text help frame these questions most clearly so that evidence can be considered and some answers can be found. At the end of the day it is up to us to understand the information this book presents and use it wisely.

If I haven't convinced you that the content of this book is as important to you as the latest clinical information let me introduce you to yet another compelling concept, that of healthcare as social justice. The Nobel laureate Amaryta Sen was asked to deliver the keynote address to the third conference of the International Health Economics Association in 2001. What he said to the economists present at that meeting is in itself a good policy guide for healthcare providers.

> "Any conception of social justice that accepts the need for a fair distribution as well as efficient formation of human capabilities cannot ignore the role of health in human life and the opportunities that persons, respectively, have to achieve good health—free from escapable illness, avoidable afflictions and premature mortality"*

---

* Sen, A. (2002). Why health equity? *Health Economics.* 11: 659–666.

In his address Sen makes the important point that a just society must be one that does not tolerate profound health inequities. What about our society—what do we tolerate? The Commonwealth Fund provides important evidence to us concerning this issue in its 2012 report *Rising to the Challenge, Results from a Scorecard on Local Health System Performance.* This report examines access to care, quality of care, and health outcomes in 306 local health care areas known as hospital regions. The authors of the report found wide variations in all three indicators, often a two to three-fold variation between leading and lagging health systems on these key indicators. There is a familiar saying in real estate: "location, location, location". Apparently where you live is not only important for your real estate values but also for your life. How long we live, how well we live, and how successful we are going to be in life is significantly determined by where we locate ourselves geographically. I suggest you read this report before you dismiss the idea that health disparities are somebody else's problem in someone else's location. Unfortunately the report suggests that we have met the enemy—and it is us. Our cities and towns often present far less than optimal performance on access, quality, and outcomes. Even the best performing systems do not perform consistently well across all three indicators. Regardless of where you live and where you practice there is significant room for improvement. Even the best of us can sometimes be the worst of us and we need knowledge and skills beyond clinical competencies to fix the problem.

As this book suggests, the situation we find ourselves in has been evolving over time into a complex tangle of interrelated components. We might fix one and make another worse. For example, as we improve the electronic medical records systems in our hospitals, we find that the infrastructure for data exchange between hospital and ambulatory care provider is in need of improvement and that patient privacy concerns require costly system safeguards that may impede data exchange and increase overall costs. Sorting out these relationships and understanding these trade-offs requires the skills you will learn as you explore the economic frameworks presented to you and take the new knowledge forward into your professional life. Yogi Berra observed that "The future ain't what it used to be" Moreover the future seems to become the present so much faster these days. Most healthcare providers want a future that gives them the opportunity to deliver care to people who need it without the nagging fear that many are completely excluded and some are lost before any results can be achieved. If we are to realize that future we need more knowledge than we have now. I recommend this book to you as a way to begin.

Mary A. Paterson, PhD, MSN
Ordinary Professor and Director, Assessment and Evaluation
School of Nursing
The Catholic University of America

References

Bipartisan Policy Center and Center for the Study of the American Electorate. (2012). Report on the turnout and registration in the American election, 2012. Washington, D.C., Bipartisan Policy Center.

Carroll, A. (2012). *JAMA* forum: the iron triangle of healthcare: access, cost, and quality. The *JAMA* Forum http://newsatjama.jama.com/category/the-jama-forum/ October 3, 2012.

Commonwealth Fund. Commission on a High Performance Healthcare System. (2012). Rising to the challenge: results from a scorecard on local health system performance. New York, Commonwealth Fund.

Conklin, A., Morris, Z.S., and Nolte, E. (2010). Involving the public in healthcare policy: an update of the research evidence and proposed evaluation framework. Santa Monica, CA, Rand Corporation.

Sen, A. (2002). Why health equity? *Health Economics.* 11:659–666.

Preface

You might be wondering *why* you spend your scarce time and energy reading about an economic analysis of the healthcare crisis and healthcare reform. Former President Clinton placed the political catchphrase "It's the economy, stupid" on his desk to remind him of the importance of this topic. Why would a president think economics is so important? Or more to the point, why might it be worthwhile for you invest time and effort to understand some basic economics? In a nutshell: practicing healthcare professionals are facing and will continue to face unprecedented change—in payment systems, patient and provider roles, the role of information technology in healthcare, and healthcare resource constraints. These changes stem from the Patient Protection and Affordable Care Act (PPACA), private-sector initiatives in the United States, private-sector initiatives in other countries (that are spurring the growth of "medical tourism"), and changes in both information technology and healthcare technology, according to the U.S. Department of Labor, Employee Benefits Security Administration (2011). Understanding the pressures driving this change, and the economic analysis of the changes that are currently underway, can help you navigate the turbulent waters that lie ahead.

Health economics provides an evidence-based framework for organizing and understanding information about the changing healthcare landscape. Media coverage of health policy typically reports isolated pieces of evidence; this book will help you fit those pieces into a more coherent whole. It will also help you assess the strength of the evidence that underlies each component of the puzzle.

What are the top ten reasons for reading about health economics?

1. The healthcare crisis is real. It is posing significant long-term and even moral questions about equity and intergenerational fairness. This book will explain what is meant by the rather ambiguous phrase "healthcare crisis," evaluate some key reforms designed to ameliorate the crisis, and examine other possible improvements. The crisis—and the resultant reforms—will generate uncertainty, change, and even opportunities for the astute healthcare professional. We will provide a macro-level overview of some of these opportunities—to help you assess the issues, identify career options, and navigate the changes. As Rahm Emanuel, President Obama's former chief of staff, said, "It is a shame to waste a crisis."

2. Our discussion of health economics will show there are no simple answers to the problems driving the healthcare crisis. Simply adopting the British model, or the Canadian model, or any other model, will not make the healthcare crisis disappear. These countries are all dealing with similar long-term challenges. As the economist Thomas Sowell points out, there is always scarcity, and there are always trade-offs. Part of the problem is good—people around the world are living longer—but in these added years they need more healthcare. Another part of the crisis that is good—compared to medicine in the 1950s (when it was much cheaper)—is that there are many more effective interventions and informative diagnostic measures, although (the bad news is) someone has to pay for these. Part of the crisis is bad—all too often Americans are leading problematic lifestyles (poor exercise, diet, obesity, smoking, drug abuse) that significantly contribute to healthcare costs. An understanding of healthcare economics will help clarify the magnitudes of these problems, the proposed solutions, and the trade-offs that must be made.

3. Understanding health economics concepts and empirical evidence will allow you to leave behind simplistic models of the healthcare crisis based on notions that there are a few bad actors (insurance executives, politicians, doctors, managed care utilization and review workers, etc.) who are spoiling what would otherwise be a perfectly good healthcare system. The current crisis is not caused simply by pharmaceutical profits, the salaries of insurance executives, or greedy physicians. You generally believe that you are not a bad apple, and if we could crawl inside the skin of other economic actors, we'd find that they are not either. It is an axiom of economics that all people respond to incentives. Sometimes systems have perverse incentives (sometimes also called *moral hazards* by economists), and the key to designing effective

solutions is identifying and changing these perverse incentives rather than vilifying specific economic actors.

4. Healthcare reform will not be a one-shot deal, regardless of the advent of Obamacare. The healthcare system is facing complex and intractable problems. A vast array of economic interests are involved. Current healthcare reforms might have some beneficial effects (as well as unintended negative effects), but will not be a final one-shot panacea. The conversation over healthcare reform will, in all likelihood, be an ongoing component of your professional life. It might be useful for you to understand this, as it will not be going away.

5. This book will examine major trends in our healthcare industry and delivery system, to help healthcare professionals understand the implications for the current debates about policy solutions. For example, we increasingly live in a global economy: new types of competition are impacting many industries, including the healthcare industry (e.g., medical tourism is increasing—entrepreneurs and health insurers are making it easier for Americans to go to places like India for cheaper surgeries at Joint Commission–accredited hospitals). Investing time to explore health economics can give a glimpse of the future and reduce uncertainty; examining the forces that are reshaping the U.S. healthcare industry (and the impact of new types of global competition) can help you analyze how these changes will affect you. Understanding these can allow you to be proactive instead of just reactive. There are and will continue to be opportunities.

6. Economic forces are like gravity: they are omnipresent, and the processes and principles that mold these forces are not suspended simply because we prefer to ignore them. (Economics is a bit like fire—it is real—and wise foresters understand and respect it.) Many healthcare professionals feel more than a bit adrift—economic forces are buffeting them, and they feel confused and frustrated. They might think that their informal analysis of the problem (e.g., get rid of managed care, might solve all their problems). However, ignorance is rarely bliss. Understanding healthcare economics may help you navigate the changes with a stronger feeling of awareness and control.

7. A better understanding of economics may expand your thinking about career options. As policy makers grapple with the cost, quality, and access problems facing our healthcare system, it is clear that behavioral change will be an essential component of meaningful reform. Patients will assume increased responsibility for preventing and managing

chronic conditions, and providers will be asked to think—and work—in new ways. The patient-centered medical home movement is an example of this. These new roles for patients and new responsibilities for providers are creating opportunities for new types of careers in the healthcare industry. Healthcare will be embracing new technologies such as the electronic health record and new practices, team-based practice, that will attempt to increase quality and lower costs. Healthcare professionals will be forced to practice in this new world—and some will see opportunities to create new types of practices delivering new types of services.

8. One important opportunity is health policy. Many healthcare professionals have not engaged in the policy debates that will shape healthcare in the decades to come, leaving key decisions to politicians, lawyers, and business people (who respond to their own unique incentives). Understanding healthcare economics would equip more healthcare professionals to play a stronger role in the reform process.

9. Understanding health economics will also help you address practical issues that affect you personally. Economic analysis can help you understand what is happening to your paycheck. The demand for your services and the supply of competitors and alternatives will largely determine your wages: buggy makers made a good living years ago, but it would be tough to earn a living as a buggy maker now, because consumers prefer to travel by car. We are seeing rapid change in our healthcare industry. Some healthcare products and services may go the way of buggies, while others will see increased demand. Economics helps us think strategically by increasing our understanding of economic forces and the trends these produce: for example, do you want to increase the demand (or access to) your services? Most businesses have only two options for increasing customer purchases: either cut price or make the product more attractive to customers. How can you increase the value proposition for your consumers, while maintaining the financial viability of your practice? Exploring your options will require careful consideration of a series of questions:

   ■ Will a new lower price or new strategy for offering your service attract more patients, contracts, or referrals?
   ■ Will your productivity increase, so you can see larger numbers of patients?
   ■ Will a new strategy help you develop synergistic partnerships with other healthcare professionals—to deliver better care for patients?

10. Finally, economists provide a conceptual framework and empirical evidence to help you explore interesting and important big-picture questions:
    - Why has the price for an hour of psychotherapy been decreasing in recent decades?
    - Why did managed care come into existence in the first place?
    - Why is the healthcare field moving away from fee-for-service?

U.S. healthcare policy—and the U.S. healthcare system—is undergoing significant changes; as this evolution continues, we will face a stream of new questions. Familiarity with the evidence-based analysis provided by health economists will help you assess these issues, as they arise.

As you explore the economics conceptual framework and evidence presented in this book, you will probably encounter new and surprising information about the forces that are shaping our health policy debates and our healthcare industry. These ideas can help you organize—and focus—your thinking. The economists' models and empirical evidence will equip you to think about evidence-based health policy in the same way you think about evidence-based practice in healthcare.

Acknowledgments

We thank Ann Wilson, Natalie Bennett, Katie Scully, and Brian Leetch for their skilled copyediting and reference checks.

Introduction

> It is not the strongest of the species that survive, nor the most intelligent, but the one most responsive to change.
>
> **—Charles Darwin**

Health economics will be an increasingly important topic for healthcare professionals in the coming years because substantial changes are expected to radically alter the ways Americans obtain and finance healthcare. The way we pay for, and obtain, healthcare has always been changing: consider the advent of Medicaid and Medicare in 1965, the rise of managed care in the 1980s, the incentives for increased reliance on electronic health records (embedded in the 2009 American Reinvestment and Recover Act), and the sweeping changes specified in the Patient Protection and Affordable Care Act (PPACA). However, the pace and magnitude of change will probably increase in the coming decades. Healthcare is scarce—in the words of economist Thomas Sowell (1993): "there is never enough of anything to satisfy all those who want it." And because it is scarce, it comes at a cost—thus, the key economic questions become: How much healthcare? How much will it cost? Who should pay for it? How will it be delivered? How will we provide, and fund, safety-net services?

What Is Driving These Dramatic Changes?

While the 2010 Patient Protection and Affordable Care Act (PPACA) addressed some important access issues, it did not directly address the looming problems posed by dramatic increases in cost, which are projected to continue in the foreseeable future. The trend lines indicate the cost increases are "unaffordable" in the sense that our society will not have sufficient resources to pay for healthcare (in its current form) as technology continues to advance. However, the 2009 American Recovery and Reinvestment Act allocated almost $50 billion to strengthen health information technology. This funding was designed to support a long-term cost-control effort focused on electronic health records and health information technology. Compared with paper charts, electronic records can:

■ Support more efficient retention and retrieval of health information.
■ Provide new types of decision support tools, such as improved access to evidence-based guidelines.
■ Provide efficient communication among providers, which is needed to avoid redundancies (such as duplicate tests), improve continuity of care, and improve the efficiency of care.

But there are trade-offs. The cost to purchase, implement, and maintain these systems is high, and the systems vary in their user-friendliness, reliability, and ability to support healthcare provider workflows.

In addition, public-sector and private-sector initiatives are working to reduce cost increases by fundamentally altering the systems for delivery of healthcare. These initiatives include

■ Accountable care organizations (ACOs) and patient-centered medical homes (PCMHs)—to decrease ER visits by extending primary care hours and to organize and coordinate care more efficiently by harnessing the potential offered by electronic health records
■ Reexamination of scope of practice and licensure laws, in response to retail clinics, telemedicine, and medical tourism
■ Integrated behavioral and physical healthcare
■ Chronic disease outreach programs—to improve health literacy and treatment compliance and to detect and treat comorbid problems such as depression
■ New payment strategies, such as pay-for-performance and bundled payments

This book is designed to equip the healthcare practitioner to understand evidence-based economic analysis of our healthcare crisis, the health reform strategy, and the forces that are reshaping our nation's healthcare system. We will provide key economic facts, explain the economics concepts that you need to examine the implications of these facts, and summarize the results of empirical studies regarding (1) our healthcare system's access, cost, and quality problems, and (2) six key trends that are reforming our system.

We understand that healthcare change can be confusing and even overwhelming for the practicing clinician—and actually for everyone; the issues are indeed quite complex. Practitioners, consumers, and even policy makers can feel that a tsunami of change is about to engulf them. This book will help you understand the terminology, the facts, and help you acquire a working knowledge of the types of changes that are underway.

We will address both macro-problems (such as the impact of our country's changing demographics) and micro-problems (such as the impact of problematic lifestyle choices on healthcare costs). Whether you applaud or decry specific policies, knowledge of the underlying issues will help you navigate the changing landscape in ways that best serve you and your patients. Otherwise, you will be in a position in which you will see changes but might be unsure about the likely impacts of these changes, and unclear about how to evaluate whether current trends are likely to be temporary or long lasting. Assessing these issues will help you assess practice opportunities (and threats), and identify viable strategies for adapting to the changes that optimize your practice and the care you provide. In addition, understanding economic ideas, and the empirical evidence provided by health economists, will help you assess policy controversies and identify sound policy options.

In every crisis there is opportunity, and there will be interesting opportunities for the astute, proactive healthcare professional. In fact, policy makers and politicians making these changes are depending on the cooperation (and sometimes the abdication) of healthcare professionals: careful thinking is needed to assess realistic options, the welfare of patients, and the financial viability of possible reforms.

This book is divided into two main sections. Section I identifies the pressures for change in our healthcare system. It focuses on issues related to access to care, cost of care, and quality of care. We examine hypotheses that underlie our current political debates, and the empirical evidence that validates or negates the hypotheses—to develop an evidence-based foundation for assessing issues and options. Section II examines six ongoing strategies for increasing the efficiency of our healthcare system—as dramatic improvements in efficiency and productivity are the keys to resolving the problem. For now, we can think of efficiency as getting more "bang for the buck." Efficiency will be examined as it relates to past, present, and proposed innovations. We will look at the federal government's strategies, market-based innovations that are impacting our healthcare industry, and the interaction between government policy innovations and private sector innovations.

We start Section I by identifying the pressures for change generated by the widely publicized failings of the current U.S. health system, and then we delve into the specifics over the next three chapters. Although the material is presented in three distinct categories (access, cost, and quality), these pressures for change are inextricably intertwined. In fact, the web of issues that link the cost, access, and quality problems is a major reason that the healthcare crisis has been so intractable for so long. As we examine these issues throughout this book, it will become apparent that simplistic solutions will not resolve the problems. So, let's begin!

About the Authors

William T. O'Donohue, PhD, earned a doctorate in psychology from the State University of New York at Stony Brook and a master's degree in philosophy from Indiana University. He is a licensed clinical psychologist in Nevada. He is a full professor of clinical psychology at the University of Nevada, Reno, and has directed the Victims of Crime Treatment Center, which provides free treatment to sexual assault victims at the university, for 17 years. Since 1996, he has received over $1,500,000 in federal grant monies from sources including the National Institute of Mental Health and the National Institute of Justice. He has published over 60 books, and more than 200 articles and book chapters.

Teresa Serratt, RN, PhD, is an assistant professor at the Orvis School of Nursing at the University of Nevada, Reno. She earned her doctorate in nursing from the University of California, San Francisco, with a specialty in health policy. She currently teaches courses in healthcare leadership and management, healthcare analysis, and healthcare economics. Her primary research focus is health policy, nursing workforce, and organizational analysis of economic and quality issues of acute care hospitals.

As a registered nurse for over 20 years, she has spent the majority of her career at the bedside providing care to critically ill adult patients. She has also held hospital education and administrative positions. In these various roles, she has experienced firsthand some of the failures of our healthcare system and feels it is imperative that healthcare professionals understand the healthcare reform issues and join the debate.

Jeanne Wendel, PhD, earned a doctorate in economics from Southern Methodist University. She is an economics professor at the University of Nevada, Reno, where she teaches classes in health economics and the economics of government regulation. She completed the first Intermountain

Advanced Training Program in Clinical Practice Improvement, served on a hospital design team, which implemented a hospital-wide quality improvement program, and supported quality improvement teams for 2.5 years. She also served as the initial coordinator for the Nevada health information technology work group.

PRESSURES FOR CHANGE

1

There are no solutions ... there are only tradeoffs.

—Thomas Sowell (1995, p. 142)

What is causing all these pressures to reform the healthcare system? We frequently hear that "the healthcare system is broken." What exactly does this mean? Why has the debate about healthcare reform been so complex, lengthy, and even bitter? What changes will be triggered by the Patient Protection and Affordable Care Act (PPACA)? What problems will remain?

To understand the system-wide changes that are underway, we begin by examining detailed evidence about the problems that must be solved. The specific problems are relatively well known:

- Employers, who pay healthcare premiums for many Americans, complain about large premium increases for something that is already many thousands of dollars, and indicate that they may stop offering some benefits or provide a benefit that is dramatically pared down. Unions respond by going on strike, or even attempting to recall governors who reduce healthcare benefits for public employees.
- Approximately 50 million individuals in the United States do not have health insurance. Yet they still need healthcare: they either access healthcare inefficiently (by, for example, using emergency rooms), declare bankruptcy because they can't pay their bills, or postpone— or forego—care. While society must address the issue of paying for "uncompensated" care, the uninsured individuals face unnecessary

health issues due to the fact that they obtain less healthcare than insured people. PPACA's health insurance mandate and Medicaid expansion are expected to reduce the magnitude of this problem but will not eliminate it.

■ Low-income individuals and residents of rural areas may have difficulty making appointments with health providers, if healthcare resources are not available.

■ Healthcare providers are concerned about the payment rate for their services. Medicare payment rates are scheduled—by law—to be reduced significantly. Provider surveys indicate that this will impact provider willingness to treat Medicare patients.

No one seems happy, not the policy makers, employers, consumers (and remember, we all are consumers sooner or later), or providers. What does all this mean? Fundamentally, it means there are problems with access, cost, and quality. We will explore these three issues in the coming chapters. Chapter 1 will examine access issues, with a particular focus on health insurance. As entry into the U.S. health system is facilitated (or constrained) by the possession (or absence) of health insurance, we look at people who are—and who are not—insured and explore the reasons and implications of these findings. We will use these conclusions to consider the likely impacts of PPACA's health insurance mandate, the Medicaid expansion, and health insurance exchanges (HIXs). We follow the discussion on access with a look at healthcare costs in Chapter 2. It is common knowledge that healthcare costs are rising faster than the rate of inflation, and these cost increases are creating stress on private and public insurance systems (the government pays for over half of all healthcare through Medicaid, Medicare, the Veterans Administration, military treatment facilities, and other programs). Finally, we explore the issues related to healthcare quality in Chapter 3. Media stories highlight the failure of the U.S. healthcare system, and in this chapter we will examine the evidence that our current quality is inadequate, analyses of the underlying issues, and strategies to increase quality of care.

By the time you have finished reading Section I, you will have gained a sense of the complexity of the issues facing our healthcare system. You will see that it is impossible to solve any one of these problems in isolation. Instead, a complex web of interactions links the three problems:

■ Poor access often means poor-quality treatment (the rural health provider is necessarily a generalist, but often the best care is provided by specialists, or episodic treatment at an ER does not generate the coordination needed to ensure a good outcome).
■ Low quality can generate unnecessary costs.
■ High costs often spur efforts to contain cost, which frequently limit access.

Because we focus on evidence-based analysis, each chapter utilizes standard problem-solving procedures: (1) organize background information, (2) diagnose the problem, and then (3) examine solution options.

Chapter 1

Access

Introduction

Concerns about access to health insurance and healthcare fueled support for the Patient Protection and Affordable Care Act (PPACA) provisions that mandate that individuals must obtain health insurance (or pay a fine), and employers must offer health insurance (or pay a fine). In addition, federal funds are available to help states expand Medicaid coverage, modernize Medicaid eligibility and enrollment systems, and create state-level health insurance exchanges. These exchanges will create frameworks within which individuals can purchase individual insurance and qualifying individuals can obtain subsidies. In this chapter, we will examine evidence on pre-PPACA barriers to health insurance access, understand the logic that underlies the PPACA strategy, and assess likely impacts.

The term *access to healthcare* focuses on the ability of individuals, groups, and communities to obtain needed medical services. While problems with accessing healthcare can be attributed to many factors (e.g., availability of providers in a geographic area, and barriers such as language or cultural differences) the access issue is most often associated with having or not having health insurance:

1. Despite the availability of uncompensated care, lack of insurance is associated with lower healthcare utilization.
2. Despite the availability of Medicaid, a substantial proportion of non-elderly people remain uninsured: indeed, most uninsured children who have chronic conditions are eligible for Medicaid, but not enrolled (Davidoff et al., 2005).

3. Insured people still worry that they could become uninsured due to job loss, health crisis, or an economic setback. PPACA will mitigate this problem, but it will not eliminate it. Individuals who purchase health insurance through the exchanges will be expected to pay a portion of the premium out-of-pocket. We can expect ongoing controversy about the definition of the concept of "affordable" expenditures for health insurance, currently defined as any amount up to 9.5% of income.

4. The cost shifting necessary to provide uncompensated care to uninsured individuals poses significant challenges, and these problems are expected to become more acute as providers and policy makers work to make the healthcare system more efficient. Under PPACA, undocumented individuals will not be eligible to purchase subsidized health insurance through a state-run HIX; therefore, we can expect that this reform will reduce—but not eliminate—the need for uncompensated care.

5. Disparities in access to healthcare pose salient issues because some aspects of healthcare are life saving, e.g., appendectomies, and life extending, e.g., insulin for diabetics, while others increase comfort or reduce pain, e.g., analgesics for arthritis. As a progressive society, we also worry about equitable access to housing, computers, and education, but access to these goods does not raise the same level of passion as access to healthcare, because the potential impact of healthcare on our quantity and quality of life is uniquely direct and personal. Some argue that healthcare is so uniquely important that it is a "right" and should be provided to all.

People who are concerned about the impact of healthcare costs on household budgets tend to advocate solving this access problem by shifting these expenditures to employers or government agencies. In fact, this cost shift has been occurring for several decades. During the 30 years from 1975 to 2005, the proportions of healthcare expenditures that were paid were as follows:

■ The share of expenditures covered by households, in the form of out-of-pocket payments decreased dramatically from 31% to 13%.
■ The share covered by public-sector agencies increased slightly from 41% to 45%.
■ The share covered by private insurance grew from 25% to 37%.

Indeed, the case for providing coverage for uninsured adults and children is strong:

■ The health and financial implications of lack of insurance coverage are likely to increase, as the cost of healthcare increases.
■ The public burden of paying for healthcare costs increases, as private coverage declines.
■ The demographic profile of the uninsured raises equity concerns.
■ As advances in genetic testing produce dramatic increases in our ability to diagnosis and predict health conditions, the implications of preexisting conditions clauses will be magnified.

At the same time, individuals and employers have become increasingly concerned about health insurance premiums. The premium for individually purchased coverage for a family of four averaged $13,210 in 2009 (Agency for Healthcare Research and Quality, 2011). In addition, the rate at which the price of this already high-cost item increases has generally been higher than the rate of general inflation. For example, in 2011, premiums increased 9%—three times the rate of general inflation. Nine percent of $13,210 is $1,189—a lot of money! The growth rate slowed in recent years, but this does not ameliorate the problem that health insurance is expensive relative to median household income (which was $52,762 for the years 2007–2011 (U.S. Census, 2013)).

Now that the PPACA has been passed—and is largely upheld by the Supreme Court—two questions are important:

■ To what degree will this legislation reduce the incidence of "uninsurance"?
■ What new issues will arise as PPACA is implemented?

The answer to the first question is discouraging: the Congressional Budget Office (CBO) estimated that 30 million U.S. residents will remain uninsured, even after PPACA is implemented. Answers to the second question also raise serious issues, such as the impact of PPACA enforcement on access to healthcare for children who are U.S. citizens in households in which at least one parent is undocumented. Examining these issues will require examination of the factors that impact health insurance decisions. We begin by asking a preliminary question: Why did Congress adopt this solution strategy, rather than opting for one of the alternate proposals? We will start by examining evidence available prior to the debate.

The press suggested that the debate over the Patient Protection and Affordable Care Act (PPACA) was protracted due to politician behavior and attitudes, but published research indicates that the politicians were facing incredibly complex problems, caused by the fact that health insurance coverage patterns reflect a web of decisions made by a host of actors—employers, individuals, regulators, providers, and insurers. Well-designed solutions must account for these issues: the history of regulation is replete with examples of overly simplistic "solutions" that failed to achieve their objectives because they did not consider underlying issues carefully—i.e., they were not evidence based.

Specifically, we will examine several types of pre-PPACA evidence that were available to lawmakers:

- Estimates of the impacts of alternate pre-PPACA proposals on the incidence of uninsurance
- Public and private insurance trends
- Characteristics of the uninsured
- Analyses of three critical issues that contribute to lack of insurance coverage:
    - Some employers do not offer insurance to their workers.
    - Some employees, who are eligible for employer-sponsored insurance, do not accept this offer.
    - Some individuals are not able to purchase insurance, due to restrictive insurance company practices (such as exclusions for preexisting conditions).

Background: Information Available to Lawmakers during the PPACA Debate

While the political debate that preceded PPACA certainly contained significant political and ideological elements, the debate was conducted in the context of substantive evidence about insurance markets, insurance trends, and factors that impact insurance coverage. The Congressional Budget Office (CBO) prepared a 2008 report to support evidence-based examination of these issues, and to inform Congress about the procedures it would use to estimate the impacts of proposed solutions on the federal budget (Congressional Budget Office, 2008b). It provides a detailed picture of the complexity of the issues and the evidence that was available to assess the issues.

Proposed Strategies for Increasing Access: Impacts on the Incidence of Uninsurance (Pre-PPACA Estimates)

Meara et al. (2007) provide a concise analysis of the impacts of three proposed strategies for offering coverage to the uninsured:

1. *Employer mandate with or without individual mandate.* An employer mandate will provide coverage for 33% of the individuals who are currently uninsured if it is accompanied by a mandate that every individual must obtain insurance. The impact will be smaller without the individual mandate because some employees will not "take up" the employer's offer of employer-sponsored insurance (ESI). The impact is limited by the fact that this policy will only impact workers. In addition, an employer mandate would reduce the probability of being employed by 1.2%, and it would reduce the average wage by 2.3%.

2. *Expand public programs, chiefly Medicaid.* Expanding Medicaid coverage to individuals with incomes of less than 300% of the federal poverty level would have a smaller impact on the incidence of uninsurance: it would provide coverage for 12% of the individuals who are currently uninsured. The impact is limited by the facts that:
   a. Some individuals who are eligible for public coverage do not apply.
   b. The policy would not apply to undocumented workers (illegal aliens).
   c. Coverage would not be offered to people with incomes above the eligibility threshold. In addition, 35% of the new Medicaid enrollees would be individuals who were previously covered by private insurance. (This result—typically described as crowd-out—can occur if some employers respond to the expansion of Medicaid by dropping insurance coverage for their employees.)

3. *Tax credit.* A tax credit for purchasing insurance would have the smallest impact on the incidence of uninsurance: this policy would provide coverage for 3% of the individuals who are currently uninsured. Estimates indicate that only 4% of individuals who are eligible and previously uninsured would be induced to purchase coverage in order to obtain the tax credit. The policy would apply to all taxpayers, including undocumented workers and individuals with above-average incomes. Whether it is wise to use public funds to help undocumented workers obtain health insurance depends on the specific policy goal. If the goal of reducing the incidence of uninsurance is to reduce inequity among U.S. citizens and other legal U.S. residents, then these funds are not well targeted. However, we would reach the opposite conclusion if the goal includes reducing numerous negative side effects of providing uncompensated care to uninsured individuals.

These analysts conclude that none of these approaches alone will accomplish the goal of universal coverage.

The three policies cover overlapping, but slightly different, segments of the uninsured population. No single policy will provide a comprehensive solution.

Public and Private Insurance Trends

On the surface, the access problem appears to be straightforward: 19% of nonelderly U.S. residents do not have health insurance, and the percentage of individuals with private insurance has decreased steadily since 1972. The percentage of people who are uninsured remained fairly constant throughout the 1980s and 1990s only because public insurance programs expanded to cover a growing proportion of U.S. residents (see Figure 1.1). More recently, the proportion of U.S. nonelderly residents covered by employer-sponsored insurance (ESI) declined from 68% in 1999 to 62% in 2006. During this period, the expansion of public coverage primarily focused on children; hence, the proportion of children who are uninsured declined slightly, but the proportion of adults who are uninsured increased.

Finally, we note that most discussions of the uninsured focus on nonelderly U.S. residents, because most (97%) individuals who are at least 65 years of age are covered by Medicare. We follow this precedent, and focus our discussion of insurance coverage on nonelderly U.S. residents.

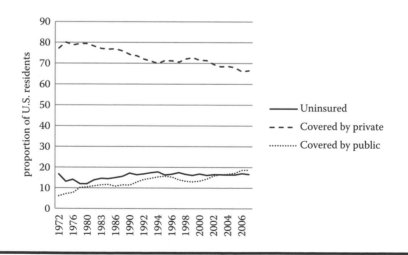

Figure 1.1   Insurance coverage trends. (From U.S. Department of Health and Human Services, National Center for Health Statistics, Centers for Disease Control and Prevention, *Health Insurance Coverage Trends, 1959–2007: Estimates from the National Health Interview Survey,* National Health Statistics Report 17, 2009.)

Who Was Uninsured Prior to PPACA?

Nearly two-thirds of nonelderly U.S. residents were covered by private insurance prior to the passage of the PPACA: over 90% of these individuals obtained insurance through their employers, while 10% purchased insurance as individuals (U.S. Bureau of the Census, Bureau of Labor Statistics, 2005). Of those who were not covered by private insurance, slightly more than half were covered by public insurance, primarily Medicaid, while the others were uninsured. Medicaid, which provides coverage for low-income individuals and individuals with specific healthcare requirements, specifically expanded coverage for children. As a result, the proportion of children who were uninsured (10%) was less than half the proportion of adults who were uninsured (23%) (see Table 1.1).

The relationship between citizenship and lack of health insurance among nonelderly U.S. residents may become an important issue. The pre-PPACA proportion of U.S. citizens without health insurance was 16%, while the proportion of noncitizen residents who lacked health insurance was much higher: 48%. However, most U.S. residents were citizens: 92% of residents were citizens, while only 8% of U.S. residents were noncitizens. Therefore, the problems posed by lack of health insurance fell primarily on citizens: 80% of the uninsured were citizens (Ku and Waidmann, 2003). For more detail, see Table 1.2.

The likelihood of being uninsured was relatively high among adults with low education and low income, noncitizens and individuals who were either self-employed or employed by small companies. The relationship between income and insurance status plays an important role in policy discussions and policy formulation: 35% of residents with income less than

Table 1.1   Pre-PPACA Insurance Status of Demographic Groups of Nonelderly People

		% of U.S. Residents	% of Children	% of Adults
Private insurance	Employment based	57	51	59
	Individual	5	4	6
Public insurance	Medicaid	17	33	10
	Other	3	1	3
Uninsured		19	10	23

Source: U.S. Bureau of the Census, Bureau of Labor Statistics, Current Population Survey Annual Social and Economic Supplement, 2005, retrieved from http://www.census.gov/apsd/techdoc/cps/cpsmar05.pdf.

Table 1.2   Lack of Health Insurance and Citizenship

	All U.S. Nonelderly Residents			Uninsured Nonelderly Residents
	Number in Each Group, millions	Percent in Each Group	Percent Uninsured in Each Group	Percent of Uninsured That Belongs to Each Group
Citizens	244	92%	16%	80%
Noncitizens	80	8%	48%	20%

Source: Adapted from Kaiser Family Foundation, The Uninsured: A Primer— Supplemental Data Tables, 2010, retrieved from http://www.kff.org/ uninsured/upload/7451-06_Data_Tables.pdf.

139% of the federal poverty level were uninsured, compared with 5% of residents with income at least 400% of this level. (The 2012 federal poverty level was $23,050 for a family of four and $11,170 for individuals (Federal Register, 2012).)

Thus, we have the following profile of the uninsured:

■ 17% were children, and another 40% were younger than 35.
■ 52% had incomes less than 139% of the federal poverty level.
■ 80% of the uninsured were citizens, and 90% of uninsured children were citizens.

In addition, the proportion of nonelderly who do not have insurance coverage was substantially higher among minorities than among whites. In 2010, 14% of non-Hispanic whites were uninsured, compared with 22% of blacks and 32% of Hispanics (Holahan and Chen, 2011).

PPACA is expected to reduce, but not eliminate, these disparities.

Insurance Markets: Three Critical Access Issues

Because many people are covered by insurance purchased in the private sector, it is important to understand how these insurance markets work. In this section, we will use some analytical techniques to examine key economics concepts about insurance and insurance markets. Don't worry—we realize that you might not have majored in economics, so we will walk through the economics analyses step by step. Your investment of time and effort will pay off in a deeper understanding of the trade-offs that must be considered to design workable and equitable health insurance policy.

How Do Insurance Markets Work?

Health insurance—and uninsurance—patterns reflect complex interactions between government policies, insurance company strategies, employers' human resource policies, and individual decisions. Remember that under PPACA, most nonelderly people are expected to continue to obtain health insurance through employers—at least initially. (Some employers may elect to stop offering health insurance and pay the fine instead.) The employees of these firms may be eligible for Medicaid; if not, they might purchase health insurance through the state exchanges—possibly at subsidized rates. While PPACA will not affect the large-group and small-group health insurance markets directly, it may exert important indirect effects. Therefore, we need to consider the question: How do these markets work?

Basic Insurance Concepts

Insurance is a mechanism for managing risk. When we purchase insurance, we essentially shift the risk to the insurance company. The insurance company can bear the risk efficiently, because it pools the risk of many participants. To understand how this works—and then explore the implications for health policy—we begin by considering a simple example from the perspective of the individual who faces risk, and from the viewpoint of the insurance company.

Suppose Bill owns a house in an area that is at high risk for earthquakes. Bill is considering purchasing insurance. His options are summarized Table 1.3.

Table 1.3 Bill's Insurance Purchasing Options

	Bill Does Not Purchase Insurance	*Bill Purchases Insurance*
No earthquake	No damage.	No damage. Bill pays monthly premium to purchase insurance.
Earthquake occurs	Bill spends $100,000 to repair structural damage.	Structural damage requires extensive repairs ($100,000). Bill pays monthly premium to purchase insurance, and he also pays the deductible specified in the policy. Much of the cost is covered by the insurance company.

Bill's Perspective

If Bill buys the insurance, and then the year is quiet with no significant earthquakes, Bill will simply pay the monthly insurance premium. In this case, he bought "peace of mind." He could relax and sleep soundly, because he knew that if an earthquake occurred, he would only have to pay the deductible, and the insurance company would cover most of the cost of the structural repairs.

The Insurance Company's Perspective

This company provides insurance coverage to thousands of homeowners—in many areas of the country. Some of the houses will experience earthquakes, and the insurance company will then cover the cost of the structural repairs. Others will not sustain any damage. The insurer will collect premiums from each homeowner, and these pooled funds must be sufficient to pay for:

1. The claims filed by homeowners that sustain earthquake damage
2. The insurance company's administrative expenses
3. A return on the company's invested capital

This means that, on average, each homeowner must pay his or her fair share of the cost of the earthquake damage plus administrative expenses, which include marketing, preventing fraud, and complying with government regulations. An insurance company that does not charge sufficient premiums to cover the cost of paying claims plus administrative expenses will go out of business. This means that insurance will *not* make earthquake repairs more affordable. Instead, it *spreads* the cost of earthquake repairs across a large group of homeowners, and shifts costs from unlucky homeowners who experience earthquakes to lucky homeowners who do not experience earthquakes. But importantly, it *adds* to the cost of paying for earthquake damage, because the insurance company cannot operate on thin air.

Bill's Decision to Purchase Insurance

Bill faces a diverse array of risks: his house could be damaged in an earthquake, his television could be damaged if his house is hit by lightning, his car may need oil changes, his new household appliance may be defective, and his daughter might lose a library book. Each of these events has two important characteristics: the probability that the event will occur, and the cost that Bill will face *if* the event occurs. Some of these bad events have low probability (lightning could hit the house, but this is a rare event), while

Table 1.4   Insurance Purchasing Decisions

Event	Probability	Cost	Decision to Purchase Insurance
Bill's car will need regular oil changes	Very high	Low	No
Household appliance might be defective	Medium	Medium	Maybe—the decision will depend on the price
Earthquake might cause structural damage	Low	Very high	Maybe—the decision will depend on the price

others occur more often (Bill's daughter might lose library books frequently). In addition, some of these bad events are very costly (repairing structural damage after an earthquake), while some are inexpensive (replacing a lost library book). Bill is faced with the question: How should I manage these risks? Should I buy the earthquake insurance? Should I buy the extended warranty next time I purchase a household appliance? Should I search for lost library book insurance? Bill could create a chart to help him sort out these issues, as illustrated in Table 1.4.

When Should Bill Buy Insurance?

Bill will not, or at least *should* not, buy insurance for oil changes for his new car. Think about his logic. Based on the number of miles he typically drives each year, Bill expects that his new car will need four oil changes next year. Each oil change will cost $35, so Bill expects to spend $140. If Bill buys oil change insurance, the premium will have to cover this expected cost *plus* Bill's share of the company's administrative expenses, *plus* some money for the insurance company's return on invested capital, which implies that the premium would be higher than $140. Bill will not buy this insurance, because the oil change expenditure is highly predictable. It doesn't make sense to pay the insurance company to pool the "risk" when there is very little risk because the expenditure can be predicted, with minimal uncertainty.

If Bill buys the extended warranty for his new dishwasher, he will pay a premium that will cover his share of claims for all defective dishwashers *plus* his share of the insurance company's administrative expenses and profit (the term *price* of insurance refers to the portion of Bill's premium that will cover these administrative costs and profit). Bill will only be willing to pay this premium if he values the peace of mind associated with shifting the risk that the dishwasher might be defective. This is unlikely, because Bill's annual income is much larger than the price of a new dishwasher (and he could wash the dishes by hand if he had to live without a dishwasher for awhile). He can afford to manage these relatively small risks on his own.

In contrast, the possibility of earthquake damage involves genuine risk of a substantial financial loss. Buying insurance could make sense if Bill believes that the extra peace of mind is worth the price embedded in the premium. Typically, this means that people buy insurance for events that are:

■ Risky in the sense that the event cannot be predicted with minimal uncertainty

■ Expensive, which implies that peace of mind is an important issue for this event

The Price of Health Insurance

The notion of the *price of health insurance* is a construct that requires careful definition. When insurance companies analyze pricing decisions, they begin by estimating the expected value of the claims that they will need to pay. We explain expected value in Box 1.1. The premium must cover this expected cost of claims plus the cost of the company's overhead plus the profit on the firm's invested capital.

Apply This Information about Insurance to Examine the Market for Health Insurance

Now that we have a basic understanding of insurance, we are ready to examine health insurance. Healthcare expenditures, as a whole, meet the rational criteria for insurance coverage:

■ Medical care expenditures involve substantial risk, in the sense that expenses vary significantly from year to year (even if we know what Bill spent last year, it would be difficult to predict his expenses for next year).

■ Medical care expenses can be very high (tens of thousands of dollars for some chronic diseases or even hundreds of thousands of dollars for serious illnesses or injuries).

However, the Nobel Prize winner, economist, author, and statistician Milton Friedman (2001) cautioned that we should look more closely before we conclude that we should insure all healthcare expenditures. Some expenditures (routine dental cleanings) are highly predictable and relatively low cost, while others have low probability and high financial impact (heart

BOX 1.1 EXPECTED VALUE

Expected value: This is a useful concept for thinking about situations that involve risk. To illustrate the concept, let's think about a lottery. Suppose we have a lottery ticket. If our ticket is a "winning" ticket, we will win $50. If we don't have a winning ticket, we will not receive anything. Suppose the total number of tickets sold was 100, so our chance of winning is 1/100 and our chance of going home empty-handed is 99/100. The expected value of the ticket is equal to $1. Here is the detailed computation:

Amount we might receive	probability	Amount multiplied by probability
0	99/100	0
100	1/100	1
	sum	1

How should we interpret this expected value? We don't expect to receive $1 on any one lottery: instead, we will either receive $100 or zero. However, if we bought individual tickets in 1000 similar lotteries, then we expect that—on average—we would win $1 per lottery.

The concept of expected value allows us to think about average results—if we consider events that may be repeated numerous times. This idea is useful for thinking about insurance premiums because the insurance company does not know how much it will spend to provide care for any one individual. However, the company will insure thousands of individuals, so it can focus on the average expenditure per individual.

surgery). Milton Friedman argued that insurance should cover events in the second category, but it should not cover events in the first category. In fact, catastrophic insurance coverage implements this idea by only providing insurance coverage for high-cost healthcare expenditures.

Health Insurance for Preexisting Conditions: Risk vs. Subsidy

The issue of insurance coverage for preexisting conditions is complex, but becomes clearer if we apply the principles of insurance that we just discussed. Let's begin by considering the issue from Bill's perspective. Suppose he generally pays $10,000 in medical expenses each year due to the fact that he suffers from a costly chronic condition; suppose further that he learns that his neighbor pays $6,000 for a health insurance plan that would cover all of his medical expenses. What will Bill want to do? Of course, Bill will attempt to purchase this insurance coverage, so he can save $4,000. It makes financial sense from his perspective. If the insurance company refuses to sell him that policy, he will complain that they are denying him the opportunity to save $4,000.

But does it make sense from the insurance company's perspective? The insurance company is willing to sell a policy to Bill's neighbor for $6000, because that amount will cover the neighbor's expected healthcare costs plus administrative expenses plus return on investment. However, Bill's expected costs are higher. If the company sells this policy to Bill for $6000, it will lose money on the policy - and it has a fiduciary responsibility to its stockholders and current employees to maintain the fiscal health of the company. The fact that Bill faces higher expected costs than his neighbor does not represent risk, because the diagnosis is known and the extra costs are predictable.

Clearly, the concept of insurance to spread risk of unknown future events doesn't really make sense in this situation. The general notion of fairness— that the general population of insured people should help cover the costs incurred by the unlucky individual who has a preexisting condition— indicates that instead we should be discussing the concept of *subsidy* to provide assistance to low-income or high-cost individuals. This distinction, between the function of insurance to spread risk and the equity argument for some types of subsidies to help people who are dealing with difficult health problems, plays an important role in health policy debates.

Insurance only *appears* to make healthcare more affordable for an insured group if some entity outside the group contributes to purchasing that insurance. This is an important point that helps explain why the access problem has been so intractable, why the PPACA debate was so contentious, and why the debate continues.

We will see below that the health insurance companies and health insurance regulators traditionally segment the health insurance market into three components:

- The large-group market, in which large employers purchase health insurance for large groups of employees,
- The small-group market, in which small employers purchase insurance for groups of 1–50 or 2–50 employees (the definition varies across states)
- The individual market, in which individuals purchase insurance

When we examine this issue in detail, we'll see that the problem described above is much more salient in the individual market than in the large-group market.

Three Critical Issues

Public debate about health insurance focused on three critical issues that impact access:

1. Some employers do not offer insurance.
2. Some individuals do not accept or take up employer-sponsored insurance, and some individuals who are eligible for public insurance do not enroll.
3. Insurance companies use restrictive practices to avoid selling insurance to people with serious health conditions.

The optimal solution strategy hinges on the relative magnitudes of each of these issues. While the solution embedded in PPACA seems straightforward on the surface, e.g., prohibit restrictive practices, mandate that employers provide insurance, and mandate that individuals have insurance, research indicates that these policies must be carefully designed because they may generate unintended consequences. While we recognize that insurance company restrictive practices played a central role in the political debate preceding passage of PPACA, we will begin by examining employer decisions to offer insurance, and individual decisions to accept or decline this offer, because these analyses will provide a strong context for examining the issues posed by restrictive practices.

Issue 1: Some Employers Do Not Offer Health Insurance

In order to examine this issue, we need to understand the economic analysis of employer-sponsored insurance (ESI). These ideas are abstract, but they will:

- help us understand why analysts have shifted from using the term *employer-provided insurance* to *employer-sponsored insurance*,
- provide a foundation for analyzing the proposal to mandate that all employers offer insurance,
- help us predict some of the outcomes of the PPACA employer play-or-pay policy.

Employers Don't Actually Pay for Employer-Sponsored Healthcare

Employer-sponsored insurance *appears* to reduce the workers' cost of healthcare, because it *appears* to shift the cost from the individual to his or her employer. Unfortunately, however, the empirical evidence is clear: workers actually pay for employer-sponsored insurance, and this indirect payment occurs in the form of reduced wages. The 2008 CBO report summarizes the available evidence: "employees, as a group, ultimately bear the costs of any payments an employer makes for health insurance" (CBO, 2008b, p. 5). Therefore, analysts have shifted from using the old term *employer-provided healthcare* to the more accurate term *employer-sponsored healthcare* (ESI). (See, for example, Emanuel and Fuchs, 2009.)

This conclusion that workers bear the financial impact of ESI may seem surprising: we do not typically observe employers cutting wages in order to pay for rising health insurance premiums. Instead, the process is more subtle. Wages may remain flat or are reduced, instead of increasing, even in the context of productivity increases, because the benefits of the productivity increases are used to fund rising health insurance premiums. Or, alternatively, we may see the dollar amount of wages remain flat during periods of inflation, which means that real inflation-adjusted wages have fallen, in response to rising health insurance premiums.[1] This bears repeating: when the costs of so-called employer-provided insurance increase faster than the general rate of inflation, workers' take-home pay is likely to stagnate or decrease.

In unionized industries, the trade-off between wages and health insurance may occur during bargaining sessions. Representatives of the autoworkers' union pointed to this trade-off when they protested cuts in retiree health insurance benefits:

> The retirees can claim ownership to this benefit legitimately; when they were working they had their union accept lower wages in bargaining in return for retiree health care benefits. (The Editors, *The New York Times*, 2009)

When these workers have less take-home pay, they not only experience problems paying for their rent, food, or cars, but in spending less they create less demand in other sectors of the economy. They may also spend less money on activities that contribute to a healthy lifestyle: fresh produce, gym memberships, apartment in a safe neighborhood, and car maintenance that contributes to auto safety.

This Is Complex: How Can We Understand the Forces That Shift the Cost of Employer-Sponsored Health Insurance onto Workers?

Economists use abstract logic to understand the reasons why this process occurs, and we can illustrate that logic with a graph of supply and demand. Be patient—this picture *is* worth 1,000 words. We will use a supply and demand graph to examine the relationships between employers and employees, and between wages and health insurance. It doesn't matter whether you enjoyed your college economics class or whether you had a college economics class: we'll do "gentle economics" and walk through the logic step by step.

In preparation for our examination of employer-sponsored health insurance, we need to consider our basic economic tools: supply and demand. Figure 1.2a and b illustrates a supply curve and a demand curve for a

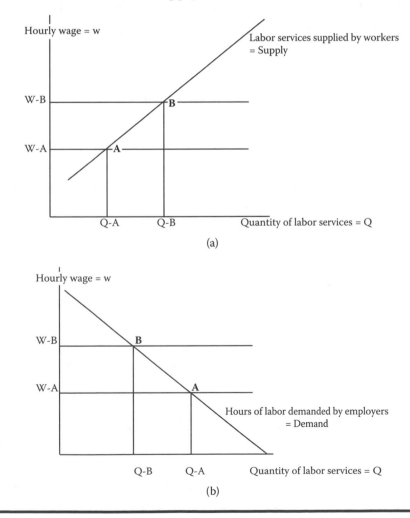

(a)

(b)

Figure 1.2 (a) Supply of labor. (b) Demand for labor.

specific type of labor service, such as unskilled labor, or nursing services, or behavioral health services. Notice that the vertical axes are labeled "hourly wage," and the horizontal axes are labeled "quantity = hours of labor services." The workers supply these services and employers "demand" or purchase these services.

The supply curve describes the workers' willingness to offer these services. Consider point A on the supply curve illustrated in Figure 1.2a. Economists offer two equivalent ways to describe the workers' opinions. Consider, for example, point A.

■ First, when the wage is W-A, workers are willing to offer exactly Q-A hours of labor services. If you want to purchase more labor services, Q-B, for example, you will have to offer a higher wage. If you offer W-B; then workers would be willing to supply Q-B hours of labor services.
■ Alternately, we could describe the same information by reversing our perspective. If you want to employ Q-A hours of labor services, then W-A is the lowest wage at which workers will be willing to contract with you. They would, of course, be delighted to provide Q-A hours of labor services for a higher wage, but you do not need to offer more than W-A.

The demand curve illustrated in Figure 1.2b summarizes the views of employers. When the wage is equal to W-A, then employers will want to purchase Q-A hours of labor services. If the wage increases to W-B, then employers will reduce their purchases of labor to Q-B. At the higher wage, W-B, the employer might find that it is beneficial to invest in labor-saving equipment that was not cost-effective when wages were lower. We can also describe the same information from the reverse perspective. If an employer is considering purchasing Q-A hours of labor services, then W-A is the highest wage the employer will be willing to pay. Of course, the employer would prefer to pay a lower wage; however, the wage W-A is the highest wage the employer is willing to pay.

Equilibrium: Quantity Supplied = Quantity Demanded—Because the supply and demand curves are drawn against the same pair of axes (wage on the vertical axis, quantity on the horizontal axis), we can overlay the two graphs to examine the interaction between workers' views summarized by the supply curve and employers' views summarized by the demand curve. Figure 1.3 illustrates the equilibrium wage, which occurs at the intersection

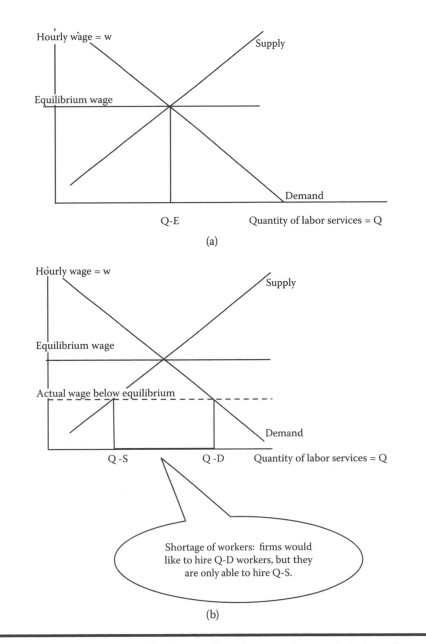

Figure 1.3 **(a) Equilibrium wage and quantity. (b) Actual wage is below the equilibrium wage. (c) Actual wage is above the equilibrium wage. (d) Familiar example: stadium seats.**

of the supply and demand curves. The equilibrium wage is an important concept: at this wage, there is no pressure for wage to change—either upward or downward. Firms want to purchase Q-E hours of labor services, and workers want to supply that quantity. Both groups are able to complete their desired transactions.[2]

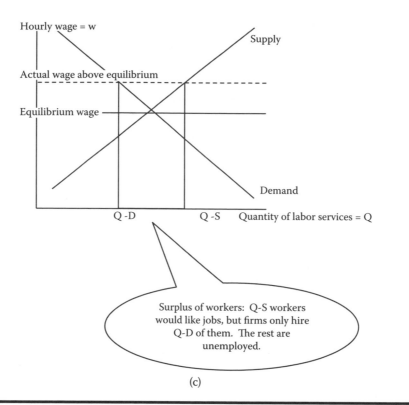

Surplus of workers: Q-S workers would like jobs, but firms only hire Q-D of them. The rest are unemployed.

(c)

Figure 1.3 (continued)   (a) Equilibrium wage and quantity. (b) Actual wage is below the equilibrium wage. (c) Actual wage is above the equilibrium wage. (d) Familiar example: stadium seats.

What Do We Mean When We Talk about the Equilibrium Wage?—When the wage is above or below the equilibrium level, suppliers and demanders begin taking actions that push the wage toward equilibrium, as illustrated in Figure 1.3b and 1.3c. In Figure 1.3b, the dashed wage line representing the actual wage is below the solid equilibrium level. Notice that workers want to supply Q-S hours of labor services at this wage, while firms want to buy Q-D hours. The gap between these two quantities represents a shortage of willing workers: firms are not able to purchase all of the labor that they would like to buy at the current wage W-A. As firms try to fill these unfilled positions, they will begin offering higher wages. As this bidding process pushes wages up, the number of unfilled positions will shrink: workers will offer more of their services as the wage increases, and firms will reduce their demand for services. The upward pressure on wage will continue until the wage reaches the equilibrium level.

In Figure 1.3c, the dashed wage line is above the solid equilibrium level. At this high wage, workers want to supply Q-S hours of labor services, while firms want to buy Q-D hours. The gap between these two quantities represents unemployment: workers who want to work at the going wage face a game of musical chairs, where there are not enough "chairs" for all of the hopeful workers. As the unemployed workers realize that they cannot find jobs at the going wage, they will offer to work for slightly lower wages or fewer benefits. As firms realize that they can hire qualified workers at these lower wages, the going wage will fall. When it reaches the equilibrium wage, all interested workers will have jobs, and there will be no further downward pressure on wages.

Why Is the Equilibrium Concept Useful?—Even though real-world markets are obviously not always in equilibrium, the concept of the equilibrium wage is very useful. By helping us understand the wage pressures that accompany surpluses and shortages, this concept also helps us understand the likely impacts of employer-sponsored health insurance. Let's illustrate the equilibrium concept by looking at a familiar example: the markets for concert and sports tickets. Prices for major events are frequently set below the equilibrium level illustrated in Figure 1.3d. In this case the supply of seats is simply equal to the number of seats in the stadium, so the supply curve is a vertical line. Fans are the buyers in this market, so the demand curve represents their willingness to pay for tickets. If fans anticipate that the price will be set below the equilibrium level, they know that they will face the musical chairs game: the number of interested buyers will exceed the number of seats. The shortage at the official price is labeled on the familiar example found in Figure 1.3d: shortage of concert tickets. The result is predictable: fans line up early in an attempt to buy tickets.[3]

Now you can begin to see that economics focuses on the wisdom of Goldilocks. If the price or wage is too high, adjustments will occur. If the price or wage is too low, adjustments will occur. If the wage is *just right*, the market is in equilibrium—in the sense that buyers do not have any reason to bid the price up and sellers do not have any reason to bid the price down.

How Does Employer-Sponsored Health Insurance Affect the Equilibrium Wage?—Now that we understand the interactions between the workers' willingness to offer labor services and the employers' interest in buying these services, we can use Figure 1.4a and 1.4b to analyze the impact of employer-sponsored health insurance on the equilibrium wage. The decision to provide health insurance will impact both the workers and firms; hence, it will impact both the supply curve and the demand curve.

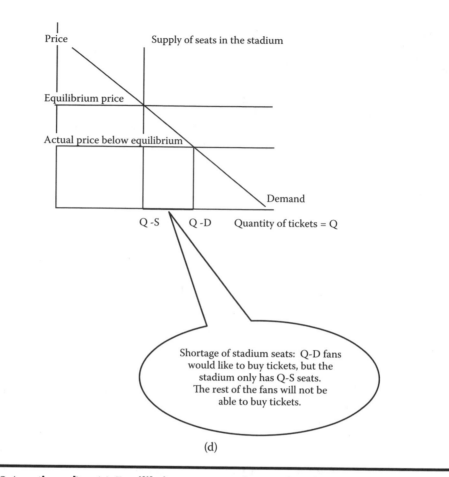

Price

Supply of seats in the stadium

Equilibrium price

Actual price below equilibrium

Demand

Q -S   Q -D   Quantity of tickets = Q

Shortage of stadium seats: Q-D fans
would like to buy tickets, but the
stadium only has Q-S seats.
The rest of the fans will not be
able to buy tickets.

(d)

Figure 1.3 (continued)   (a) Equilibrium wage and quantity. (b) Actual wage is below the equilibrium wage. (c) Actual wage is above the equilibrium wage. (d) Familiar example: stadium seats.

Let's begin by examining the impact of the decision to provide health insurance on the demand curve. The demand curve shows the maximum wage that firms are willing to pay for each quantity of labor services. If firms are currently hiring Q-E labor services, as shown in Figure 1.4a, then W-E is the maximum amount the firms are willing to pay to hire this quantity of labor services. When firms begin providing health insurance, they split this amount, W-E, into two buckets. Some of the payment will be called wage, while the other component will be called health insurance. Firms are indifferent about this split, because the total amount they pay remains unchanged, and it is this total amount that affects their bottom line. This means that the demand curve, which represents the amount the firm is willing to pay as wage, shifts down, as illustrated in Figure 1.4a. The vertical distance between the original demand curve (no insurance) and the new

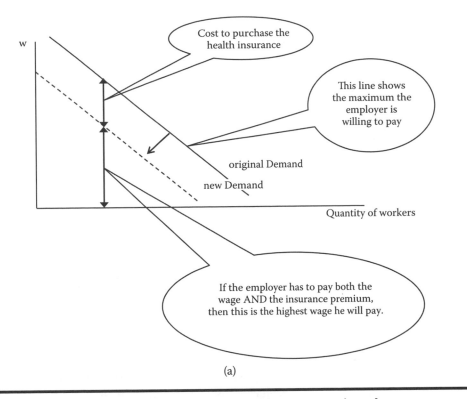

Figure 1.4 **(a) When an employer provides health insurance, it makes two types of payments for labor services: wages and health insurance. (b) When the employer provides health insurance, the worker receives two types of payments: wages and health insurance.**

demand curve (with insurance) is equal to the amount the firm pays for health insurance. A detailed analysis of this issue was conducted by Baicker and Levy (2007) when health insurance premiums averaged $3 per hour; hence, we use that estimate for our discussion (see Box 1.2).

Most workers value health insurance, so the employer's decision to provide health insurance will also impact the supply curve. This supply curve shows the lowest wage at which workers will be willing to supply their labor. If the wage will be augmented with health insurance, then workers will be willing to supply labor services at lower wages, and the supply curve will shift out, as illustrated in Figure 1.4b. The vertical shift in the supply curve reflects the wage cut workers are willing to accept in order to obtain health insurance. Consider, for example, people who specifically choose jobs or stay with a specific employer because the employer offers health insurance. In order to keep their health insurance, these people are giving up opportunities for higher wages, more interesting work, or better possibilities for promotion. Economists call this *willingness to pay*.

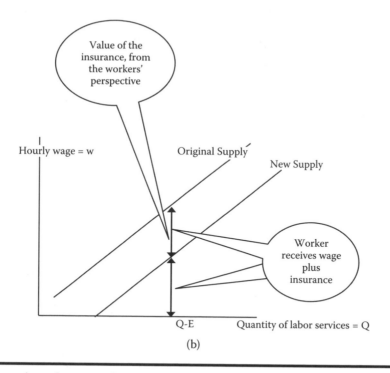

(b)

Figure 1.4 (continued)   (a) When an employer provides health insurance, it makes two types of payments for labor services: wages and health insurance. (b) When the employer provides health insurance, the worker receives two types of payments: wages and health insurance.

It is important to note that the health insurance cost shift from employers to workers hinges on the relationship between the employers' cost to purchase health insurance and the workers' willingness to pay for health insurance (by accepting lower wages). For any specific quantity of labor services, workers will be willing to accept lower wages if the employer offers health insurance. Two key questions are: How much do workers value health insurance? How does worker willingness to pay for health insurance compare to the employer's cost to purchase insurance? The answers to these questions will determine the magnitude of the shift in the supply curve. Two possibilities are illustrated in Figure 1.5a and b.

Scenario 1—We'll begin with the widespread assumption that workers place a high value on health insurance (see Figure 1.5a). In this case, the shift in the supply curve is substantial: workers are willing to accept a significant reduction in wages in exchange for health insurance. To find the impact of health insurance on the equilibrium wage, we show the initial situation (no insurance) with solid supply and demand lines, and the initial

> ## BOX 1.2 AVERAGE COST OF HEALTH
> ## INSURANCE PER WORKING-HOUR
>
> Among large employers, the average premium in 2009 was $4,674 for single coverage and $13,210 for coverage for a family of four.
>
> A full-time worker is typically paid for 40 hours per week, for 52 weeks per year. This implies that a full-time worker is paid for 2,080 hours per year.
>
> Thus, the average premium per employee costs between $2.25 per hour and $6.35 per hour, depending on the ratio of employees electing single vs. family coverage. The weighted average premium is nearly $5 per hour (using the U.S. Census estimate that the average household size is 2.59 and the Employee Benefits Research Institute (EBRI) estimate that 79 million individuals and 77 million dependents have employer-based coverage). If employees pay a portion of this cost, the employer's average hourly expense would be lower than the range computed here.
>
> A detailed analysis of the impact of this issue was published in 2007, when the average premium paid by employers was approximately $3 per hour; hence, we use that number in our discussion.
>
> The PPACA employer mandate specifies that if an employer does not offer insurance, the penalty is $2,000 per year for every employee after the first 30. For a large employer, this penalty raises the cost of hiring an employee by approximately $1 per hour. Based on existing evidence, we should anticipate that this penalty will exert some downward pressure on wages or jobs. Therefore, employees will bear some (and possibly most) of this cost. However, the penalty will not shift the supply curve because employees do not directly benefit from the penalty.
>
> **Source:** Claxton and Damico, *Snapshots: Employer Health Insurance Costs and Worker Compensation*, Kaiser Family Foundation, 2011. http://kff.org/health-costs/issue-brief/snapshots-employer-health-insurance-costs-and-worker-compensation/

(no insurance) equilibrium wage. Then we show the new situation (with insurance), using dashed supply and demand lines. We locate the intersection of these dashed lines, which marks the level of the new (with insurance) equilibrium wage. Next, compare the change in the wage (arrow A) with the money spent by the employer to purchase the insurance (arrow B):

Scenario 1: workers place a high value on health insurance

- Insurance is a bargain for workers: the wage cut A is smaller than the workers' perception of the value of the health insurance C
- Insurance is a bargain for the employer: the wage cut A is bigger than the cost to purchase the health insurance B

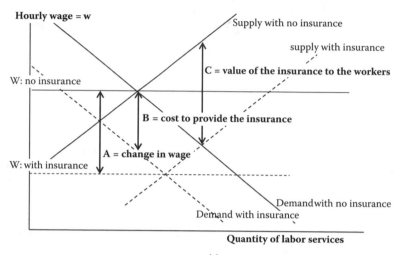

(a)

Scenario 2: workers place a low value on health insurance

- Workers do not want insurance: the wage cut A is bigger than the workers' perception of the value of the health insurance C
- The employer does not want to offer insurance: the wage cut A is smaller than the cost to purchase the health insurance B

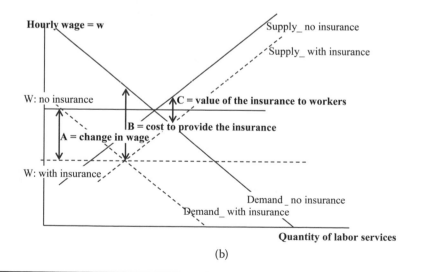

(b)

Figure 1.5   (a) Health insurance impacts wage: Scenario 1. (b) Health insurance impacts wage: Scenario 2.

the drop in the wage is *bigger* than the cost to purchase the insurance! This means that *the employer benefited from providing insurance*!

Did the employer gain this benefit at the expense of the workers? No. Compare the magnitudes of the wage reduction with the value of the insurance as perceived by the workers. The workers obtained insurance—the value is measured by the height of arrow C—at a bargain. They only paid an amount measured by the height of the shorter arrow A, in the form of lower wage. How did this happen? The key is the relationship between the cost to buy the insurance and the value of the insurance to the workers: arrow A is taller than arrow B.

This scenario, which is illustrated in Figure 1.5a, is consistent with the statements made by the autoworkers' union—that they explicitly accepted lower wages when they bargained for increased health benefits for the union members. Figure 1.5a provides an important insight: when workers place a high value on health insurance, and this value exceeds the actual cost to purchase the health insurance, the reduction in the equilibrium wage also exceeds the cost to purchase the health insurance. In this case, the employer actually saves money by providing health insurance. Thus, providing health insurance is a profitable strategy for an employer if the firm's employees place a high value on health insurance. Because this is a surprising insight, we will review:

1. the economic logic that produces this result and,
2. the underlying causes of this result

As we work through these details, remember that this is one possible scenario. We will consider the alternate scenario below. Empirical analysis indicates that we should consider this scenario carefully: evidence indicates that employers pass the cost of health insurance on to their employees. In response to evidence that workers pay completely for health insurance—in the form of reduced wages—analysts have dropped the term *employer-provided insurance* in favor of the more accurate term *employer-sponsored insurance.*

Logic That Produces This Result for Scenario 1—Let's examine Figure 1.5a again, to be sure we understand the logic. Look at the supply and demand for labor services when the employer provides health insurance, and locate the new equilibrium wage where these lines intersect. Here is the first important point: the new equilibrium wage is lower than the original (no health insurance) equilibrium wage. Firms expect to pay lower wages because they are now splitting the total payment into two categories (wages and health insurance), and workers are willing to accept lower wages because they are now receiving part of their payment in the form of health insurance.

Figure 1.5a also provides a second important insight: the decision to provide health insurance *increases* the firm's profit, because the difference between the original wage and the new wage is *bigger* than the cost to provide health insurance. The vertical distance between the two demand curves (arrow B) represents the cost to provide health insurance. You can see that the difference between the two equilibrium wages (arrow A) exceeds the length of arrow B. This occurs in our first scenario because the large shift in the supply curve reflects the high value that these workers place on health insurance. Assuming that the firm spends approximately $3 per hour to purchase health insurance, the firm's decision to purchase health insurance reduces the workers' wages by more than $3.

Workers benefit from employer-sponsored health insurance because the wage cut is smaller than the value of the health insurance that the workers receive in exchange for that wage cut. Arrow C measures the wage cut that workers are willing to accept in exchange for health insurance. You can see that the actual wage reduction is smaller than the amount measured by arrow C. Therefore, these workers will view the employer-sponsored health insurance as a bargain.

How Can the Decision to Provide Health Insurance Yield Benefits for Both the Employers and the Workers?—Employer-sponsored health insurance can offer this bargain for two reasons. Large employers (more than 50 employees) purchase insurance in the large-group market and pay substantially lower premiums than the workers would face if they purchased insurance as individuals. We will explore the reasons for this difference in premiums when we examine issue 3.

All employers purchase health insurance with pretax dollars, while—until very recently—individuals typically purchased health insurance with after-tax dollars. Consider the tax implications of splitting workers' compensation into two buckets. When the employer labels the compensation "wages," the worker pays income tax on that amount and purchases goods and services with the remaining after-tax dollars.

■ Suppose, for example, a worker receives $100 in wages and pays income tax equal to 20% of this income ($20). Then he has $80 in his pocket, and he can use this money to buy goods and services such as food, gas, clothing, and health insurance. If he could buy health insurance for $20, he would have $60 to spend on other goods and services.

■ In contrast, if the employer relabels some of this compensation "health insurance," the employer purchases the health insurance and deducts that cost as a business expense. The worker does not pay income tax on the value of the health insurance policy. The worker receives taxable income equal to $100 − $20 = $80, and he pays 20% of this amount in taxes ($16). After he pays this tax, he has $66 to spend on other goods and services.

The inequity of the historic discrepancy between the tax treatment of employer-sponsored insurance and the tax treatment of individual-purchased health insurance has been widely discussed. The 2010 PPACA included measures to attempt to reduce this inequity. However, PPACA does not change the fact that large employers typically purchase health insurance in the large-group market, and prices are lower in the large-group market than in the market for individually purchased health insurance.

Scenario 2—This scenario focuses on workers who are not willing to accept the wage cuts that would be necessary to pay for health insurance. This attitude could reflect several underlying factors. Low-wage workers may place higher priority on keeping the money instead of accepting wage cuts to indirectly purchase health insurance, in three types of circumstances:

■ Low-wage workers might place higher priority on housing, food, and transportation than on healthcare. A full-time minimum wage worker who earned the federal minimum wage of $7.25 per hour in 2012 would earn $14,500 per year. If this worker is faced with paying the average health insurance premium of $6,800 per year, his take-home pay would be reduced to $7,700 per year, or $642 per month. In this case, the average health insurance premium is almost 47% of the worker's annual earnings.

■ Individuals who are eligible for Medicaid may place low value on private-sector health insurance.

■ Individuals who work for small employers may be likely to fall in this category, since small employers typically pay higher rates for health insurance than large employers. We'll discuss the reasons below; here we are interested in the implication. The downward shift in the demand curve will be larger for small employers than for large employers. Therefore, worker wage cuts will be larger in small firms than in large firms.

■ Young healthy adults typically incur lower average healthcare expenditures than older adults. Thus, young workers are likely to place a lower value on health insurance than older workers and exhibit a lower willingness to pay. This is a rational response for individuals who are comparing the health insurance premium with expected annual healthcare expenditures. If all members of an employee group incur the same wage penalty because the firm pays the same premium per employee, these young workers are on average subsidizing older workers. Since young workers are also, on average, earning lower salaries than older, more experienced workers, this implies a wealth transfer from lower-income workers to their higher-income coworkers. This intergenerational transfer is a concern to those who want to make sure that health reform enhances social justice. Some argue that the intergenerational transfer is fair, because the young workers will gradually grow older. Our current demographic situation demonstrates, however, that this logic is *only* correct if the ratio of younger to older workers remains constant. It is clear instead that this ratio changes substantially over time. The current trend is clearly toward fewer younger workers supporting more and more older individuals, which imposes a burden on the younger generation.

Empirical evidence indicates that these issues are important. One-third of uninsured individuals have incomes within $3 of the minimum wage (after adjusting for state-level variations in the minimum wage) (Baicker and Levy, 2007). While these facts are well known, our analysis of Scenario 2 indicates a surprising conclusion: mandating that all employers must sponsor health insurance could impose of hardship on these low-wage workers. Under PPACA, the low-wage workers' employer must either pay a fine of approximately $1 per hour per employee for a large employer or purchase health insurance at a cost of at least $3 per hour. Either way, the employer faces higher costs per worker; hence, the demand for workers shifts down. This will put downward pressure on the wages (or employment) for these already low-wage workers.

Figure 1.5b illustrates the implications of these issues. The wage cuts that workers are willing to accept (arrow C) in exchange for health insurance are smaller than the employers' cost to purchase health insurance (arrow

B). The change in the equilibrium wage is smaller than the employers' cost to provide health insurance and larger than the value workers receive from health insurance. Employers do not want to provide insurance in this scenario, and the workers agree with this decision. That is, workers do not want employer-sponsored health insurance—in the sense that they are unwilling to accept the consequent reduction in wages. While the policy discussion of health insurance typically assumes that everyone wants employer-sponsored health insurance, this assertion ignores the marketplace reality that workers actually trade wage reductions for health insurance. Two types of workers may be particularly reluctant to make this trade: low-wage workers and young workers.

The Stark Implication of Scenarios 1 and 2—In Scenario 1, the employer offered health insurance pre-PPACA because employers and workers *both* benefit from ESI. The PPACA employer mandate only applies to employers facing Scenario 2. These employers do not offer insurance because neither the employer nor the workers are willing to make the dollars vs. insurance trade-off. Pre-PPACA evidence indicates that:

- These firms predominantly employ low-wage workers.
- Most of the cost of the health insurance or the penalty will translate into downward pressure on wages for these already low-wage workers. For workers earning the minimum wage, the downward shift in the demand curve implies downward pressure ont he number of jobs.

Use These Scenarios to Examine Important Policy Issues—Now that we have explored the underlying factors that influence employer-sponsored health insurance decisions and the consequent wage adjustments, we are ready to examine three factors that cause strain in the markets for private insurance.

An Inefficient Healthcare System Means Lower Wages for Workers— Healthcare expenditures have been increasing faster than the general level of inflation for many years. This implies that healthcare expenditures account for an increasing percent of our national economic output, as illustrated in Figure 1.6. It also implies that the wage–health insurance trade-off cannot typically be accomplished by simply foregoing wage increases. Instead, actual wage cuts will be required. This causes strains in labor markets because it counters the reasonable expectation that workers should share in productivity gains by receiving pay increases. Part of the healthcare crisis is exactly this: a costly inefficient healthcare system means lower wages for workers.

Source: National Health Expenditure Data, Table 1.
http://www.cms.gov/Research-Statistics-Data-and-Systems/
Statistics-Trends-and-Reports/National Health Expend Data/
downloads/tables.pdf

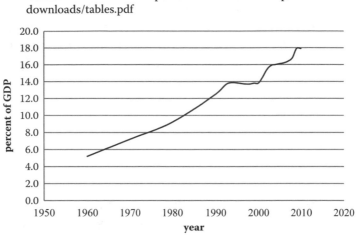

Figure 1.6 Healthcare expenditures as a percent of gross domestic product (GDP).

Healthcare Mandates Lead to Higher Costs for Health Insurance and Lower Wages—Our logic and our graphs are based on the implicit assumption that the employer can choose the types of healthcare services that will be included in the health insurance package, i.e., to define the package that maximizes the net value—the difference between the value generated for the workers and the cost to purchase the insurance. In recent years, state and federal mandates have reduced employer flexibility to shape the package of services that will be covered (Jensen and Morrisey, 1999). For example, prior to PPACA 40 states mandated that ESI must include coverage for psychologists' services, 39 mandated coverage for chiropractors' services, and 35 mandated coverage for dentists' and optometrists' services. While all of these professionals provide valuable services, empirical studies indicate that these coverage mandates lead to increased premiums for health insurance.

The typical news media discussion of these mandates starts from the implicit assumption that all workers want comprehensive health insurance, and therefore the key issue is a power struggle between employers and workers. Our logic implies that employers want to provide insurance when they have workers who value insurance enough to accept the wage cuts necessary to cover the cost of health insurance. This implies that private sector health insurance decisions reflect workers' wishes on average. This also implies that mandates to make coverage more comprehensive may harm low-wage workers by pricing them out of the insurance market, unless the mandate is accompanied by a subsidy to finance the additional costs. That is, these mandates may result in increased unemployment and reduced health insurance coverage for low-income workers.

Some Workers Complain That Their Employers Don't Offer Enough Insurance—We will examine two explanations for this seemingly irrational behavior:

1. Pauly (2001) offers a thought-provoking analysis of complaints about insufficient insurance that focuses on the fact that a single employer is likely to have employees with a diverse array of preferences. Large firms typically employ a diverse workforce that includes both young, healthy workers (with lower healthcare costs) and older workers (with higher healthcare costs). When the typical large employer is considering whether to add a specific benefit to the health insurance package, it probably has some workers with Scenario 2 preferences and other workers with Scenario 1 preferences. How will the employer decide whether to add the benefit to the firm's health insurance package? If the employer views the health insurance package as a tool to reduce worker turnover, the firm would be most concerned about the preferences of workers who are most likely to quit and seek jobs elsewhere. Because young workers are more likely to seek new jobs than older workers, we expect large employers to place priority on these workers' preferences—and young workers generally prefer less generous benefits because they are typically healthier than older workers, and they have lower incomes.

   States are currently facing this issue, as they define the basic benefit packages that will be offered in the state health insurance exchanges.

2. Employers will not provide insurance if the wage is within $3 of the minimum wage. In this case, the minimum wage law prevents the wage from falling to the equilibrium level. In this situation, the employer will not offer insurance. Because these workers have relatively low income, this is likely to be a situation in which workers would not be willing to accept lower wages in exchange for health insurance, as we discussed in Scenario 2.

The results of the 2013 health insurance exchange that Aon Hewitt operated for 100,000 employees of Sears Holdings Corp. and Darden Restaurants, Inc. indicate that employees within an employee group *do* have diverse preferences. Each employer offered a fixed amount of money to each employee, and employees were permitted to "spend" that money purchasing insurance in the exchange operated by Aon Hewitt. Some employees (42%) chose plans that were more expensive than their previous plans, while others (26%) chose plans that were less expensive than their previous plans (Mathews, 2013).

Issue 2: Some Individuals Are Uninsured, Even Though They Are Eligible for Public Insurance or ESI Because They Do Not Take Up the Insurance Offer

While it may seem incredible to analyze the proportions of individuals who decline ESI or do not apply for free public coverage, in the context of concern about the problems posed by lack of insurance coverage, substantial analysis has documented the importance of this issue. For example, Buchmueller et al. (2005) noted that 6 million children who were eligible for public coverage under State Children's Health Insurance Program (SCHIP) remained uninsured because their parents or guardians did not apply for the coverage. Sommers (2006), Aizer and Grogger (2003), and Aizer (2007) analyzed factors that influence these parental decisions and conclude that information and administrative hurdles such as asset tests and mandatory waiting periods exert significant influence on Medicaid take-up rates. (The term *take-up* is used to describe a decision to accept an insurance offer.)

Employees also make decisions to accept or reject employer offers to sponsor insurance: 20% of uninsured workers were eligible for an employer's ESI but were not enrolled. The proportion of workers who decline an employer's offer of ESI is related to income: 29% of workers with income less than the federal poverty level are eligible for ESI but decline the offer. In contrast, 16% of workers with income greater than 400% of this level decline ESI offers (Kaiser Family Foundation, 2004). Vistnes and Monheit (2011) investigated whether the decline in ESI coverage stems from a decline in employers offering ESI or a decline in the rate at which individuals take up the offer. They concluded that patterns differ by firm size. They found that both insurance offers and take-up decisions declined at small firms. At large firms, the take-up rate declined, but the proportion of large employers offering insurance remained stable. These authors also make one more important point: the nature of ESI is also changing—fewer firms offer dependent coverage, and the proportion of individuals who take up dependent coverage is declining.

Interactions among these factors add another layer of complexity. Abraham and Feldman (2010) reported that workers are less likely to take up an employer's insurance offer when their children are eligible for Medicaid. In addition, Buchmueller et al. (2005) and Herring (2005) reported that fewer employers offer coverage when charity care is available and employers raised the workers' contribution for family coverage as SCHIP expanded. These findings suggest that the impacts of PPACA on private insurance markets should be monitored carefully, because they indicate that Medicaid coverage can crowd out private coverage—in the sense that individuals will not purchase private coverage and firms may not offer coverage if public coverage is available. Bansak and Raphael's 2006 study of insurance decisions concluded:

> We find that between one-quarter and one-third of the increase in public health insurance coverage for SCHIP-eligible children is offset by a decline in private health coverage.[4]

This places an additional burden on state Medicaid/SCHIP programs, as some families and employers substitute public for private insurance. The results pose a challenge to states: if a state provides funds to add four children to the SCHIP program, only three of those children were previously uninsured, while one child simply switched from private to public coverage. While the opportunity to switch to public coverage is a boon to that family's budget, it is a burden to the state's budget. Anecdotal evidence indicates that some state Medicaid program analysts assume that some employers will drop coverage when the Medicaid expansion is implemented, and they factored this into their cost estimates.

Individuals will also consider the cost of the monthly premium when deciding to take up employer-sponsored health insurance. The *Wall Street Journal* reported (Thurm, 2013) that chain restaurants estimate that some of their employees will apply for Medicaid coverage.

Economists use the concept of *price elasticity* to measure the sensitivity of purchase decisions—for any good—to changes in price:

$$\text{Price elasticity of demand} = \frac{\%\ \text{change in quantity purchased}}{\%\ \text{change in price}}$$

Okeke et al. (2010), for example, concluded that the probability an employee will decline an employer's offer of insurance increases by 1% for every 10% increase in the out-of-pocket premium. Thus, the price elasticity of the demand for health insurance is equal to

$$\frac{1\% \text{ decrease in quantity}}{10\% \text{ increase is price}} = -0.1$$

They also find that married workers are more price sensitive than single workers, presumably because these workers may have the option of enrolling in their spouses' plans, and lower-income workers are more price sensitive than higher-income workers.

The fact that price elasticity is estimated to be low (the magnitude is less than one) has two implications for health policy:

1. Small premium subsidies may not be an effective strategy for addressing the problem of the uninsured: a subsidy equal to 10% of the out-of-pocket premium will only increase the take-up rate by 1%.
2. Mandating more generous coverage, such as coverage for mental health conditions, will induce some individuals to drop coverage if the mandate leads to health insurance premium increases. However, the impact of these mandates on insurance take-up decisions is likely to be modest: a 10% increase in out-of-pocket premiums is likely to induce 1% of workers to drop coverage.

Analysis of the high proportion of Hispanic workers who do not have insurance highlights additional issues. Dushi and Honig (2005) and Waidmann et al. (2004) analyzed the key question: Do minorities have lower rates of insurance coverage because:

1. they are less likely to receive an ESI offer, or
2. they are less likely to take up ESI offers?

Dushi and Honig (2005) concluded that minorities are less likely to receive an ESI offer, but once an employee receives an offer, the likelihood of accepting the offer is not correlated with race or ethnicity. Waidmann et al. (2004) took this analysis a step further and concluded that subtle details are important to inform policy design and support estimation of the impacts of policy innovations. Waidmann et al. (2004) found that:

- Hispanic workers are more likely to receive an ESI offer when the analysis controls for job skills, immigrant status, and employment characteristics.
- Take-up rates are lower for immigrant Hispanics than for nonimmigrant non-Hispanics, but among nonimmigrants, the take-up rates for Hispanics and non-Hispanics are comparable.

Individual attitudes about risk taking and the value of insurance also influence take-up decisions. Vistnes and Monheit (2011) analyzed data from the 2001 Medical Expenditure Panel Survey (MEPS) that provides large-sample data on individual attitudes about insurance and coverage status. These authors used econometric techniques to control statistically for two-way causality issues, and they concluded that worker attitudes about insurance are an important factor influencing job search decisions and insurance take-up decisions. They concluded that adults who do not place a strong value on insurance are more likely to be uninsured because they are: less likely to obtain job offers from employers who offer insurance, and less likely to enroll in insurance when coverage is offered. In addition, Polsky et al. (2005) report that willingness to pay for insurance also depends on the type of coverage: married workers are more likely to decline coverage if the employer offers only a health maintenance organization (HMO).

Issue 3: Restrictive Insurance Company Practices Make It Impossible for Some Individuals to Purchase Insurance

Some people argue that we should repeal parts of PPACA, while others argue that the components of this complex plan are inextricably linked. To explore this issue, we will examine the issues posed by restrictive insurance company practices. Several industry practices that have been standard in the market for individual insurance are prohibited by PPACA. In this section, we examine:

1. Industry reasons for using those practices
2. Previous federal law to limit the use of the practices, e.g., 1996 HIPAA
3. Issues related to the new limitations in the PPACA

Industry Reasons for Using Restrictive Practices

To streamline the discussion, we will focus on one common practice: exclusions for preexisting conditions. (Another widely discussed practice is refusing to renew policies after the policy holder is diagnosed with a high-cost condition. The two practices pose similar issues, from a regulatory perspective. Therefore, we focus on preexisting conditions exclusions as a well-known example.) Preexisting conditions clauses in health insurance policies remove the responsibility of the health insurance company to pay for conditions that were in existence (usually within a 12-month period) prior to the policy implementation. A preexisting condition could be evidenced by documentation of symptoms, diagnosis, or treatment of the condition. The 1996 Health Insurance Portability and Accountability Act (HIPAA) limited the types of situations in which insurance companies could impose preexisting conditions restrictions, but it did not eliminate these clauses. PPACA further restricts preexisting conditions clauses. While this may present good news for patients with these conditions, we will see below that this policy *only* makes sense if it is coupled with an enforceable health insurance mandate.

You might be thinking that the reasons for preexisting conditions exclusions are obvious: profits and greed. However, the health insurance market has specific characteristics that make the situation more complicated. A Stanford economist, George Akerlof, provides a clear analysis of the underlying issues and subsequently won a Nobel Prize, in part for these ideas.

Background Information: The "Lemons Problem"

The lemons problem plays a critical role in health insurance markets and health policy debates, but the problem is not unique to the health insurance market. In fact, Akerlof focused on the used-car market as the key example to illustrate the problem, and he used the common term *lemon* to describe a car with persistent repair problems. We'll start by examining Akerlof's description of the used-car market, and then apply the concept to the health insurance market (Akerlof, 1970).

Akerlof (1970.) provided a logical explanation for the fact that the warning "buyer beware" (*caveat emptor*) seems to be particularly important in the market for used cars. The fundamental problem has two components:

1. The quality of used cars varies dramatically.
2. Buyers cannot always directly observe the quality of the car.

A buyer who is looking at a specific car, say in good condition, can research the Blue Book average market price for this type of car. However, even cars in good condition range in quality, and many buyers do not have sufficient mechanical skills to assess where a specific car falls within that range. We will assume that our buyer does not have these skills. Even if the seller tries to assure the buyer that his specific car is at the top of that range, the buyer will not believe the seller's assertions—largely because the buyer cannot verify them. This buyer will not be willing to pay any price above the Blue Book average price.

Suppose further that this particular seller is telling the truth: this car's quality is at the top of the good range, and the seller knows it. He may not be willing to sell at the average price, because he knows the car is worth more. He may decide to withdraw his car from the market, and drive it himself for a few more years. If owners of above-average-quality cars decide to keep their cars because the Blue Book price seems too low, then the average quality of cars for sale will fall, and the average Blue Book price will fall. Once again, owners will withdraw cars for which the quality is above the new lower average. Pretty soon, the only used cars that are for sale will be the lemons that no one wants to buy. This process is generally known as a market "death spiral."

Used-car buyers and sellers have developed numerous solutions: car title information that specifies whether the car has been in an accident, mechanics offering second opinions, and used-car lots that offer warranties.

The Lemons Problem in Health Insurance Markets

The lemons problem also occurs in the health insurance market—with a very important twist. In this market, the quality of health insurance buyers varies across individual buyers, and sellers cannot directly observe all aspects of this quality. Healthcare expenditures vary substantially across individuals: in general, 20% of individuals account for 80% of healthcare expenditures (O'Donohue and Cucciare, 2005).

Firms selling health insurance can discover *some* information about a potential buyer's health by requiring a physical and requiring the buyer to disclose information such as health history and current risky behaviors; however, the individual buying health insurance always has more information about his or her health than the company selling the health insurance. Therefore, health insurance companies worry: Is this individual buying insurance today because he or she knows about an expensive diagnosis or condition that has not been disclosed? Why today? He or she didn't purchase health insurance yesterday. What changed? What new information spurred this decision?

Figure 1.7 illustrates the problem. If all individuals are initially in the market, and health insurance firms cannot observe any information about

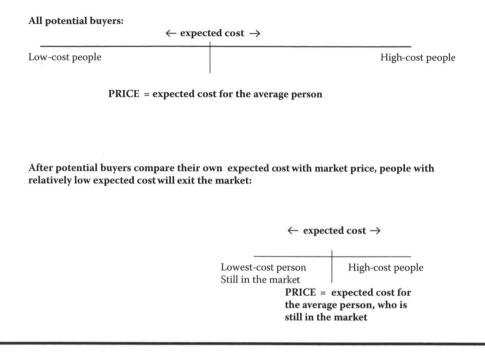

Figure 1.7   The lemons problem.

individual health status, the equilibrium premium will be equal to the average health claims plus overhead plus return on investment. When relatively healthy individuals compare their expected expenditures with the premium, some will drop out of the market because they will think that the insurance premium exceeds their future healthcare costs. Thus, the average health-care expenditures of the people who remain in the market will increase. Therefore, even more individuals will realize that their expected expenditures are lower than the premium and drop out of the market. Eventually, the only people who will remain in the market will be the extremely high-cost people—as the market experiences a death spiral. Current efforts to convince young, healthy individuals to buy insurance in the new exchanges reflect substantial concern over the issue.

Employer-Sponsored Health Insurance Mitigates the Lemons Problem

Employer-sponsored group health insurance provides a solution for this problem, particularly in a large-group market: individuals are buying coverage today indirectly, through employers, simply because they are employed. Thus, insurance purchases are tied to employment status, rather than health status and expected healthcare expenditures. This solution is not perfect:

health status can be correlated with employment status, and high-cost individuals may be more likely to accept employer offers of insurance than low-cost people. In addition, employers can attempt to screen applicants on health status as a way to maintain some control over the costs of insurance premiums. However, this solution allows the market for employer-sponsored group health insurance to function reasonably well, particularly for larger employers.

The U.S. health insurance industry therefore has three clearly defined segments: the large-group market generally defined as having at least 50 members, the small-group market of 2–50 members, and the individual market (Fronstein 2010). Prices are lowest in the large-group market, because risk spreading is most effective in this segment, and because marketing to large employer groups is relatively efficient. Prices are substantially higher in the individual market because the lemons problems is an important issue for individually purchased insurance, and because marketing costs are highest in this segment of the industry—partly due to the cost for the insurance company to acquire and verify information about the individual's health status.

Employer-sponsored insurance was not initiated as a strategy to solve the lemons problem. Instead, this inadvertent solution to the lemons problem was developed during World War II as a solution to the problem posed by U.S. government wartime wage and price controls (notice that this is an example of unintended effects of government intervention). During World War II, U.S. firms increased production dramatically to supply weapons, ships, planes, uniforms, and other war materials to the U.S. government. At the same time, a substantial portion of potential young workers were not available to work because they were serving in military units. As a substantial buyer of U.S. manufacturing output, the U.S. government was concerned about upward pressure on wages due to this increased demand and reduced supply. To forestall this problem, the government imposed wage and price controls. The wage controls created a serious problem for firms with large government contracts: they were not able to hire all of the workers that were needed to deliver the contracted outputs because workers were not motivated by these artificially low wages; the free market would have provided a much higher wage. These firms wondered: "What can we do to attract more workers, since we cannot offer higher wages?" Blue Cross and Blue Shield health insurance, developed in New England during the 1930s as a strategy to facilitate collection of healthcare bills, provided the solution. The 1942

Stabilization Act ruled that firms could offer health insurance benefits without violating the wage controls (Wisconsin Policy Research Institute, 2006).

Employers continued to offer health insurance benefits after the war—and the wage controls—ended, because purchasing health insurance indirectly through an employer offered two benefits. In addition to mitigating the lemons problem, employer-sponsored health insurance offered a tax benefit: it was a tax-deductible business expense for the employer. While the employer enjoyed the direct tax benefit, workers also benefit from this policy indirectly.

Legislation to Restrict the Use of Preexisting Conditions Exclusions

Title I of HIPAA: Prohibit Restrictive Practices in the Markets for Small-Group and Large-Group Health Insurance—Title I of the 1996 Health Insurance Portability and Accountability Act (HIPAA) limited the use of restrictive practices in the large-group market and in the small-group market, but it did not apply these restrictions to the individual market. Congress debated this issue before passing the 1996 HIPAA, in which Title I outlaws the use of specific practices in the group markets. HIPAA is more famous for the section on health information privacy and security Title II, but the name of this law (the Health Insurance Portability and Accountability Act) reflects the content of Title I.

The debate yielded interesting and important information about this issue. Table 1.5 provides an overview. Both sides agreed that banning the restrictive practices would lead to higher premiums as people with high-cost conditions obtain coverage, and these higher premiums would exacerbate the affordability problem. It is interesting to note that the two sides only disagreed about the magnitudes of the impacts. Surprisingly, advocates argued that banning restrictive practices would have minimal direct impact, and hence the unintended cost impact would be small. Opponents argued that the direct impact would be substantially larger, which would produce a larger impact on premiums. As shown in Table 1.5, HIPAA banned the restrictive practices in the group markets, but did not extend the ban to the individual market. This was a reasonable step, given that the lemons problem is more salient in the individual market, which constitutes approximately 10% of the health insurance market. PPACA extended the ban to the individual market, which was reasonable because PPACA mitigates the lemons problem by mandating that individuals must have insurance.

Table 1.5   Overview of HIPAA

	Health Insurance Market		
	Individual	*Small Group*	*Large Group*
Guaranteed renewability	Yes	Yes	Yes
Limit time excludes preexisting condition	No	Yes	Yes
Portability	No	Yes	Yes
Certificate of creditable coverage	Yes	Yes	Yes
Nondiscrimination		Yes	Yes
Special enrollment period		Yes	Yes
Guaranteed access/availability	Only for some individuals leaving group coverage	Yes	No

Source: Scanlon, W. 1998. Health Insurance Standards: New Federal Law Creates Challenges for Consumers, Insurers, Regulators. 1998. US. General Accounting Office. GAO/HEHS-98-67, p 30.

Title I of HIPAA and PPACA target insurance industry practices that were designed to deal with the lemons problem: preexisting conditions clauses, health status disclosure requirements, and provisions that rescind coverage if the individual fails to disclose relevant health information. These "restrictive practices," which are viewed by insurance companies as reasonable efforts to deal with the reality of the lemons problem, are often viewed by consumers as unethical. Why did the legislators who voted for PPACA feel comfortable extending the ban on these practices to the individual market (when their predecessors who crafted HIPAA did not do this)? The PPACA includes an essential component: the individual health insurance mandate/tax. The concept of relying on the combination of these two policies was based on evidence from pre-PPACA state-level reforms.

State Reforms That Preceded PPACA Reforms at the State Level

Beginning in the 1990s, several states enacted reforms to expand health insurance coverage that were expected to be the successful pilot demonstrations to guide federal reform, but the results were problematic. Three primary mechanisms for state reform efforts included mandated guaranteed issue, constrained rate setting, and individual coverage mandates. Guaranteed issue regulations required health insurance companies that sell individual health insurance policies to make those plans available for purchase to any individual, regardless of their health condition. As of 2011, five states (Vermont, New Jersey, New York, Massachusetts, and Maine) required health insurance companies to guarantee issue to all individual policies in their state. Another seven states require guaranteed issue for some plans or some individuals. According to Kaiser Family Foundation 2011a, those states are Idaho, Michigan, Ohio, Oregon, Rhode Island, Utah, and West Virginia. Constrained rate setting regulations impose limits on how health insurance companies can set rates within the individual health insurance market. Community rating is a mechanism used by insurance companies to spread risk evenly across a group of insured individuals. Rather than calculating the risk for an individual age, health status, or geographical location, they calculate the risk of the group as a whole. New York is the only state that still mandates a pure community rating, while six states utilize an adjusted community rating (Maine, Massachusetts, New Jersey, Oregon, Vermont, and Washington), permitting rates to vary based on demographic characteristics such as age. Other states limit the variation in premiums, by specifying rating bands. A rating band equal to three, for example, means that an insurance company's highest premium can only be three times that company's lowest premium. Rating bands have been used in numerous states (Idaho, Indiana, Kentucky, Louisiana, Minnesota, Nevada, New Hampshire, New Mexico, North Dakota, South Dakota, and Utah). Finally, several states (California, Maryland, Maine, and Washington) have considered individual mandates, but Massachusetts is the only state that enacted it. While Massachusetts' initiative did increase the number of insured individuals, it did not achieve universal coverage. Estimates indicate the uninsured decreased from 10.4 to 2.6–5.4% of the population (Nardin et al., 2009).

Much can be learned from these state-level attempts to intervene in the insurance market in an effort to increase health insurance coverage. Guaranteed issue and constraints on rate setting were implemented with the goal to ensure that those who typically could not access health insurance due to preexisting conditions, age, or other factors had the opportunity to purchase affordable health insurance policies. However, this action ultimately drove overall policy costs up, and those who deemed themselves at low risk for needing health care opted out of the market—leaving those "high-risk" individuals in the pool. Insurance companies unable to make a sound business case for staying in the market opted out, leaving some states with few companies willing to sell individual health insurance. Those that stayed in the market offered fewer benefits at a much higher cost (Wachenheim and Leida, 2012).

In Massachusetts, the cost of reforms exceeded projections, and the cost of medical care has escalated (Tuerck et al., 2011). Some of the funds to finance this reform came from fines assessed to individuals and employers not in compliance with the mandate to purchase or offer health insurance. However, the majority of the needed funding has been diverted from the state's "free-care pool," money that had previously been given to safety-net facilities and providers. Access to care for the low-income has declined; instead of free care, they have to meet deductibles and copays, with modest improvements for other segments of the population (Nardin et al., 2009).

These early reform experiences pose an important caution as policy makers design the detailed rules that will govern the health insurance subsidies and the HIX policies. Current policy suggests vaguely, at this point, as the regulations are still evolving, that the state HIXs will ensure that the prices of the individual insurance policies are "reasonable." Early rate-regulation experience indicates that this task should be approached with humility. Identifying a reasonable premium is difficult, because health insurance is a multifaceted product. It may be more realistic to focus on competition as a strategy for ensuring that premiums will reasonably reflect cost. However, it may be necessary to expand our concept of insurance markets from state-regulated and state-defined markets to a broader national concept, in order to generate effective competition.

The Supreme Court Decision—In March 2012, the Supreme Court heard arguments for and against the constitutionality of the government mandate for purchasing health insurance or paying a "fine" contained in the PPACA. Proponents argued that the individual mandate is necessary to create more stability in the health insurance market that was lost with the provisions that banned preexisting conditions clauses and lifetime benefit caps. Opponents cited infringement of personal freedom, enforcement difficulties, and the fact that this provision will not ensure that the entire U.S. population will have health insurance coverage. However, the court upheld the requirement that individuals must have health insurance.

Consider the ramification to the health insurance industry if the Supreme Court had ruled that the individual mandate was unconstitutional, but allowed the rest of the PPACA to stand—specifically the bans on preexisting conditions clauses and the lifetime maximum benefit. You can predict the impact this would have had for insurance providers and buyers: the always-fragile market for individually purchased health insurance would have been hit with an increased lemons problem. Early reform experience in a small number of states indicated that this could be expected to trigger a market death spiral.

A study conducted by the Urban Institute (Blumberg et al., 2011), a non-partisan economic and social research organization, estimated that only 3% of the nonelderly U.S. population would be affected by the individual mandate, as the other 97% either already have ESI, have health coverage through a government program, have an income below the threshold set for those subject to the mandate, or would qualify for partial subsidies that would help pay for their health insurance premiums. The researchers conclude that a small number of people will be affected by the mandate, but there is a large benefit for the overall population.

While the problem of restrictive industry practices is significant for the individuals who are specifically impacted, it is not the main issue for the majority of uninsured individuals. Hence, outlawing these practices, by itself, will not solve the problems faced by uninsured individuals. Based on analysis of ESI, the solution must include subsidy to help low-income individuals purchase insurance.

In addition, scientific advances in the field of genetics may also be exerting subtle pressure to address this issue. Lack of insurance will be more problematic, and restrictive practices will impact larger numbers of people, as these advances make it increasingly possible to predict which individuals will experience high-cost conditions (Chen, 2002).

Solution Options: What Do We Learn from Examining the Three Critical Issues?

Thus, we see that:

- Nearly 20% of nonelderly U.S. residents are uninsured
- Private coverage rates have steadily declined while public coverage has been increasing
- Coverage patterns and trends are the result of numerous decisions made by individuals and families, employers, insurers, and government agencies
- A complex array of demographic and employment factors influence these decisions

Designing a policy to work toward the goal of universal coverage requires careful attention to these decisions and the factors that influence them in order to ensure that the policy succeeds with minimal unintended consequences.

In order to think about solutions, we return to the discussion at the beginning of this chapter, to recall the key point that health insurance cannot, by itself, make healthcare more affordable. In fact, insurance does not make anything more affordable. Instead, insurance is only designed to manage risk by spreading risk, which simply means that it spreads the costs incurred by people with costly diagnoses across the entire insured group. However, individuals also bear additional costs to participate in this risk-spreading system, because the premium must cover the average healthcare expenditures incurred by members of the group, plus administrative costs.

Some advocate replacing this system with single-payer public coverage. Medicare provides this type of coverage for most seniors over age 65. We will discuss the payment issues faced by Medicaid in Section II. However, at this juncture it is safe to say that economists generally take a dim view of monopolies in terms of their inefficiencies, inability to innovate, and lack of incentives to satisfy customers (think of the post office or DMV). For an interesting perspective on this issue, see Newhouse and Sinaiko (2007).

Insurance only appears to make healthcare more affordable for the insured population as a whole if an entity outside the population contributes to purchasing that insurance. Given that workers actually pay for ESI and taxpayers pay for government-sponsored insurance, the population as a whole cannot make healthcare more affordable by purchasing insurance through one of these entities. This is an important point that helps explain why the access problem has been so intractable, why the 2010 PPACA debate was so contentious, and why we should probably expect ongoing evolution of PPACA policies.

Insurance companies set premiums to cover the expected cost to provide healthcare and also cover overhead expenses and profit. This means that we routinely pay insurance premiums that are higher than the expected cost of the claims—because the cost of "doing business" needs to be added. We are willing to do this because the expected cost of claims is an average that applies to all insured people—as a group. We might incur actual expenses that are substantially lower than this average—or substantially higher. We pay an insurance premium that is higher than the average cost in order to avoid the risk that we might incur a very large expense. Therefore, shifting the risk to the insurance company allows us to plan and manage our household budgets and assets. The difference between the premium and the expected cost of claims is the price that we pay in order to shift the risk to the insurance company. This leads to five important conclusions about insurance:

1. The price of insurance is equal to the difference between the premium and the expected cost, and the price is always greater than zero.
2. It makes sense to buy insurance for high-cost events that do not occur frequently. It does not make sense to buy insurance and pay to shift risk for events that are relatively low cost.
3. Insurance is a mechanism to manage risk by paying to shift risk. It does not make healthcare more affordable. In fact, the opposite is true—it makes healthcare more expensive because we pay a premium to cover the expected cost of claims plus the price to shift risk to the insurance company.
4. If a group of employees is covered by an insurance policy and each employee pays the same monthly premium for that coverage, younger employees, on average, subsidize the older employees. The expected cost of claims is higher for older employees, on average, than for younger employees. If we do not adjust the premium to account for this, then the younger, typically lower-wage employees subsidize the older, typically higher-wage employees.

   The same logic leads to a more uncomfortable conclusion. Suppose two employees pay the same premium. One has a known health condition that will require expensive treatment this year. The other does not have any known health conditions. In this scenario, the more healthy employee subsidizes the less healthy employee. You might be thinking, yes, that is the purpose of insurance. That is true. However, the healthy person may also resent this fact if he or she is paying the predictable healthcare costs of someone who smokes, doesn't exercise, and eats Twinkies for breakfast. We need to keep this in mind: we will see important implications as we explore this issue further.

   This logic also helps us think about the types of risks for which we buy insurance. Do you buy auto insurance for collision or oil changes? If you don't buy oil change insurance, consider the reason. According to the information presented above, the premium for oil change insurance would have to cover the average price of expected oil changes plus overhead expenses to administer the policy plus sufficient profit to yield a reasonable rate of return on the company's invested capital. This means that oil change insurance premiums would be higher than the average annual cost of predicted oil changes. Thus, oil change insurance would not make oil changes more affordable; instead, it would make them more expensive. This explains why we typically buy insurance for risky events that will be expensive if they occur, but that have a low probability of actually occurring. It only makes sense to buy insurance for events that are financially substantial but unlikely, because we are paying for the privilege of sharing our risk with the insurance company. This issue has clear implications for discussions of *what* should be included in the basic benefit plan, and whether we should applaud or oppose the shift toward high-deductible consumer-directed plans coupled with catastrophic insurance.

5. This discussion highlights the importance of the distinction between insurance, which transfers and pools risk, and subsidy, which provides financial assistance to low-income or high-cost individuals. If health insurance is simply a tool that allows us to reduce our exposure to risk, the public discussion of access to health insurance would focus on catastrophic insurance, and it would not include debate about comprehensive inclusion of preventive care. However, the debate about mini-med policies suggests that most advocates of increased access to health insurance would probably not be satisfied with universal access to catastrophic insurance. For a summary of this issue, see Box 1.3.

We must conclude, therefore, that public passion about universal coverage does not focus on access to health insurance. Instead, this debate is really focused on universal access to healthcare, and health insurance is viewed as a good strategy for financing the subsidy that will be needed to accomplish this goal. This point has one important implication: there won't be any shortcut solutions to the access issue. Subsidies will be needed. We can't all be subsidy recipients, so the key policy question is how to pay for the subsidy. You might be thinking, "That's easy—government, employers, hospitals, insurance companies, and pharmaceutical companies can provide the subsidy." We'll see below that the answer won't be that simple, particularly because these costs must eventually be paid by someone; they simply can't be perpetually passed on. So the question becomes, who will pay? Box 1.4 provides some perspective on this issue. We also have traditionally assumed that it is important to ensure universal access to telephone service. Analysis of strategies for financing universal access to health insurance echoes the issues raised by the telephone service subsidy.

BOX 1.3 MCDONALD'S AND MINI-MED POLICIES— SHOULD THIS COUNT AS PROVIDING INSURANCE?

A recent story reported by *The Wall Street Journal* brings this debate into the public discourse by highlighting two issues with limited-benefits plans, commonly referred to as mini-med plans, that the health-care reform regulations will raise. These plans are typically offered by companies with a high turnover of employees, like McDonald's, whose typical employee is young and earns a low income. These employees would not be able to afford high-premium health insurance.

First, mandates in the healthcare reform law require insurers to spend 80–85% of the premiums on payments for healthcare. Advocates of the mini-med health insurance plans find this regulation problematic, as the overhead to administer these types of policies for companies with a high turnover of employees is higher than that of other types of policies.

Additionally, these plans impose annual expenditure caps that are not compatible with PPACA requirements. For example, McDonald's employees in Montana pay $56 per month for basic coverage that provides up to $2,000 in benefits per year. These plans currently operate under waivers, but it is expected that these plans will not be permitted after 2014.

This issue raises two questions: what qualifies as health insurance, and whether or not the United States wants to mandate health insurance if it comes at the cost of jobs. As the policy debate continues and each stakeholder lobbies for its service or provider to be included, care must be taken to avoid adding more and more coverage mandates that would make premiums too costly for most Americans to purchase.

Source: Healthamburglar, *The Wall Street Journal*, October 2–3, 2010; Fuhrmans, More Employers Try Limited Health Plans: Cheap 'Mini-Medical' Policies Cover Drugs and Doctor Visits, but Little Hospitalization, *The Wall Street Journal*, January 17, 2006; What Is a Mini-Med Plan? Kaiser Family Foundation, July 5, 2011, http:// healthreform.kff.org/notes-on-health-insurance-and-reform/2011/july/ what-is-a-mini-med-plan.aspx.

BOX 1.4   THIS PROBLEM IS NOT UNIQUE TO HEALTHCARE

We also have a social goal to ensure universal access to telephone service to make sure everyone could dial 911 in an emergency. For many decades, this goal was accomplished via a cross-subsidy system. When AT&T provided regulated monopoly telephone service, regulators set prices to ensure that business customers subsidized residential customers, and urban customers subsidized rural customers. This permitted regulators to set relatively low residential rates, which permitted a large proportion of households to purchase telephone service. When MCI applied for permission to compete with AT&T, by providing microwave transmission of business telephone service between St. Louis and Chicago, the regulators faced a dilemma. The new competitor offered lower prices for those business customers. The application was initially denied, however, because the new competition threatened the profits generated when AT&T served business customers who were needed to subsidize the low rates charged to residential customers. It was clear that the telephone industry could not enjoy the benefits of competitive innovation and—at the same time—maintain the cross-subsidy pricing system. If we want to support the social goal of universal telephone service, we must utilize a more direct and transparent strategy to finance that social goal.

Source: MCI WorldCom Inc., 1999.

Conclusion: Equitable Access to Healthcare Is an Important Social Goal, but Health Insurance Is Just a Tool to Achieve a Larger Goal—Health

Healthcare is only one of several factors that help individuals produce "health." The twentieth-century gains in life expectancy also reflect improvements such as public health measures (clean drinking water and vaccinations) and auto safety measures (limited-access interstate highways). In addition, strong evidence indicates that education and income are positively correlated with health status.

This raises the question: Equitable access to what?

- Health insurance?
- Healthcare?
- Health?

Insurance is an important tool: people who don't have health insurance get less healthcare than people with insurance, and they have higher mortality risk. In fact, "catch-up care" occurs when previously uninsured individuals become eligible for Medicare; however, it is not clear that this extra care can completely ameliorate health deficits acquired during previous episodes of uninsurance. A study conducted by McWilliams et al. (2007) found that previously uninsured adults with diagnoses of hypertension, diabetes, heart disease, or stroke who enroll in Medicare at age 65 had significantly higher numbers of physician visits and hospitalizations, and higher medical expenditures, than people with these diagnoses who had previously been insured. This increased utilization and cost continued up to age 72 (McWilliams et al., 2007).

However, insurance may not be enough to eliminate health disparities. Evidence indicates that the relationship between socioeconomic status (SES) and health involves a range of factors beyond the connection between SES and health insurance. Some of these factors are well recognized but not well understood, such as the correlation of SES with smoking and obesity, and the impact of income and education on health. This may reflect an array of factors, such as the ability to choose safer jobs and safer housing locations.

Finally, as we conclude our discussion of access, we note that discussion of universal coverage tends to gloss over the critical issue of defining the package of benefits that will be included in the mandated insurance package. *Health insurance* is an umbrella term with a variety of meanings that differ from person to person. How we ultimately decide to define the components of health insurance has significant cost and access implications.

Can we agree on a basic benefits plan? What should be included? What should be excluded? Will we be willing to accept a two-tier system? Medicare already utilizes a two-tier system: some Medicare recipients purchase supplemental insurance policies Medicare Part C, while others do not. (Payment for Part C is covered by Medicaid or by retiree health plans for some individuals.) Are we comfortable with health insurance addressing just catastrophic events, or should all insurance plans be required to cover some types of preventative care—and if so, which ones? Some have suggested that the employer mandate should permit provision of a high-deductible health insurance plan with health savings accounts to cover noncatastrophic health bills. Is this good enough coverage?

Before we move on to exploring possible large-scale solutions, we need to look at the other two pressures for change: cost and quality. In Chapter 2 we will build upon what we've learned in this chapter to include issues related to healthcare costs.

Endnotes

1. Inflation means that the purchasing power of a dollar decreases over time. Suppose I have $1,000 to spend in year 1 and another $1,000 to spend in year 2. If inflation is 5%, my year 2 dollars will not stretch as far as my year 1 dollars. In year 2, I can only buy 95% of what I could in year 1, even though I still have the same number of dollars. Inflation varies tremendously, but it tends to be 3–4% per year, over long periods of time.
2. Despite the plethora of jokes about economists who disagree with each other, economists largely agree on core ideas. One of these core ideas is that price ceilings create shortages, and price floors create surpluses. Impacts of price ceilings have been widely documented in the housing market. To read more, go to http://www.fee.org/library/books/roofs-or-ceilings-the-current-housing-problem/. This article discusses the California housing issue at two critical time periods within the context of price controls.
3. You might wonder why the concert promoter sets the ticket price below the equilibrium price. This is a good question. Setting a low price creates a line of fans waiting to buy tickets, and this may boost the group's popularity.
4. SCHIP is sometimes also known as CHIP (Children's Health Insurance Program). It is a federal and state insurance program designed to provide health insurance to families with modest incomes, who do not meet the criteria for Medicaid eligibility.

Chapter 2

Cost

The first lesson of economics is scarcity: There is never enough of anything to satisfy all those who want it. The first lesson of politics is to disregard the first lesson of economics.

—Thomas Sowell (1993, p. 131)

Introduction

Healthcare expenditures have been high and increasing rapidly for decades. Why is this issue so particularly important, urgent, and ominous now? Healthcare spending has increased substantially over the past four decades. Americans spent an average of $984 inflation-adjusted dollars (per capita) on healthcare in 1960, and they spent six times that amount in 2004. During these years, healthcare expenditures also increased as a proportion of gross domestic product (GDP), from 5% to 16%. More importantly, healthcare expenditures have been increasing faster than inflation, as detailed in Table 2.1.

Before we proceed, we should note three overlapping terms: cost, price, and expenditures. We tend to use the word *cost* in a variety of situations: sometimes we use this word to describe the price per item, while in other situations we use this word to indicate the amount of our total expenditure. If we were complaining about increased cost of gasoline, for example, we might be referring to increased price per gallon, or if we just bought a new gas-guzzling vehicle, we might be referring to increased cost of commuting to work (because we need more gallons of gas). When we say that

Table 2.1 Healthcare Expenditures per Capita Have Increased Substantially

	1960	2004
Health expenditures[a] per capita		
Adjusted to 2004 dollars[b]	938	6,497
Health expenditures as % of GDP	5.2	16

Source: Table 1, http://www.cms.gov/Research-Statistics-Data-and-Systems/Statistics-Trends-and-Reports/NationalHealthExpendData/downloads/tables.pdf.

[a] National health expenditures include public and private funding for personal healthcare, administration, public health, structures, and R&D.
[b] Adjusted using U.S. city average CPI, all consumers.

"healthcare costs are increasing," we are typically referring to total healthcare expenditures. These expenditures could increase as a function of increases in price, increases in quantity, or increases in both price and quantity.

Background Information: What Does It Mean to Say, "The System Is Not Sustainable?"

Spending on health-related programs accounted for 22% of federal expenditures in 2006 (Stanton and Rutherford, 2006). Continued increases in healthcare expenditures, combined with the aging of the baby boomers, are expected to fuel substantial (and what many see as simply unaffordable) increases in the Medicare budget.

The annual Medicare trust fund report (Centers for Medicare and Medicaid Services, 2010), presents the trustees' financial projections, along with an actuarial analysis of these projections. Figure 2.1, which is constructed from data provided in the trust fund report's supplemental tables, illustrates two important points:

■ Current Medicare payroll tax collections and Medicare premiums do not cover current Medicare expenditures. In 1967, Medicare payroll taxes and Medicare premiums covered 76% of Medicare expenditures; in 2012, they covered 53% of expenditures, and they are projected to cover only 44% of Medicare expenditures by the year 2050.

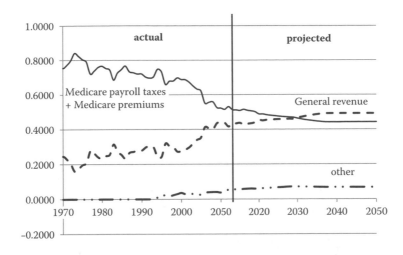

Figure 2.1 Medicare sources of noninterest income and expenditures as a percentage of gross domestic product. (From Centers for Medicare and Medicaid Services, Trustees Report and Trust Funds, Expanded and Supplementary Tables, Medicare Sources of Income as a Percentage of Total Income, 2012, http://www.cms.gov/Research-Statistics-Data-and-Systems/Statistics-Trends-and-Reports/ReportsTrustFunds/index.html.)

■ The gap between Medicare expenditures and Medicare income from payroll taxes is filled by payments from general federal tax revenues: general fund revenues accounted for 25% of Medicare expenditures in 1967, and they currently account for 42% of Medicare expenditures.

However, David Walker, the then comptroller general of the United States, warned in a 2007 statement to Congress:

If the American people understand that there is no magic bullet—if they understand that

■ we cannot grow our way out this problem;
■ eliminating earmarks will not solve the problem;
■ wiping out fraud, waste and abuse will not solve the problem;
■ ending the "Global War on Terrorism," exiting from Iraq, or cutting way back on defense will not solve the problem; and
■ letting the recent tax cuts expire will not solve this problem;

then they can engage with you in a discussion about what government should do; how it should do it; and how we should pay for it without unduly mortgaging the future of our country, children, and grandchildren. (Walker, 2007)

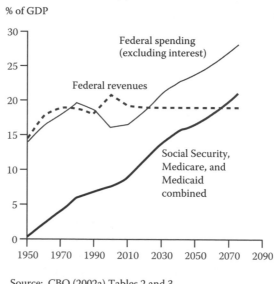

Total spending, entitlement spending, and revenues, 1950 to 2075

Source: CBO (2002a) Tables 2 and 3.
Note: Actual data until 2000, CBO forecasts afterward.

Figure 2.2   Total spending, entitlement spending, and revenues, 1950–2075. (From Congressional Budget Office, Tables 2 and 3, 2002.)

State and local governments are facing similar issues, as they examine the impacts of increasing Medicaid expenditures on state budget options. States, on average, spend 16% of their budgets on Medicaid, 46% on education (including elementary, secondary, and higher education), and 38% on corrections, transportation, public assistance, and all other programs and activities (Kaiser Family Foundation, 2011b). If Medicaid expenditures continue to grow faster than the general rate of inflation, the state will face tough choices: maintaining the current level of Medicaid coverage would require either substantial cuts in funding for education and the correction system or substantial tax increases, or both.

Continued growth in healthcare expenditures, as a proportion of GDP, also has serious implications for consumer budgets. The circular flow in Figure 2.4a and b illustrates the logic. Members of households go to work every day, to produce goods and services. Their employers pay wages and salaries to these workers, and then offer the goods and services for sale. Workers use their income to purchase these goods and services. Thus, average output per person determines the average standard of living per person. Therefore, this diagram highlights a key point: *we cannot be a nation of consumers unless we are first a nation of producers*—and productivity, measured

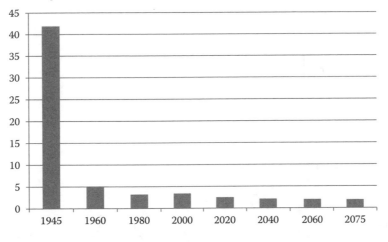

Source: Government Accountability Office 2010. Strategic Plan: Serving the Congress and the Nation, 2010-2015. GAO-10-559SP:

Figure 2.3 Number of workers per retiree. (From U.S. Government Accountability Office, *Strategic Plan: Serving the Congress and the Nation, 2010–2015*, GAO-10-559SP, 2010.)

by output per worker, determines our standard of living (consumption per person) over the long-run. If you are thinking, "But we buy our consumer goods from China," remember that we have to produce something to sell in the international market if we want to continue to buy goods in that market. Participation in this market necessitates a two-way street of both buying and selling. A nation cannot participate as a consumer only. As the healthcare industry expands, the proportion of our nation's productive resources that are employed in the healthcare industry will grow, and the proportion employed in other industries will shrink. Unless average worker productivity grows faster than healthcare expenditures, we will produce fewer non-healthcare goods and services (per capita). The non-healthcare portion of our standard of living will fall. The concern that individuals may view this as a decline in real wages generates political pressure for healthcare "cost containment."

In order to consider strategies to accomplish cost containment, we must (1) understand the forces that are currently causing the cost increases and (2) assess the implications of cost containment. While the idea of cost containment sounds good in the abstract, implementation of serious cost containment measures will impose other types of costs. We must consider our options carefully, and this means that we must start with a correct diagnosis of the underlying causes of the upward trend in healthcare expenditures.

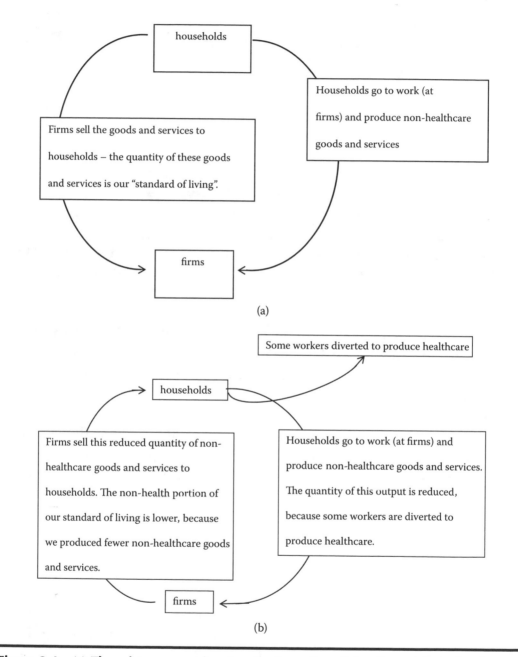

Figure 2.4   (a) The microeconomics circular flow: the minimalist version. (b) The microeconomics circular flow: impact of expanding healthcare sector.

Diagnosing the Problem: What Is Fueling the Cost Increases?

Numerous factors contribute to healthcare cost increases. Public discussion of this issue has included:

- Aging of the population (older folks use healthcare more than younger folks)
- Lifestyle factors (obesity, smoking, sedentary lifestyle)
- Medical malpractice claims (which represent as a cost of doing business)
- Profits (insurance company, pharmaceutical companies, healthcare providers)
- Healthcare billing fraud
- Advances in technology (better medicine, such as hip replacements and improved cancer treatments)

Detailed multivariate econometric analyses conclude that the primary cause of the long-term trend of increasing healthcare costs has been technological advancements. By "technological advancements" we do not simply mean devices, or software like Electronic Medical Records (EHR) systems or cardiac shunts—however, these are also certainly included in the definition. We also mean "softer" medical advances, like drug therapies for cancer, hospice care, new pain medications, or intensive therapeutic treatments for autism. Basically, any healthcare advance is technology. The second most important contributing factor is the aging of the population. Older folks use more medical resources than younger folks, and generally the more we prolong life—from people living into their 50s, 60s, 70s, and beyond—the more costly it is, as these later years are usually associated with high medical costs. Other issues, such as malpractice claims or pharmaceutical company profits, may contribute to the high level of healthcare costs, but they cannot explain the long-term upward trend (because they have not been increasing at a rate that could explain the rapid *increase* in healthcare expenditures); thus, we will focus our discussion on technology in healthcare.

Technology

Okunade and Murthy (2002) provided a big-picture overview of the impact of new technology on our healthcare system, as illustrated in Figure 2.5.

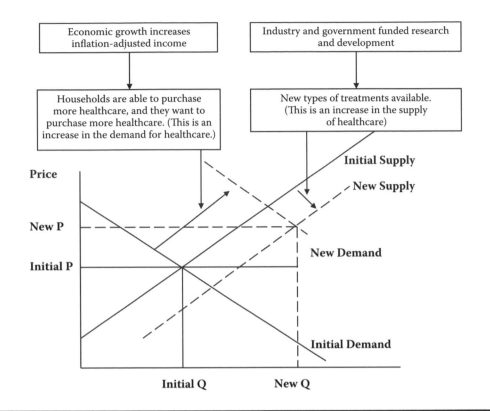

Figure 2.5 Increased healthcare expenditures reflect increases in both average production cost and demand.

There is no sinister plot here. Instead, it is reasonable to say that all of the characters in this story are "good guys": private and government entities funded successful research and development (R&D) that increased the supply of effective—and usually expensive—treatments. No one wants to return to less advanced healthcare—we can more effectively treat many illnesses than we could, say, 40 years ago—but all this comes at a cost. Remember, economists love to say "there is no free lunch." During the same years, U.S. economic growth provided increased per capita income, and this increase in income spurred increased demand for the new treatments. The simultaneous increase in the average cost of producing new treatments, along with the increase in demand for these treatments, generated increases in both the price and the quantity of healthcare services.

We will examine evidence below, to assess whether the new treatments have generated value for patients.

While Okunade and Murthy (2002) concluded that healthcare cost increases are driven by increases in both supply (due to increased technology) and demand (due to increased income and population aging), policy discussions focus on the role of technology. Federal policy can influence R&D spending through changes in tax policy, patent policy, and government grants. Government policy initiatives to influence the demand-side variables (per capita income and population aging) are less feasible (and less desirable).

You may be thinking: "The information you are presenting doesn't sound like the information we see on the news. Are you sure this is correct?" This is a good question. Politicians and journalists may have difficulty compressing discussion of complex issues into appealing mass media sound bites. (Notice: Our discussion occupies dozens of pages!) The information presented here summarizes the results of careful studies published in government documents and economics journals. While the news is not cheerful, we ignore it at our peril. After all, the force of gravity impacts us, whether we agree with gravity or not, or whether the press includes this in its coverage of the news. Wise people hire engineers to design bridges that will withstand this force instead of trying to ignore it. Former Soviet Premier Nikita Krushchev famously summarized our predicament: "Economics is a subject that does not greatly respect one's wishes" (Khrushchev, 2011).

International experience offers an opportunity to check our conclusion that technological progress is the primary force that is generating the steady increase in healthcare expenditures. The technological advances are available worldwide. Therefore, if technology is the primary cause of increases in U.S. healthcare expenditures, then we should logically expect to see a similar rate of increase in European countries, even though European countries have different levels of healthcare expenditures per capita. The Kaiser Family Foundation notes that more recent data indicates that the U.S. growth rate was high relative to the growth rate in other industrialized countries, but these countries face the same fiscal dilemma that challenges the U.S.: "Health spending is rising faster than incomes in most developed countries, which raises questions about how countries will pay for their future health care needs." (Kaiser Family Foundation. Snapshots: Health Care Spending in the United States & Selected OECD Countries, Apr 12, 2011. http://kff.org/health-costs/issue-brief/snapshots-health-care-spending-in-the-united-states-selected-oecd-countries/)

Other nations are also developing strategies to address the resulting financial pressures. Great Britain announced major reforms in 2010 (Timmins, 2010). Under the new system, general practitioners will control most of the healthcare budget, and they will be responsible for purchasing healthcare (including hospital care) for their patients. This reform has sparked concern that the general practitioners will become the agents who must ration limited dollars among patients. Some European countries are trimming the range of services covered under the public health insurance plans, and increasing the role of privately purchased supplemental insurance (Gechert, 2009).

Because Technological Advancement Is the Root Cause of the Unsustainable Cost Increases, Maybe We Should Reduce Our Investment in Research

The conclusion that technology is the major driving force behind healthcare cost increases has an important implication: regulatory solutions that target profits or prices will not work. Instead, solution strategies must be designed to reduce the quantity of healthcare (rationing), reduce the average cost of delivering some types of healthcare (increase efficiency), or reduce the rate of production of new technology. We will consider the first two strategies in Chapter 3, on healthcare quality. We will focus here on the question of whether we should reduce spending on research and development (R&D). The federal government has policy levers to accomplish this:

- The federal government could reduce government funding for healthcare research.
- The federal government could modify tax and patent policies to make industry-funded research investments less attractive.

The federal government provides substantial funding for healthcare research: industry provided 57% of biomedical research funding, and the federal National Institutes of Health (NIH) provided 28% of this funding. However, the federal commitment to biomedical research declined slightly in recent years. Inflation-adjusted funding doubled between 1994 and 2003, which is an annual rate of increase of 7.8% per year. Since 2003, however, inflation-adjusted funding provided by NIH decreased 2.2% per year after

2003. The U.S. commitment to biomedical research has global implications, because U.S. spending accounted for 70 to 80% of total global biomedical research funding in 2003. In this year, the United States spent 5.6% of its total health expenditures on biomedical research (Dorsey et al., 2010). Recent evidence indicates that research spending is increasing in other countries, such as China and India.

Before we can assess the solution option "reduce R&D to slow the rate of healthcare technological advancement," we consider the evidence regarding two critical questions:

- Do the new treatments improve health?
- Are the new treatments a good investment as measured by cost per life saved (or cost per life-year saved)?

Do the New Treatments Produce Good Value for the Dollar?

New treatments, such as the vaccine Provenge™, developed to treat meta-static castration-resistant prostate cancer, are highlighting the importance of this issue. This treatment costs an estimated $50,000–100,000 per patient, and it increases survival for 4–4.5 months (Landau, 2010).

Three types of studies provide the starting point for our examination of the question: Do the new technologies produce good value for the dollar?

1. Nordhaus (2003) noted that Americans benefited from both increased life expectancy and increased consumption of (non-healthcare) goods during the twentieth century, as detailed in Table 2.2. Life expectancy of white males increased from 50 to 77 years (an astonishing 60% increase), while our annual consumption of non-healthcare goods quin-tupled from $4,000 per person to $20,000 per person.

   Nordhaus (2003) conducted an informal poll and posed the question of whether each respondent would prefer:
   - Option A: 1948 health conditions and 1998 nonhealth living standards
   - Option B: 1998 health conditions and 1948 nonhealth living standards
   The respondents to this survey were evenly split. Nordhaus concluded that Americans value the innovations in healthcare as much as we value

Table 2.2   1900–2000: Increased Life Expectancy[a] and Increased Standard of Living

	1900	2000
Life expectancy (white males)	50	77
Standard of living, measured in constant dollars (consumption of goods other than healthcare)	$4,000	$20,000

Source: Jones, *Federal Reserve Bank San Francisco Economic Letter: More Life vs. More Goods, Explaining Rising Health Expenditures*, San Francisco Federal Reserve Bank, 2005.

[a] Life expectancy varies by race and gender. We report only for white males to simplify the comparison of the change in life expectancy to the change in standard of living.

Table 2.3   More Years of Life vs. Higher Standard of Living: Nordhaus's Survey

	1948	1998
Option A		
Healthcare	Year 1948 healthcare	
Non-health consumption		Year 1998 non-health consumption
Option B		
Healthcare		Year 1998 healthcare
Non-health consumption	Year 1948 non-health consumption	

the increase in non-healthcare goods and services that we have enjoyed since 1948. (see Table 2.3).

2. Cutler and McClellan (2001) examined the increase in healthcare expenditures and the increase in life expectancy that occurred between 1950 and 1990:

   ■ The present value of expected lifetime healthcare expenditures increased by $35,000 per person, and life expectancy increased by 7 years.

   ■ On average, we paid $5,000 per extra life-year. Relative to other ways we can spend money to increase life expectancy, this has been a bargain.

3. Similarly, Hall and Jones (2007) estimated that the marginal cost of saving a life (via healthcare) was $1.9 million in the year 2000. Federal agencies routinely implement policies that spend substantially greater amounts per life saved. In fact, these analyses indicate that as a life-saving strategy, healthcare is a bargain, which suggests, surprisingly, that healthcare expenditures might actually be *too low*.

4. Three studies indicate that some of the new treatments offer significant improvements over older treatments:

   ■ Cutler and McClellan (2001) focused on the cost and life-saving impact of one specific treatment. They note that the average cost of treating a heart attack increased in inflation-adjusted dollars from $12,100 in 1984 to $21,700 in 1998, and the life expectancy of heart attack victims increased from 4 years 11 months to 6 years during that time period. Essentially, the $10,000 cost increase purchased an extra expected year of life for the average patient. The studies mentioned above indicate that this was money well spent.

   ■ A study of claims data for a large sample of Medicare patients concluded that patients who used newer generations of drugs lived longer than patients who used older generations of drugs (Lichtenberg, 2003).

   ■ Lichtenberg (2009) concluded that life expectancy increased faster in states with more rapid increases in the proportions of diagnostic imaging and prescription drugs that were newer, and the proportion of physicians who graduated from more highly ranked medical schools.

Can We Assess Whether $1.9 Million Is Too Much (or Too Little) to Spend in Order to Save a Life?

Several federal agencies face analogous decisions: How much should we spend to save lives by increasing highway safety or drinking water quality? These agencies have developed strategies for answering these questions, and we are beginning to see increased use of these strategies for analyzing healthcare issues. Studies of routine decisions that involve trade-offs of money vs. risk indicate that people, on average, would be willing to pay $100,000 for an extra statistical life-year, or give up a statistical life-year if they could receive $100,000. Restating the same results in terms of lives saved, these studies indicate that individuals are willing to trade—in the aggregate—$7.4 million for one statistical life saved.

Before we consider situations in which these results are used by agencies in the United States (e.g., the U.S. Department of Transportation and the U.S. Environmental Protection Agency (EPA)) and in other countries, it is important to be clear about the term *statistical life-year* or *statistical life saved*. No one is suggesting that people offer to be killed 1 year early in exchange for money. Instead, analysts observe that people make numerous decisions to save money by accepting a slight increase in risk, or to spend a little more money in order to reduce risk. For example, we save money by accepting risk when we take a more risky job (because the pay is better), buy a small car (which increases our risk of dying in an accident), or decide to drive an extra year on those somewhat worn tires. When we make these decisions, we don't seriously believe that we are shortening our lives. Instead, we are accepting risk. We understand that out of every 100,000 people who make similar decisions, a small number will have an accident, but we don't know the identity of the future accident victims, and we don't believe that we will necessarily be those victims ourselves. We understand that there is a statistical risk, a statistical life-year lost, or a statistical life lost, but the identity of the victim is not known.

Federal regulatory agencies, such as the U.S. Environmental Protection Agency and the U.S. Department of Transportation, make numerous regulatory decisions that involve trade-offs between dollars and lives. Are these dollars best spent to:

- Install a stoplight to make an intersection safer?
- Require side airbags in cars?
- Tighten the limit for permissible exposure to a chemical?
- Require infants to have a seat on an airplane (instead of allowing them to ride on their parents' laps)?

These decisions generate substantial controversy. For a discussion of the last example, see Box 2.1.

These agencies make decisions that affect all of us. To estimate what we would decide in the aggregate, they look at thousands of decisions made by individuals. (Examples of individual decisions that require this trade-off are listed in Box 2.2. Studies cited by the EPA examine decisions to accept the risk of driving a small car (because the small car is cheaper) or working at a more dangerous job (to obtain the hazard pay differential).) Based

BOX 2.1 SHOULD PARENTS BE REQUIRED TO BUY AIRPLANE TICKETS FOR INFANTS AND TODDLERS?

The Federal Aviation Administration considered mandating that each airline passenger be restrained in a separate seat, including children under the age of two, who are currently permitted to fly on their parents' laps. Newman et al. (2003) analyzed the likely impacts of this policy. They concluded that requiring young children to sit in seats with appropriate restraints would prevent 0.4 deaths (from air crashes) per year. However, mandating that parents purchase tickets for young children would make air travel more costly, and some parents may choose to drive, rather than fly. The probability of death per mile of auto travel is higher than the probability of death per mile from air travel; hence, this substitution could lead to a *higher* rate of travel-related deaths for young children. The analysts also considered a scenario in which parents do not switch from air travel to car travel. In this case, the cost per death prevented was estimated to be $6.4 million.

BOX 2.2 DO YOU MAKE DECISIONS TO TRADE DOLLARS FOR RISK?

■ Did you drive to work (or school) today in a Hummer? If not, why not? Have you compared the death rate (per million miles driven) in your car to that in a high-curb-weight Hummer?
■ Did you ever hold your toddler on your lap on an airplane, instead of buying a ticket for your child?
■ Or maybe you have accepted risk in exchange for nonmonetary values:
  – Hang glide? Ride motorcycles? Ride a bicycle without a helmet— just to feel the wind blowing through your hair? Played racquetball without goggles?
■ Do you have a fire extinguisher in your car—within reach from the driver's seat?
■ When was the last time you checked your home fire extinguisher? Smoke alarm batteries? Have you tested for radon? Carbon monoxide?

on these analyses, the EPA website states that measures should be adopted if a statistical life can be saved for less than $7.4 million (in 2006 dollars), or a statistical life-year can be saved for less than $360,000 (National Center for Environmental Economics 2013). If you are thinking that this statement sounds overly precise, you are right. The criteria establish a reasonable rough order of magnitude, rather than a precise dollar cutoff. If we are considering a policy that will reduce risk for $8 million per life saved, we will not feel comfortable opposing the policy simply because the cost per life saved is slightly above the cutoff level. Indeed, we might advocate further study before making the decision. However, we will feel comfortable supporting a policy that increases safety at $50,000 per life saved or opposing a policy that will require $400 million per life saved.

You may still be thinking that this type of cost-risk trade-off should not be applied to healthcare decisions. If so, you have identified an important issue: the trade-offs cannot be avoided completely, but there is controversy about the appropriate strategy for addressing this issue. We will examine the implications of this issue for development of treatment guidelines in Chapter 3.

Solution Options: How Can We Make the System More Sustainable?

From the big-picture perspective, there are only three types of solution options:

1. We could continue to spend more on healthcare every year, and accommodate this by spending less on other goods.
2. We could take steps to restrain the quantities of healthcare services that are utilized annually in the United States.
3. We could implement measures to increase the *efficiency* of our healthcare system (so we could use more cost-effective strategies to produce healthcare services).

Each of these strategies poses costs and benefits. None can be implemented easily, cheaply, or painlessly. The third strategy, to develop a more efficient healthcare system, clearly makes the most sense—and we will focus on this strategy in Section II. However, we will see that this will require substantial adjustments by healthcare providers and healthcare consumers. At this point, we will consider the pros and cons of each of the three strategic options.

Option 1: We Could Continue to Spend More on Healthcare Every Year, and Accommodate This by Spending Less on Other Goods

While this sounds grim, it might be a wise reallocation of spending, to reduce spending on nonessentials such as entertainment (or more housing square footage than our grandparents enjoyed) in order to increase spending on healthcare. This is the classic "guns or butter" trade-off economists talk about. Given the improved quality of healthcare (compared with the options available to our grandparents when they were our age), this might be a wise choice. However, it will be a painful choice, for often "we want it all"—we want to ignore the sad fact of scarcity. However, if we cannot pay for current healthcare, and if we, as a nation, borrow money to pay for our current expenditures (our current national debt is $15.6 trillion, and is increasing by about $4 billion per day), we are simply "living large" and asking our children and grandchildren to pay the bill for our lifestyle. Many consider this irresponsible and even unethical.

Option 2: We Could Restrain the Quantities of Healthcare Services That Are Utilized Annually in the United States

The generic term for efforts to restrain the quantity utilized is *rationing*. Three basic strategies have been discussed:

■ We could ration by price.
■ We could ration by wait time.
■ We could set priorities—by either (1) creating and enforcing treatment guidelines or (2) asking healthcare professionals to adopt a population health perspective and allocate scarce resources to patients.

Let's consider each strategy.

We Could Ration by Price

Yachts and luxury vehicles are rationed by price—and consequently most of us do not purchase these items. Their high price is an effective rationing mechanism. While we accept price rationing for most goods, this approach is often viewed as unacceptable for healthcare. However, when we don't have universal health insurance coverage for *all* types of healthcare (e.g., all the physical therapy visits that produce value for the patient), we are implicitly rationing by price. Rationing by price means that people who are not willing or able to pay the price are not able to purchase the good. If some types of healthcare increase life expectancy, price rationing would imply that life expectancy would be correlated with income: people with more income and assets would be able to purchase greater life expectancy, while low-income people would have shorter life expectancy. (While this correlation is clear when one examines rich vs. poor nations, this correlation generates more controversy and concern when it is examined *within* one country).

While most people do not support the idea of rationing healthcare by price, we should remember two things:

1. Health status and life expectancy are correlated with income in the United States: Singh and Siahpush (2006) found an additional 2.8 years of life for those people in the most affluent group compared to those categorized into the most deprived group in 1980–1982. By 1998–2000, that number increased to 4.5 years of additional life. However, Murray et al. (2006) show that the connection between socioeconomic status (SES) and health is not straightforward—there are clearly additional factors at work.
2. In addition, it is important to remember that we allow rationing by price on a number of other products and services that contribute to health, such as food, housing, and education.

We Could Ration by Wait Time

Concert and sports tickets are frequently rationed by wait time: individuals who are willing to wait in long lines, perhaps camping overnight, are able to purchase tickets, while others do not get tickets. We hear that Canadian patients may wait weeks or months for some procedures—and that some Canadians seek care in the United States to avoid this wait time—but the idea of adopting this mechanism as a cost-control strategy has not been seriously considered in the United States (O'Neill and O'Neill, 2007; Gravalle and Siciliani, 2009).

We Could Ration by Setting Priorities

Defining a basic benefit package that should be available to everyone sounds like a commonsense solution to the cost problem. Oregon implemented this strategy for its Medicaid program, to determine which services would be covered and which services would not. The state prioritized treatments and provided Medicaid coverage for high-priority treatments (and denied coverage for low-priority treatments). While this sounds straightforward, the system encountered legal and political challenges. This strategy is politically difficult because it implies a two-tier system. Given the fact that the new technology saves lives, a system that provides basic care to everyone (while denying high-tech care to all Medicaid enrollees) will not solve the fairness and access issue. If high-tech care is not available to everyone, then we can still expect that people with higher ability to pay for healthcare will have longer life expectancy (Tengs, 1996).

Managed care in the 1990s did slow the rate of cost increases, in part by denying coverage for low-priority treatments. However, these coverage limitations created a backlash that resulted in legislation that tempered cost-containment efforts.

Option 3: We Could Make Our Healthcare System More Efficient

At this point, many people would like to choose "none of the above." The only way to avoid the options listed above is to increase system efficiency. Increased efficiency would deploy resources more effectively, permitting us to increase access and contain cost—and this effort plays a central role in current federal policy. Of course, the impact on quality will depend on our definition of *quality*, and on the strategies used to increase efficiency. We will examine strategies for achieving this goal in the second half of this book. Quality issues form an important backdrop to the discussion surrounding efficiency: some hope that we can increase both quality and efficiency, while others fear that these two goals are not congruent.

Conclusion: Given the Challenges Posed by Strategies to Ration or Prioritize, We Should Pay Serious Attention to Strategies for Increasing the Efficiency of Our Healthcare System

Our current healthcare system is not financially sustainable. It is becoming increasingly clear that we will have to face the grim fiscal implications of the prediction that healthcare may account for 30% of GDP by 2050. The federal government funds a significant share of healthcare in the United States. We face a limited set of options. From a fiscal perspective, we must either:

- Slow the rate of healthcare cost increases by adopting policies to reduce R&D spending
- Recognize that the healthcare system will continue to offer increasingly expensive (and sometimes effective) treatments—and develop a coping strategy such as:
  - Develop strategies to restrict, or ration, access to care.
  - Allow the federal government budget to increase (higher taxes or more borrowing, or both) substantially (as a proportion of GDP).
- Dramatically increase the efficiency of the healthcare system. (While strategies to increase efficiency generate some controversy, this is probably the strategy with the least negative implications—if we can increase efficiency without reducing quality.)

At this point, we should note that public policy discussions include numerous other suggestions for solving the healthcare cost problem, such as:

- Implement measures to reduce profits earned by pharmaceutical companies.
- Import cheaper prescription drugs from abroad.
- Provide basic care for everyone, and require out-of-pocket payment for higher levels of care.
- Adopt a system similar to Canada, Great Britain, Switzerland, Singapore, and Germany.

None of these strategies have sufficient power to solve the healthcare cost problem because this problem is generated by two fundamental forces that would not be ameliorated by these strategies: technological innovation (i.e., increased supply) and expansion of the retired population (i.e., increased demand for services covered by Medicare). In addition, each of these strategies has limitations. Consider, for example, two tactics that have been suggested to reduce prescription drug prices.

Two of the Numerous Suggestions That Sound Good, but Have Limited Potential for Solving the Problem

Modify Tax or Patent Policies to Reduce Pharmaceutical Profits

Pharmaceutical profits are not above average compared to similar businesses, given the level of risk and expense required to develop new products.

Therefore, tax or patent policies designed to reduce profits below this level would probably lead to reductions in future research and development (R&D). The evidence indicating that we have benefited from recent R&D raises questions about the wisdom of reducing incentives for future R&D. Reducing pharmaceutical company profits would also reduce their incentive to invest in R&D. Do we really want (as an unintended consequence) to have less R&D and fewer and smaller companies (or no companies) producing new medications?

Facilitate Importation of Prescription Drugs from Lower-Price Non-U.S. Sources

Prescription drug prices are higher in the United States, Europe, and elsewhere due to a sophisticated price discrimination system. How can a poor person in Africa buy AIDS drugs? A price discrimination system charges lower prices to people with less ability/willingness to pay—it is the ultimate sliding scale. People in a low-income country can pay prices that just cover production costs only if people in higher-income countries pay prices that are high enough to cover production cost plus the up-front cost of R&D. This is essentially a subsidy for the poor paid for by the rich. For this system to work, it cannot permit buyers in the high-price countries to import from the low-price countries. You might be wondering: How does this explain the lower prices in Canada and Europe? GDP per capita is higher in the United States than in Canada and Europe, but the difference is probably not sufficient to explain the price differences. The United States has been discussing this issue with EU countries, asking them to pay a greater share of R&D costs.

General Conclusions

We conclude that there are no easy shortcut solutions, and the options of rationing care, allowing healthcare costs to continue to grow (as a share of GDP), or reducing R&D raise serious concerns. Our remaining option is to focus on strategies to increase efficiency—without sacrificing quality by redesigning healthcare. Many people believe that this is possible. In fact, these people believe that our current level of quality is too low (a classic source for this is the Institute of Medicine's *Crossing the Quality Chasm*), and they recommend strategies to increase both efficiency and quality.

In Chapter 3, we explore the third source of pressure for change: concerns about inadequate quality of care. That will be our concluding chapter on the discussion of pressures for change. In the second half of the book, we will explore the public- and private-sector innovations that are designed to increase efficiency, access, and quality.

Chapter 3

Quality

Introduction

The Institute of Medicine's classic study *To Err Is Human: Building a Safer Health System* (Kohn et al., 2000) set off a chain reaction across the U.S. healthcare system (this study is available free on the web; we recommend that you at least scan it). The study concluded that avoidable medical errors occurring in U.S. hospitals cause 44,000–98,000 deaths annually. The follow-up report 10 years later, *To Err Is Human—To Delay Is Deadly* (Jewell and McGiffert, 2009), found little had changed in improving patient safety, and that preventable medical errors were still causing significant numbers of deaths each year. The report concluded that systemic change would be necessary to improve a healthcare system that is plagued with quality issues, while we spend more on healthcare per capita than any other industrialized nation (Committee on Quality of Health Care in America and Institute of Medicine, 2001).

Americans might tolerate rampant healthcare cost escalation if they believed that these dollars were deployed efficiently and effectively, but news stories document healthcare quality issues as frequently as they document access and cost issues. Stories of surgeries gone wrong, diagnostic test results not reaching the patient or provider, providers ordering unneeded tests because they are worried about litigation, and medication errors are recurring themes. Additionally, too little treatment is evidence based. This leads to high variability in care and inconsistent quality. Finally, comparisons with other industrialized nations seem to indicate these other nations have better health outcomes while spending less on healthcare.

If we are not getting value for our dollars, the critical question is: Why not? Some argue that the fundamental problem is that our system is built on the diagnosis and treatment model rather than prevention. Public health and healthcare professionals argue that chronic diseases are the most costly, yet the most preventable. "Despite the evidence that prevention works, the focus in our health care system over the past century has not been on prevention of chronic disease, but on treatment of short-term, acute health problems. As a nation, we have emphasized expensive cures for disease rather than cost effective prevention" (Centers for Disease Control and Prevention, 2003, p. 7).

Nearly half of Americans have one or more chronic conditions, and these conditions are the leading cause of illness, disability, and death in the United States and account for the majority of the healthcare expenditures (Hoffman et al., 1996).

Untreated mental health problems. Depression is often missed, and other disorders, such as attention deficit disorder and bipolar disorder, are overdiagnosed. Too often behavioral health interventions are not evidenced based (Fisher and O'Donohue, 2006).

Economists describe the same issue from a slightly different perspective. Individuals and societies can use a diverse array of tools or inputs to produce health. Healthcare is one set of tools; other inputs that contribute to health include public health measures such as sanitation and vaccination, environmental protection, and individual behaviors, such as healthy eating and exercise. Some inputs that produce health are clearly outside our traditional notion of the healthcare system, including traffic safety, education, and anti-gang violence programs. This diversity of factors that influence health makes it difficult to define and assess the quality of our healthcare system.

In this chapter, we will explore the evidence that the U.S. healthcare system does not provide quality care and examine the solutions that have been implemented to address these issues, as well as some of the controversies these solutions have created.

Background Information: Three Types of Evidence Indicate That Quality Is Not Consistently High

Three types of evidence indicate that quality is not consistently high:

- International comparisons indicate that other countries are doing more with less.
- Published studies document the occurrence of preventable medical errors.
- The Dartmouth Atlas documents significant variations in treatment patterns across geographic areas.

We will examine each type of evidence.

International Comparisons Indicate That Other Countries Are Doing More with Less

The United States has the highest healthcare cost per capita, while countries with lower expenditure levels have better infant mortality statistics and longer life expectancies. On the surface, this evidence seems to point to a clear conclusion: our healthcare system is not delivering value for the dollar. Infant mortality and life expectancy are "summary statistics" in the sense that these statistics provide a quick, high-level overview of population health; therefore, the low U.S. performance on these measures could signal fundamental problems. We will focus here on a study that compared U.S. and Canadian data, conducted by the U.S. National Center for Health Statistics and Statistics Canada (O'Neill and O'Neill, 2007). Garber and Skinner (2008) place the issues in a larger context, in their interesting comparison of the United States with Canada, France, Germany, Japan, and the United Kingdom.

The O'Neill and O'Neill (2007) comparison of U.S. and Canadian data indicated that comparisons of these types of summary statistics should be viewed with caution—for two reasons. First, healthcare is only one factor that influences population health. The authors of this study present cancer incidence and mortality data that highlight three key points:

1. The cancer-related mortality rate is higher in the United States than in Canada.
    - In the United States, 163 women died from cancer each year (for every 100,000 women), but the comparable number in Canada is only 149.
    - The situation is similar for males. For every 100,000 males, 239 die from cancer each year in the United States, but only 220 die from cancer in Canada.

This seems to raise questions about the quality of the U.S. healthcare system.

2. The probability of getting cancer is higher in the United States than in Canada.

   ■ For every 100,000 women 415 are diagnosed with cancer each year in the United States, compared with 350 in Canada.

   ■ For every 100,000 men 562 are diagnosed with cancer each year in the United States, compared with 464 in Canada.

   The authors of the study point to another difference between the two countries as a possible explanation: the obesity rate is higher in the United States than in Canada. If the obesity rate is indeed the primary explanation for the higher U.S. cancer-related mortality rate, then we should reconsider our interpretation of the two countries' mortality rates. Instead of providing a measure of the quality of the two health systems, the comparison of the cancer-related mortality rates may be signaling the importance of lifestyle issues that lie outside the healthcare system.

3. The probability of surviving a diagnosis of cancer is higher if you receive the more aggressive U.S.-style treatment.

   ■ For women, the U.S. mortality per case is 0.39, while the Canadian mortality rate is higher: 0.42.

   ■ For men, the U.S. mortality rate is 0.42, while the Canadian mortality rate is higher: 0.47.

The authors of the study conclude that you are more likely to contract cancer if you live in the United States, but the relatively aggressive treatment provided in the United States offers a higher probability of survival.

Thus, while life expectancy is an important measure of population health, we must be cautious about using life expectancy as a measure of healthcare quality. Healthcare is only one of a large set of factors that influence health, and these factors can vary systematically across populations and nations. Violence causes more deaths in the United States than in Canada. Data from the Centers for Disease Control shows homicide accounted for 3.3% of deaths in the United States in 2008. Another study (Lemaire, 2005) exploring the impact of firearms on life expectancy found that the U.S. firearm homicide rate is 5.5 times higher than the country with the next highest rate, Italy. Homicide and suicide rates due to firearms account for a loss of 103.6 days of life for the average American. This is a social factor that is clearly outside the scope of the healthcare system, yet it influences the summary statistic of life expectancy. For example, life expectancy of males between the ages of 20 and 24 in the United States is much lower than that of males in Canada, and the gap is largely due to differences in the accident and homicide rates. The study authors conclude: "Although the overall mortality rate is higher in the U.S. at all age groups, the importance of non-disease related factors (accidents and homicides) is much greater in the U.S." (O'Neill and O'Neill, 2007).

Second, international comparisons of summary statistics, such as infant mortality, can be impacted by differences in treatment options available to residents of the two countries and differences in the definitions that are used to create the data. Infant mortality is an important issue in the United States. Racial disparities, teen pregnancy, and gaps in prenatal care access and utilization pose troubling issues. Nonetheless, the O'Neill and O'Neill (2007) comparison of U.S. and Canadian data raises two important points about international comparisons of infant mortality statistics.

The overall infant mortality is higher in the United States *because* the rate of multiple births is higher in the United States. The data indicate that infant mortality rates are *lower* in the United States for single births (compared to Canada). The same comparison holds for multiple births. However, the United States has a higher proportion of multiple births, and the infant mortality rate is higher in both countries for multiple births than for single births.

One contributing factor to the higher rates of multiple births in the United States is greater access to elective fertility treatments among insured individuals. Access to fertility treatments indicates greater wealth and is certainly important to those would-be parents who value having children. However, treatments that stimulate ovaries to produce eggs and treatments that involve the implantation of embryos increase the likelihood of multiple births, which are associated with lower birth weight and prematurity. Although premature babies are more likely to survive if born in the United States, prematurity increases the risk for infant death (Kramer et al., 2005).

In addition, definitions for infant mortality rely on the reporting country's measure of live birth. Many European countries and Japan record a live birth only if the baby takes a breath upon delivery or is at a certain gestational age or weight. This definition differs significantly from the definition used by the World Health Organization and by the United States. International differences in definitions of live birth make it difficult to compare infant mortality rates (defined as deaths per live birth) across nations (Grady, 2009).

What Can We Conclude about This Evidence?

All of this does not prove that the U.S. system is efficiently and effectively producing high-quality care. Instead, it demonstrates that international comparisons must be approached with caution. And they do not, by themselves, provide the evidence needed to diagnose and solve our problems. More detailed work is needed to understand the issues. However, examination of the international evidence does raise an important question: How do we define the boundaries and responsibilities of the healthcare system? Is the healthcare system anything that produces health (anti-gang violence programs, produce selection, and prices in grocery stores)? Or, should we define healthcare to be steps to produce health that are implemented by a well-defined set of healthcare providers? What about cosmetic plastic surgery? This activity is implemented by those providers, but is it healthcare? Do we consider fertility treatment for the first child healthcare? What about the third child? Are elementary school smoking prevention programs examples of healthcare or education? What about redesigning bridges to reduce highway deaths? Where should we draw these lines?

Diagnosing the Root Cause of the Quality Problem

Two major efforts to document, analyze, and diagnose quality problems point to a clear diagnosis: the root cause of our quality problem is our failure to implement systematic procedures. Let's take a closer look at this evidence.

Evidence Documents the Occurrence of Preventable Medical Errors

The Institute of Medicine report on quality and medical errors (Kohn et al., 2000) (see Box 3.1) provides the second type of evidence that the U.S. healthcare system needs improvement. This report documents the magnitude of the problem, estimates the numbers of resulting deaths, and analyzes the underlying causes. It also presents a clear diagnosis: medical errors do not simply result from greed, laziness, incompetence, or gaps in medical science. This is good news, because it is difficult to solve problems that require eliminating greed and laziness. Instead, this report points to a clear solution strategy: the report argues that a substantial portion of medical errors could

BOX 3.1   INSTITUTE OF MEDICINE'S QUALITY INITIATIVES

Phase 1 of the Institute of Medicine's (IOM) quality initiative produced the report, "America's Health in Transition: Protecting and Improving Quality." This report emphasized that quality must be monitored and improved. Phase II produced two widely publicized reports: "To Err is Human: Building a Safer Health System" and "Crossing the Quality Chasm: A New Health System for the 21st Century." These reports highlighted the importance of quality issues, and generated widespread public discussions of the failures of the current healthcare system. Phase III of this initiative encompasses efforts to operationalize the recommendations made in these reports - to increase safety and quality while also being effective, equitable, timely, efficient and patient-centered. A summary of the key priorities from these reports can be found on the website: http://www.acmq.org/education/iomsummary.pdf

be prevented by developing stronger systems for implementing and monitoring systematic care processes.

The IOM report argues that medical errors arise when:

■ Pharmacists misread handwritten prescriptions
■ Test results are lost or misdirected
■ Critical information is not shared accurately among members of the healthcare team
■ Patients are not given proper treatment, as defined by evidence-based protocols

Electronic information systems, decision support tools, and other strategies for building systematic processes can be designed to mitigate these problems. Toyota focused on systematic processes to minimize automobile manufacturing defects (Lean manufacturing), and healthcare organizations have been adapting these methods to strengthen healthcare processes using adaptations of Toyota's process for improvement, called Lean Six Sigma or Six Sigma.

Following the IOM report on medical error and patient safety issues in U.S. hospitals, the Joint Commission on Accreditation of Healthcare Organizations (JCAHO) strengthened requirements for systematic processes to improve the quality of care provided in U.S. hospitals, including:

- Patient identification that included two means to identify patients, such as name and birth date
- Medication safety that included mandates for medication labeling, patient education regarding their medications, and reconciling a patient's medication at the time of admission and discharge with his or her list of prehospitalization medications
- Infection control methods that prevented and identified postoperative infections and prevented central line and urinary catheter infections
- Elimination of surgical mistakes that resulted from misidentification of patient or surgical site

Following this report The Joint Commission (JCAHO) began requiring hospitals to report any event that resulted in "unexpected occurrence involving death or serious physical or psychological injury, or the risk thereof. Serious injury specifically includes loss of limb or function" (The Joint Commission, 2002). These events have been termed "sentinel" as they require immediate investigation and action to prevent further events. Sentinel events include things like falls, infant abductions, surgery performed on the wrong site, inpatient suicides and other severe events. Additionally, the JCAHO published National Patient Safety Goals that focused on eliminating known causes of medical errors such as incorrectly identifying patients, poor communication between care providers, and double-checks for high risk medications prior to administration.

Evidence Documents Variations in Regional Treatment Patterns

Beginning in 1973, a group of researchers has been documenting a startling fact: the composition of healthcare varies dramatically across U.S. cities, states, and regions. Medicare patients in high-spending regions are receiving more diagnostic tests and are being diagnosed with more diseases. According to Song et al. (2010), the typical patient in a high-spending region is "in fact, less sick than average" (p. 1). The likelihood of having hip, shoulder, or knee replacement surgery varies by a factor of 10, depending on where a Medicare patient resides (Fisher and Bell, 2010). The variation is notable even within states; for example, hip replacement surgery rates ranged from 2.7 per 1,000 in Los Angeles, California, to 6.7 in San Luis Obispo, California (during 2005–2006). In addition to these diagnosis and treatment variations, healthcare spending differs markedly across the United States. Per capita spending ranged from $4,000 in Utah to nearly

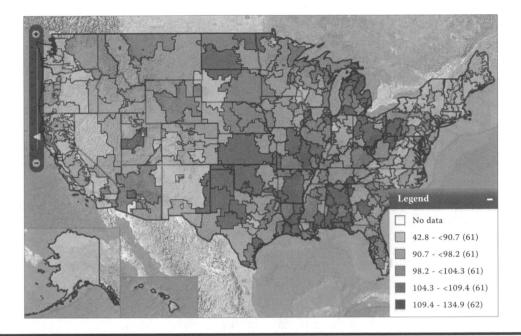

Figure 3.1   Variation in surgery rates. Courtesy of the Dartmouth Institute for Health Policy and Clinical Practice. All surgical discharges per 1,000 Medicare enrollees by race. In The Dartmouth Atlas of health care. http://www.dartmouthatlas.org/data/map.aspx?ind=60 (accessed June 17, 2012).

$6,700 in Massachusetts in 2004 (Fisher, Wennberg, Stukel, Gottlieb, and Lucase, 2003). A comparison of similar Medicare patients in low-spending and high-spending regions estimates that those living in high-spending areas receive 60% more services, equating to nearly 29% more healthcare spending (Fisher et al., 2003). For example, Figure 3.1, reproduced from the Dartmouth Atlas website, illustrates the variation in surgery rates across the United States.

Multivariate statistical analysis indicates that these variations are not explained by observable differences in demographic or health system variables; hence, the Dartmouth Atlas evidence raises fundamental questions:

What Is Influencing Physician Decisions?

Researchers at RAND reviewed 50 published studies of specific types of care, and concluded that patients, on average, only receive half of the recommended and appropriate care. (Think what this would do to total healthcare expenditures if this problem were corrected. Providing additional care would, by itself, push healthcare costs up, but providing more appropriate care could generate net savings.) This gap between scientific evidence and actual practice probably leads to over 19,600 additional deaths each year when we just look at two preventive diseases, pneumonia and colorectal cancer. There is great variability in the quality of care provided irrespective of whether the care is preventative, acute, or for chronic conditions. These authors concluded that we should define, measure, and monitor quality of healthcare in the same ways that we measure the quality of products, and these measures should be made publically available, and on a national level (McGlynn et al., 2003).

Doyle et al. (2008) offer a different perspective. These analysts analyzed outcomes for 30,000 patients who were randomly assigned to clinical teams. Patients treated by physicians at the higher-ranked institution spent fewer days in the hospital and incurred lower costs than patients treated at the lower-ranked institution, but the health outcomes were not significantly different. The analysts suggest that the physicians trained at top-ranked institutions had superior ability to apply judgment in clinical situations, but the other physicians substituted more time and diagnostic tests to reach a similar outcome.

Does Higher Utilization Reduce Mortality?

A study conducted by Fisher et al. (2003) found that the risk of death *did not* differ across regions with different healthcare spending. Those patients in the highest-spending quintile received nearly 60% more care than those in the lowest-spending quintile. This higher spending was attributed to more hospitalizations, physician visits, subspecialty visits, diagnostic tests, and minor procedures.

Are the Regional Differences Large Enough to Be Important?

One analysis (Fisher et al., 2009) estimated a cumulative savings of $1.42 trillion by 2023 if annual growth in per capita Medicare spending were reduced from the 3.5% annual average (from 1992 to 2006) to 2.4% (the rate in San Francisco). This is a rough computation, of course, and the details are controversial.

The magnitude of the geographic variation that is not currently explained by differences in population, socioeconomic status, or health characteristics is substantial. This suggests that patterns of care are influenced by a variety of factors that are not related to scientific evidence. This leads to a much broader conceptualization of the problem: improving healthcare system quality requires more than reducing errors related to bad judgment or negligence. To ensure that healthcare decisions are evidence based, it will be necessary to develop more systematic processes of care, and new types of research to ensure that strong evidence is available to support provider decisions.

Solution Options: How Can We Make Our Healthcare System More Systematic?

This set of evidence spurred substantive efforts to utilize Total Quality Management (TQM), clinical pathways, and clinical guidelines to strengthen quality by institutionalizing systematic processes.

Applying Total Quality Management Principles to Healthcare

Dr. Donald Berwick (president and CEO, Institute for Healthcare Improvement, Boston, Massachusetts) and Dr. Brent James (executive director, Intermountain Health Care Institute for Health Care Delivery Research, Salt Lake City, Utah) established research and training programs to develop strategies for applying industry Total Quality Management (TQM) methods to strengthen systematic processes in healthcare. Both argued that investing time and effort to develop and maintain systematic processes would address two critical goals: by reducing medical errors, the processes would increase quality and, at the same time, reduce cost. These processes would reduce medical error in individual cases, and also reduce medical error in the larger sense, as documented by the Dartmouth Atlas. In addition to the effort required to apply TQM principles in specific healthcare settings, this effort would require two additional inputs. A well-developed set of evidence-based guidelines is needed to define the "right" processes, and health information technology (HIT) is essential for managing the information needed to support and monitor care coordination, guideline compliance, and systematic quality reporting. This evidence is creating pressure to develop strategies to ensure that healthcare decisions are evidence based. We will discuss TQM principles and evidence-based guidelines here; we will examine HIT in Section II.

Brief History

TQM principles were initially developed by W. Edwards Deming to improve quality in manufacturing industries. These principles were embraced by Japanese industrial leaders after World War II, and are widely credited with providing the foundation for the high-quality levels achieved by firms such as Toyota. The TQM principles articulate a philosophical approach and a pragmatic strategy for achieving high-quality output by focusing on:

1. Systematic processes designed to minimize random variation and control systematic variation
2. Evidence-based decision making ("In God we trust; all others bring data" [Hastie et al., 2009, p. 3])
3. A customer-focused definition of quality

Doctors Berwick and James have demonstrated the value of applying these ideas in healthcare to develop the systems needed to reduce medical error. Both contributed to the IOM *Crossing the Quality Chasm* report (Committee on Quality of Health Care in America and Institute of Medicine, 2001), along with individuals from industry (Henry Ford Health System, Delta Airlines, General Electric Company). It is also notable that Dr. Berwick headed the Centers for Medicare and Medicaid Services (CMS) from 2010 to 2011.

The quality improvement philosophy focuses on the importance of systematically collecting data on processes, outcomes, and customer viewpoints, and using these data to proactively improve the processes involved in producing the good or service. Deming (1993) emphasized that data should be used to support analysis; it should never be used as a weapon for punishment. (One of his 14 key principles is "drive out fear.") In this view, customer complaints provide useful data that support the analysis needed to identify opportunities for improvement. Data are also used to diagnose the root causes of process variation, to test the success of solutions designed to reduce variation, and to track outcomes.

The pragmatic strategies for achieving TQM goals focus on the importance of a team approach. The problem-solving team is essential, because evidence-based diagnosis of the root causes of process problems requires detailed frontline knowledge of the process. A broad-based team that includes individuals with specific knowledge of every process component is essential to provide this information. Teams are typically trained to use a series of quality tools, which provide specific strategies to help the team build a base of shared knowledge about the process, diagnose critical process issues, analyze sources of process variation, target specific issues for improvement, diagnose problems, and design solutions. Teams are advised to implement a series of steps, summarized by an acronym such as FOCUS[1]:

- **F**ind an opportunity for improvement (i.e., specify the problem to be solved).
- **O**rganize a team that has frontline knowledge of the process components.
- **C**larify existing information to provide a foundation for evidence-based decisions.
- **U**nderstand the sources of variation and the root causes.
- **S**olve the problem.

Notably, the team is not invited to discuss solution options until it has completed the previous steps of collecting and analyzing data to diagnose the source of the problem.

The Joint Commission on Accreditation of Healthcare Organizations (JCAHO) embraced the TQM approach to strengthening healthcare quality in the early 1990s, and produced materials to help organizations implement quality improvement programs based on TQM concepts, such as "The Measurement Mandate: On the Road to Performance Improvement in Health Care" (Joint Commission on Accreditation of Healthcare Organizations, 1993).

Recognizing that the application of manufacturing-based principles to the delivery of healthcare would require careful thought (and new types of thinking by healthcare professionals), advocates of this strategy renamed the set of ideas, using the phrases quality improvement (QI) or continuous quality improvement (CQI). The term *quality improvement* was intended to denote a significant change in strategy from the previous quality assurance programs. JCAHO began inspecting for CQI implementation in the 1995 accreditation process: hospitals were expected to demonstrate (1) implementation of CQI teams and training, and (2) use of quality tools.

While TQM programs can provide clear benefits for specific process improvement applications, they can also support the increased use of systematic evidence-based processes that are essential for strengthening healthcare quality, particularly when combined with health information technology (HIT). Current federal policy is focused on the premise that TQM's emphasis on strengthening processes can radically transform the way we think about doing our jobs and the meaning of being a skilled professional. Well-designed processes supported by HIT can potentially make it possible to systematize care for a large proportion of patients, and it is widely believed that this systematic approach can dramatically reduce medical error. Consider, for example, the treatment of a hip surgery patient that has just entered the hospital. If the physician's job is to manage every detail of this patient's care, then the physician must be alert to ensure that no detail is forgotten. If, instead, the physician logs onto a computer that is programmed with standing orders for "typical hip surgery" patients, then the physician focuses on determining whether this particular patient is typical, or whether this patient requires a customized treatment plan. In this process-oriented setting it is expected that fewer medical errors will occur due to neglected details, and the physician will be able to devote a larger proportion of his or her time to the more difficult cases. To realize these benefits of HIT and TQM, it will be necessary to have clear treatment guidelines for a broad array of diagnoses and conditions.

This of course raises questions about who will develop and update those guidelines and what constitutes scientific evidence. Large entities such as Kaiser, Cleveland Clinic, and others have been active in developing and implementing systematic protocols. They have also been active in analyzing their electronic data, and using the results to update and improve their protocols. For example, Kaiser published a press release on April 14, 2009, stating that analysis of their data on diabetic patients indicated that controlling blood sugar too tightly was associated with a higher incidence of subsequent Alzheimer's (Kaiser Permanente 2009). Based on this information, the article indicated that Kaiser intended to alter its treatment of certain diabetic patients with slightly less tightly controlled blood sugar. TQM's emphasis on data-driven decision making and in-process analysis indicates that this is the type of response that healthcare organizations and providers should be making. On the other hand, it raises questions about the role of scientific bodies and scientific consensus in developing and updating treatment guidelines (see Box 3.2).

Implement Systematic Protocols: Clinical Pathways and Guidelines

Efforts to implement systematic care processes proceeded on two levels. Clinical pathways were used at the healthcare provider level to ensure the systematic quality of care delivery. Clinical guidelines were developed by organizations such as medical associations and managed care organizations

BOX 3.2   CONTRAST THE PACE OF TECHNOLOGY DEVELOPMENT AND IMPLEMENTATION IN THE HEALTH INDUSTRY AND IN THE MICROCHIP INDUSTRY

Andy Grove, the CEO of Intel from 1987 to 1998, asserts: "There are important differences between health care and microchip industries in terms of research efficiency." During the 40 years from 1965 to 2005, the microchip industry produced remarkable technical advances, while the "war on cancer" proceeded slowly. Grove identifies several critical differences in the research processes that support these two industries: the microchip industry has more advanced techniques for early evaluation of new technology, and for adopting new technology in the workplace.

Source: Grove, A., *JAMA* 294:490–492, 2005.

to translate research results into operational guidelines for health-care providers.

Clinical Pathways

Clinical pathways (also known as critical pathways, integrated care pathways, or care maps) became prevalent in the acute care and home health settings beginning in the early 1980s. As an established management tool in the air flight and construction industries, clinical pathways were adopted and developed by interdisciplinary health team members. Their purpose was to standardize care processes based on established guidelines and evidence, thus improving the quality and coordination of care among the healthcare team. For example, interventions were designed to implement standards of care to optimize healing and control lengths of stay.

Expected patient outcomes were assessed along a sequenced time continuum to evaluate whether important milestones in the healing process had been achieved. These pathways or maps could be tailored to focus on individual patient conditions. For instance, if a postsurgical patient had complications with blood pressure control, ambulation within the first 8 postoperative hours may not be clinically appropriate, and therefore the pathway or map could be modified to reflect the specific patient issue. Several studies have identified improved quality of care and positive financial outcomes with the implementation of these pathways for specific patient populations (i.e., total knee and hip replacement surgeries, heart failure, pneumonia, etc.); however, resistance from physicians who object to the development of "cookbook medicine" and the erosion of their professional autonomy can limit the overall effectiveness of this quality and cost improvement strategy (Every et al., 2000).

Clinical Guidelines

Clinical guidelines summarize research results and identify best practices. While guidelines were initially developed to support provider decision making and help patients understand treatment options, they may also be relevant to malpractice cases and health insurance coverage decisions. Acceptance of the concept of clinical guidelines has increased since the Agency for Healthcare Research and Quality (AHRQ) (previously the Agency for Health Care Policy and Research) announced a program to develop evidence-based guidelines in 1993. Later, it established evidence-based practice centers (EPCs) to "synthesize scientific evidence to improve quality and effectiveness in health care." In addition, AHRQ partnered with the American Medical Association (AMA) and the American Association of Health Plans (now America's Health Insurance Plans) to create the National Guideline Clearinghouse.

Advocates argue that this effort to summarize and synthesize research results and articulate the implications for clinical practice is important due to the complexity and annual volume of research results. If guidelines succeed in helping physicians identify and implement best practices, they will significantly impact the healthcare provided to individual patients.

While the concept of using guidelines to summarize and synthesize available scientific evidence is straightforward, the recent controversy over new mammogram guidelines illustrates the complexity and difficulty of this task. The federally funded U.S. Preventative Services Task Force (USPSTF) announced new and revised mammogram guidelines in November 2009 (USPSTF, 2009). This touched off a storm of controversy that resulted in passage of the Vitter amendment, which requires health insurers to cover mammograms for women ages 40 to 49 without a copayment (Herszenhorn, 2009).

We will examine two underlying issues in this controversy that illustrate the issues that face the guidelines effort in general. First, the guidelines are based on the scientific evidence that was available to the panel, but that evidence was not high quality; in fact, the panel did not rate any of the available evidence as having a quality better than fair. Second, creating the guidelines required the panel to weigh the benefits of screening for breast cancer against the potential harms—and this trade-off raised serious ethical, pragmatic, and analytical issues. A set of articles (DeAngelis and Fontanarosa, 2010; Berg, 2010; Murphy, 2010; Woloshin and Schwartz, 2010; Woolf, 2010) published in the *Journal of the American Medical Association* (JAMA) details these issues.

Quality of the Evidence

We will begin by examining the quality of the science that was available to the mammogram panel, the options for dealing with this problem, and the resulting controversy. The panel made a decision to use only studies that were based on randomized clinical trials, even though this meant that the panel relied on old studies that were conducted in the 1960s and 1970s. No randomized clinical trials of mammogram effectiveness have been undertaken since that time (due to ethical questions about assigning women to control groups that would not receive mammograms). Now that screening is widely recommended, it is no longer feasible (or perhaps ethical) to have unscreened control groups. Numerous studies therefore rely on observation rather than randomized experimental designs, despite the fact that randomized clinical trial (RCT) studies are often viewed as the gold standard for medical research. The panel's decision to consider only RCT studies is controversial because these studies have two serious disadvantages. First, because the studies were relatively old, the accuracy of the screening may have been lower than the accuracy of more recent mammogram screenings, and that accuracy rate plays a key role in the comparison of the costs and potential harms of screening.

Second, the RCT studies divided women into two groups: those invited to participate in the screening and those who were in the control group and were not invited to participate in the screening. Compliance with the study instructions was only 70 to 80%, which means that some of the women who were invited did not actually obtain screenings, and some of the women in the (unscreened) control group obtained mammogram screenings outside of the study. However, a woman who was initially included in the treatment (screened) group remained in the screened group even if she did not actually have a mammogram. Similarly, a woman who was randomly assigned to the control group remained in the unscreened control group even if that woman did obtain a mammogram outside the study. The researchers used this strategy to avoid self-selection bias.

Opponents of the panel's methodology argued that the panel should have considered observational studies that would have looked at populations of women who actually did and did not obtain screenings. These studies indicated that mammography is more effective than the results presented by the RCT studies. It is possible that this reflects the fact that the observational studies are more recent, and therefore rely on more accurate mammography techniques. It is also possible that the observational studies show a higher effectiveness for mammography, if women who are at higher risk are more likely to get screened. In fact, one research study shows that women with higher risks, such as relatives who had breast cancer, are more likely to obtain mammography screenings.

The panel attempted to maximize the value of information that was available by using meta-analysis and statistical and mathematical modeling. We will explore one aspect of these models below to provide an illustration of the type of thinking that is used in these models. Here we should note the high degree of uncertainty about the estimates. The panel argued that routine screening should begin at age 50 rather than age 40 because 1,904 screenings are required to avert one death for women in their 40s, but only 1,339 screenings are required to avert one death among women in their 50s. The USPSTF recommendations published in the *Annals of Internal Medicine* (2009) state, however, that the ranges of these estimates are wide. Among women age 40-49, the best estimate of the number of women that must be screened to prevent one death is 1,904, with a confidence interval of (929 to 6,378). Among women age 50-59, the best estimate of the number of women that must be screened to prevent one death is 1,339, with a confidence interval equal to (322-7,455). The substantial overlap of the two confidence intervals raises questions about whether the difference between the two point estimates is meaningful.

Weighing the Costs and Benefits

The second controversial aspect of the panel's work focused on the methods used by the panel to weigh the benefits of screening against the potential harms. These potential harms include overdiagnosis and overtreatment triggered by false positive results, such as unnecessary biopsies. This aspect of the panel's work generated controversy about two issues.

First, questions were raised about who should make these trade-offs: Is this a scientific trade-off that should be made by a scientific body that is removed from political debate and discussion? Or, is this fundamentally a policy issue that should be debated in the political arena? While the panel argued that it was not considering or making any recommendation about insurance coverage, others viewed this position as naïve. It seems unrealistic to expect that insurers will not base coverage decisions on guideline issued by a federally funded panel. In fact, one reaction to the panel's recommendation for reduced mammography screening was passage of a bill that requires insurers to cover mammograms on the old, more frequent, schedule.

Second, the appropriate role of cost considerations in healthcare guidelines is a long-standing hot-button issue. Dr. David Eddy has been a long-time vigorous advocate of the importance of explicitly considering cost trade-offs (Eddy et al., 1988). Similarly, the British National Institute for Health and Clinical Excellence (NICE) utilizes the quality-adjusted life-years to determine the cost-effectiveness of new treatments (National Institute for Health and Clinical Excellence 2011). The NICE website states, "With the rapid advances in modern medicine, most people accept that no publicly funded healthcare system ... can possibly pay for every new medical treatment which becomes available. The enormous costs involved mean that choices have to be made. It makes sense to focus on treatments that improve the quality and/or length of someone's life." To maximize the benefits that can be achieved with available resources, the NICE website states that treatment impacts on quality adjusted life-years (QALYs) will be compared with treatment costs. Treatments that cost less than \$31,000–\$47,000 per QALY will be categorized as cost-effective. This policy, of course, generated controversy.

Example of the Statistical and Math Modeling

To examine the substance of the mammogram screening debate, we must consider a critical issue. Analysis of the value of testing and screening programs inevitably faces the substantive question: What is the value of the information produced by the test? A test may have a high degree of scientific accuracy and still produce information that is of limited value. In order to understand the underlying mechanism that causes this problem, we need to examine Bayesian statistics. We will examine the statistical concept using a straightforward example that was published in the journal *Decision Sciences*, on the issue of whether we should do random drug testing of college athletes, and then we will apply the ideas to the mammography issue (Feinstein, 1990).

The *Decision Sciences* article focused on the question: If we do random drug testing of athletes, how much information will the test results give us?

Let's assume that the test has a lab accuracy of 95%. This means that the test result will accurately reflect reality 95% of the time:

- If an athlete is actually using drugs, the test result will correctly identify the athlete as a drug user with probability 0.95.
- If an athlete is not using drugs, the test will correctly identify the athlete as a nonuser with probability 0.95.

However, if we do this testing on a population in which a very low proportion of athletes use drugs, the test results may not give us any information at all. To understand the problem, consider Table 3.1.

Supposed we administer this test to 1,000 athletes, of which 50 actually use drugs and 950 do not. Then the incidence of drug use in our sample is 5%. (This is the base rate of drug use in this student population. It is also known as the Bayesian prior probability). These numbers are shown in the last row of Table 3.1, labeled "number of students." When the 50 students who actually use drugs take the test, it will provide an accurate result for 95% of these students. This implies that the test results will show that there

Table 3.1   Test Results vs. Reality for Hypothetical Set of Student Athletes: Only 5% Actually Use Drugs

	Reality = *The Student DOES* *Use Drugs*	*Reality =* *The Student DOES* *NOT Use Drugs*	*Total Number* *of Students* *in Each Row*
Test result: The student DOES use drugs	45 Test result is **accurate** for 95% of the 50 students who use drugs	45 Test result is incorrect (**false-positive**) for 5% of the 950 students who do not use drugs	90 Students receive test results that indicate drug use
Test result: The student DOES NOT use drugs	5 Test result is incorrect (false negative) for 5% of the 50 students who do not use drugs	905 Test result is accurate for 95% of the 950 students who do not use drugs	910 Students receive test results that indicate NO drug use
Numbers of students	50 Students who— really—DO use drugs	950 Students who— really—DO NOT use drugs	1,000 Students tested

are 45 students who use drugs and 5 who do not. When the 950 students who do not use drugs take the test, it will correctly identify 905 of the students as non-drug users, and it will incorrectly identify 45 of the students as drug users. The test has produced false positive results for these 45 students.)

Taken as a whole, the test results for the 1,000 students will indicate that 90 of the students use drugs and 910 of the students do not (as shown in the last column of Table 3.1). If we look at the 90 positive results, shown in the first row of the table, we will see that half of them are accurate and half of them are false positives. This is shocking. We administered a test that, from a science point of view, is 95% accurate, and yet when we look at the test results that indicate drug use, only half of them are correct. The problem is that we administered the drug test in a population in which actual drug use is very low. We only have false positive results for 5% of the non-drug-using students, but the number of non-drug-using students is high compared with the number of drug users.

If we administer the same test to a different group of 1,000 students in which the rate of drug use is high, perhaps 50% of students use drugs in the second population, the test results yield significantly more information. In this case, 95% of the positive drug test results are accurate, and only 5% of them are wrong (see Table 3.2).

Clearly test results provide valuable information when the lab test has a high scientific accuracy rate *and* the test is performed on a population in which the incidence (or base rate) is high. This implies that screening tests, such as mammography, make sense in populations with a relatively high expected incidence, and they don't make sense in younger populations with lower incidences. The idea that we should apply this logic to analyze screening tests is not new: Louise Russell wrote an interesting book in 1994, *Educated Guesses*, that examined these issues for a series of tests such as mammography and prostate cancer. Despite this long-standing discussion, the mammogram screening guidelines announced by the U.S. Preventive Services Task Force (December 2009) generated vigorous controversy, which focused on the details of the decisions that are needed to apply this logic to a specific situation.

The panel used this Bayesian logic, as it examined trade-offs for women age 40 to 49 and trade-offs for women aged 50 to 59. The panel concluded that the harm outweighed the benefits for the younger group of women, whereas the benefits outweighed the harm for the older group of women. Opponents reject this conclusion for three reasons. First, the criteria for

Table 3.2 Test Results vs. Reality for Hypothetical Set of 1,000 Student Athletes: 50% of the Students Use Drugs

	Reality = *The Student DOES Use Drugs*	**Reality =** *The Student DOES NOT Use Drugs*	*Total Number of Students in Each Row*
Test result: The student DOES use drugs	475 Test result is **accurate** for 95% of the 500 students who use drugs	25 Test result is incorrect (false positive) for 5% of the 500 students who do not use drugs	500 Students receive test results that indicate drug use
Test result: The student DOES NOT use drugs	25 Test result is incorrect (false negative) for 5% of the 500 students who do not use drugs	475 Test result is accurate for 95% of the 500 students who do not use drugs	500 Students receive test results that indicate NO drug use
Number of students	500 Students who— really—DO use drugs	500 Students who—really— DO NOT use drugs	1,000 Students tested

weighing deaths against the harm of unnecessary treatment are not clear. Second, opponents do not believe that the panel gave sufficient consideration to the probability that mammogram screening permits women with cancer to be treated at an earlier stage, with less of a burden to the patient. Third, opponents of the revised guidelines argue that dividing the population into age groups 40 to 49 and 50 to 59 was arbitrary. The opponents argue that the number of deaths averted by mammogram screening is similar in the two groups. The panel reported that 0.5 deaths would be prevented per 1,000 screenings for women age 40–49, and 0.7 deaths would be prevented per 1,000 screenings for women age 50–59. Given the uncertainty intrinsic to these estimates, opponents of the panel's conclusion argue that it is not clear that these groups are significantly different. Similarly, the estimated numbers of women who would be overtreated are similar for the two groups: for every 1,000 women screened, the panel estimated that the number of women overtreated would lie between 1 and 5 for women age 40–49, and this number would lie between 1 and 7 for women age 50–59 (Woloshin and Schwartz, 2010).

Dr. David Eddy has argued that we should address the first issue raised by the opponents, by quantifying both the benefits and the harms in terms of dollars. This approach would permit a more straightforward and transparent comparison of benefits against harms. He developed a model in 1988 (with coauthors) that indicates that annual screening is probably not cost-effective, while benefits would outweigh costs if we screen every other year or every third year (Eddy et al., 1988). The Eddy study indicates that the cost per life saved by annual screening is $1 million. Screening every other year reduces the cost per life saved to $263,000, screening every third year reduces the cost per life saved to $185,000, and screening every fourth year reduces the cost per life saved to $10,000. The authors of the Eddy study concluded that:

■ Annual screening is not an effective use of resources (more lives could be saved with the same number of dollars if we spent those funds in other programs).
■ Screening every 2 or 3 years probably is an effective use of society's resources.

Mammography screening technology has advanced since 1988; however, the question of *whether* we should use this type of analysis during the guidelines development process is still a hot-button issue. Advocates of this approach argue that treatment guidelines should provide recommendations that are grounded in the reality that resource allocation issues can't be ignored. Others shy away from this analysis, citing concerns about the social impact of explicit decisions to accept increased risk of some deaths to save money. (The book *Tragic Choices* (1978) offers a thoughtful discussion of this view.)

This controversy is not confined to the United States. A recent *Wall Street Journal* headline describes the controversy: "Britain stirs outcry by weighing benefits of drugs versus price" (Whalen, 2005). This issue is also not unique to healthcare decisions. Significant controversies, in the 1980s, focused on the question of whether cost-benefit trade-offs should be considered when the Occupational Safety and Health Administration (OSHA) specifies occupational safety regulations. Two contentious cases reached the Supreme Court, focused on the application of these ideas to specify regulations limiting worker exposure to benzene and cotton dust.

Implications of Not Enough Science

When we don't have enough science to draw a clear conclusion about benefits and harms of a specific screening program or treatment, how should we proceed? We have two options. We could implement the screening program or treatment until sufficient evidence becomes available to make a determination of whether we should continue or discontinue the treatment. Alternately, we could follow a policy that we will never begin widespread use of the treatment or test until we have sufficient evidence to conclude definitively that the benefits outweigh the harms. As we move toward increased emphasis on evidence-based decision making, the debate between these two approaches will become increasingly salient.

One reason this debate is so contentious is that the stakes are high. If we adopt a strategy of prioritizing resources on the basis of maximizing the benefits per dollar, we will face some implications that are clear but uncomfortable. This discomfort with cost-benefit analysis underlies support for the policy that cost cannot be used to develop guidelines, elderly life-years saved cannot be valued less than others, and disabled people's life-years saved cannot be valued less than others.

Conclusion: Some Strategies for Strengthening Quality Are Clear; However, the Concept of Healthcare Quality Is Multidimensional

In this concluding chapter of Section I, we explored issues related to quality of care in the United States. We examined the evidence that supports the perception that there is room for improvement in delivering high-quality care in the United States. In evaluating the evidence, we learned that international comparisons must be used with caution, as some of the differences in life expectancy and infant mortality may reflect factors outside the control of our healthcare system.

Lifestyle factors contribute to disparities in outcomes:

■ International comparisons of infant mortality rates may not tell the whole story, as differences in definitions and access to life-prolonging technologies impact the statistics.
■ Higher rates of obesity in the United States may lead to the higher reported rates of cancer, compared to Canadian rates.

■ Greater access to firearms may help explain the decreased life expectancy rates in the United States, which are less than those of other industrialized nations.

We also noted that implementing and monitoring systematic care processes could prevent medical errors. Regional differences in healthcare utilization, expenditures, and outcomes support the necessity of basing healthcare decisions on evidence that will require systematic processes of care and new types of research that would provide support for care providers.

As our society grapples with the issues surrounding access, cost, and quality of healthcare, we will need to define what health means. Is it merely the absence of illness and disease? If that is our definition, what roles do the individual lifestyle and environment play? What will we decide about prevention activities and screenings?

We will also consider the web of relationships between health and socioeconomic factors, such as income, education, and occupational status. The federal Department of Health and Human Services report *Health, United States, 2011* (National Center for Health Statistics, 2012) includes a section focused on socioeconomic status (SES) and health. This report notes that the web of interactions between SES and health is complex, and it probably includes multiple causal factors. Income and education may impact the individual's access to healthcare resources, because these variables are correlated with health-related behaviors, and an individual's health may impact his or her ability to pursue educational opportunities and earn income. Evidence of these relationships is long-standing.

For example, researchers in the 1990s presented evidence that:

■ Low SES is associated with increased morbidity and mortality (Adler et al., 1994; Adler and Coriell, 1997)
■ Low-income individuals are two to five times more likely to suffer from a diagnosable mental disorder than those in the top SES bracket (Bourdon et al., 1994; Regier et al., 1993)

We need to define the boundaries and responsibilities of the healthcare system and develop stronger systems for implementing and monitoring systematic care processes. In Section II, we will examine strategies for strengthening the system, including:

- Consistently utilizing quality management systems like TQM
- Supporting efforts to develop scientifically sound clinical guidelines
- Leveraging health information technology to become more systematic in healthcare delivery and quality of care monitoring

Conclusion to Section I

Each of the three problems (access, cost, and quality) is complex, and the three problems are inextricably linked. Solutions that focus on just one area will always fail to deliver the results we intended to achieve. This is why the health reform bill is so complex, and why it is not realistic to expect that specific pieces of the PPACA can be repealed, without causing new types of problems. It's a jigsaw puzzle.

While the mandate is unpopular, universal access reduces distortions that hinder competitive market forces, and these forces are essential to reduce cost and increase quality. At the same time, lower cost would reduce the price tag for universal coverage. Similarly, better coordination (facilitated by continuous insurance coverage) would strengthen quality, and systematic quality would reduce cost.

In addition, examination of the difficult issues posed by the three problems points to a deeper layer of complexity: the boundaries of our healthcare system are not clear. We tend to view the healthcare system as the set of services that are typically provided by licensed medical professionals, and covered by standard health insurance policies. As we explore the access, cost, and quality issues, however, we see that healthcare is simply a tool for producing health. We don't wake up in the morning and think, "This would be a good day to get some healthcare—I would really enjoy that experience!" Instead, we obtain healthcare only as a strategy to increase our health. Further, healthcare is only one of a broad array of strategies for increasing health. One analyst concludes that 40% of early deaths can be attributed to individual behaviors, 30% result from genetic predispositions, 15% reflect social circumstances, and only 10–15% stem from deficiencies in our healthcare system (Heckman, 2012). This inconvenient truth has three important implications:

- It is difficult to measure the performance of the healthcare system (or specific healthcare providers), because healthcare outcomes are frequently impacted by factors outside the provider's control.

- We cannot address the important issue of health inequality simply by offering universal access to insurance coverage. Health inequality is clearly an important issue that is becoming more salient. Data from the Social Security Administration demonstrate increasing health inequality, based on remaining life expectancy for individuals who reach age 65:
  - For individuals born in 1912, the gap between the remaining life expectancy of 65-year-old individuals with high- vs. low-income was less than 1 year.
  - For individuals born in 1941, this gap was 5.5 years (Waldron 2007).
- Allocating increasing proportions of public funding to healthcare could be counterproductive if we "find" those funds by decreasing efforts to provide universal access to a reasonably good education, adult literacy, and job training, or measures to prevent or alleviate poverty.
- A recent article written by James Heckman (who won the 2000 Nobel Prize in economics) argues that we are seeing increasing evidence that early experiences (*in utero* and early childhood) shape important elements of the individual's subsequent experience, such as educational attainment and propensity to engage in risky behaviors (Heckman, 2012). If this set of early results turns out to be correct, it has important implications for prioritizing our efforts to build health.

Our healthcare system faces multifactorial problems. The good news is that there are efforts currently underway to begin addressing and resolving these issues. The bad news is that not all of these efforts will be successful. In Section II, we will begin to explore strategies and solutions to the pressures for change that have occurred or are being proposed in order to address the issues of our current healthcare system. Through this exploration, we will have the opportunity to apply the economic principles we've learned in Section I to identify what works and what doesn't, and examine how these efforts may influence our future as healthcare professionals.

Endnote

1. FOCUS is one of several acronyms that summarize this series of steps. While the acronyms vary, the underlying ideas do not.

STRATEGIES TO INCREASE EFFICIENCY

II

Introduction

A provocative editorial appeared in *The Wall Street Journal* on February 18, 2013, entitled: "The Coming Failure of 'Accountable Care': The Affordable Care Act's Updated Versions of HMOs Are Based on Flawed Assumptions about Doctor and Patient Behavior" (Christensen et al., 2013; Norbeck et al. 2013). This editorial argues that Patient Protection and Affordable Care Act (PPACA) envisions that accountable care organizations (ACOs) can deliver healthcare that is high quality and cost-efficient, but this vision is based on the flawed assumptions that these results can be achieved with fundamental changes in physician and patient behaviors. Instead, this editorial argues that we should revise our regulatory policies to support and encourage innovations in healthcare delivery methods, locations, and strategies. Why should we pay attention to one editorial (among many) in one newspaper? The lead author, Clay Christensen, is also the lead author of a book (*The Innovator's Prescription*, 2008) that is generating substantial discussion—and influence. In fact, the American Recovery and Reinvestment Act (ARRA) funding for health information technology will build the infrastructure needed to support some of these innovations, and a 2004 report by the Federal Trade Commission and Department of Justice recommends that states should seriously consider the regulatory issues mentioned in the editorial. If we want to understand where the system is headed, it will be useful to understand the ideas detailed in the book and summarized in the editorial.

We will tackle the task of understanding this strategic vision—and thinking about the ideas in the context of other ongoing trends and issues—by examining five strategies for making our system more efficient:

- Align incentives
- Manage care
- Prevent and manage chronic conditions
- Encourage competitive innovation
- Harness the potential offered by health information technology

This discussion will help you identify the strengths and limitations of these efforts to generate significant efficiency gains (that may also fundamentally redesign our healthcare system). We will apply lessons learned from past experience, and assess new proposals and innovations. We start with an overview of the role market forces play in the healthcare industry and how the forces may impede efficiencies.

Do Healthcare Markets Operate Efficiently?

Statistical evidence indicates that market forces do operate in the healthcare industry, but this industry has specific characteristics that create inefficiencies:

- Some healthcare market participants wield a lot of market power, including large purchasers such as Medicare and Medicaid, physicians, hospitals, and insurance companies.
- Insurance distorts normal incentives that influence both the amount of healthcare and the types of healthcare that patients want to purchase, and that providers want to provide. Milton Friedman's (2001) warning, "We spend other people's money differently than we spend our own," is important: consumers may be more careful about monitoring expenditures when they pay directly out-of-pocket than when they are essentially spending the insurance company's money.
- Healthcare providers (physicians, psychologists, and nurse practitioners) have significantly more information about treatment options and expected treatment outcomes than patients; in fact, it is fair to say that patients "hire" healthcare providers to make decisions and provide advice. In the language of economics, patients are the principals and healthcare providers are the agents—hired to act in the best interest of

the principals. Knowledge in healthcare is asymmetric—the healthcare providers have more information than patients—and this can generate incentives to overprovide care. This problem also occurs when drivers hire auto mechanics to diagnose and repair car problems, when individuals hire attorneys to handle legal matters, and when homeowners hire contractors to address home repair or remodeling issues. The principal faces the same problem in each of these situations: he or she is not sure whether the agent's actions and recommendations are also influenced by the agent's self-interest.

Kenneth Arrow, who won the 1972 Nobel Prize for his work in economics, wrote a classic paper in 1963 that detailed the plethora of market failures in healthcare. Other analysts who examined government regulatory behavior conclude that policy makers and regulators also face limitations. Therefore, it is reasonable to expect that our healthcare sector will continue to be shaped by *both* government policies and market forces (Glazer and Rothenberg, 2005).

Two Key Market Failures in Healthcare

The Principal–Agent Problem: Healthcare Providers and Auto Mechanics

The principal-agent relationship between patients and providers poses significant problems for healthcare interactions. The principal (the patient) does not have enough information to accurately assess the quality of the agent's work (the healthcare provider) and the veracity of his or her stated opinions. Because the agent knows that the principal has limited ability to assess the quality of his or her work, the incentives embedded in the payment system can influence the agent's behavior.

A provider, or an auto mechanic, who is reimbursed on a fee-for-service basis has a monetary incentive to overtreat patients or recommend unnecessary auto repair. In fact, Sears was prosecuted some years ago (Anderson, 2011) for implementing a payment incentive system in which employees in the auto repair shops could increase their earnings by increasing the number of repairs completed. The prosecutor charged that the result was predictable: recommendation and completion of unnecessary auto repairs. Sears subsequently redesigned the payment system to eliminate this incentive.

The idea that providers might systematically generate demand for their services by recommending unnecessary treatments has been controversial.

Economists describe this process with the shorthand phrase "supply-induced demand" (SID). Empirical evidence on the magnitude of SID is mixed. The statistical challenges of testing this hypothesis are formidable. However, analysis of the incentive for unnecessary auto repair provides a useful clue: this incentive is strong when the mechanic does not have enough customers to fill his schedule, and this incentive is blunted by the mechanic's concern about the impact on his reputation if "unnecessary" repairs are discovered (Darby and Karni, 1973). This implies that overtreatment probably varies significantly across physicians, and across time periods, which complicates statistical analysis of this hypothesis. Nonetheless, empirical evidence does support the basic idea that providers respond to payment system incentives (Robinson, 2001).

Insurance Reduces the Incentive for Patients to Shop Wisely

This problem is compounded by the fact that insurance reduces patient incentives to be cautious about healthcare expenditures. While patients may realize that fee-for-service (FFS) payment gives providers an incentive to overprovide care, health insurance blunts patient incentives to be skeptical.

How Should Government Address These Market Failures?

These market failures are not unique to healthcare; each type of market failure occurs in a broad array of industries. Strategies deployed to address these problems fall into two categories:

- Government can address market failure problems by developing programs or specifying regulations aimed to supplant the market process.
- Government can design market-based policies to mitigate the market failure and strengthen the market outcome.

Many of the debates about health policy are essentially debates about the optimal balance between these two types of strategies. These debates also occur in other areas; for example, Box II.1 provides an overview of the application of these strategies to increase average automobile fuel economy.

Many policies combine the two strategies. In this section, we will examine the use of these two options to address market failures that impact the

BOX II.1 ALTERNATE REGULATORY STRATEGIES TO ACHIEVE A SOCIAL GOAL: FINDING A COST-EFFECTIVE STRATEGY

Consider, for example, our current strategy for increasing average automobile fuel economy. The United States currently uses the first option: regulations mandate that automakers must ensure that their cars meet corporate average fuel economy standards. In 2007, the standard for automobiles was 27.5 mpg, and automakers must achieve an average of 54.5 by the year 2025. In contrast, the second strategy would focus on raising gas taxes to induce consumers to purchase fuel-efficient cars. While this strategy is not popular, a Congressional Budget Office report concluded that consumers would spend less overall if we implemented the gas tax strategy. According to this report, the CAFE strategy leads to increased costs because consumers and firms respond to the regulation by adjusting their behaviors. As a result, the straightforward regulatory approach is not as straightforward as it seems.

Sources: Congressional Budget Office, Fuel Economy Standards Versus a Gasoline Tax, Economic and Budget Issue Brief, March 9, 2004, http://fpc.state.gov/documents/organization/82504.pdf. Bamberger, R., and Yacobucci, B.D. 2007. Automobile and light truck fuel economy: The CAFE standards. RL33413 (January 19). http://www.fpc.state.gov/documents/organization/82504.pdf.

efficiency with which healthcare is produced. Specifically, we will examine five strategies to increase healthcare system efficiency:

- Align payment incentives
- Manage care
- Provide wellness, prevention, and disease-management programs
- Develop new types of providers and consumers
- Build an information infrastructure

Chapter 4

Align Incentives via Payment System Design

Introduction

In this chapter, we will examine Medicare policies that determine the rates paid to healthcare providers. We will also examine three policy issues:

- Medicare rate structures create inefficient silos; hence, Medicare is exploring the potential for bundled payments to mitigate this problem.
- Cost-cutting efforts may have unintended consequences for competition among healthcare providers.
- Rate-setting policies must be structured to address quality issues.

We start by exploring the role that the dominant purchaser of healthcare (i.e., the U.S. government) influences behaviors within the healthcare system, before looking at specific innovations.

Strategies to Control Cost: Rate Design Replaced Certificate of Need Programs

When the Medicare program was developed in 1963, it was structured to conform to the payment system that was widely used at the time: fee-for-service payment. In a fee-for-service system, the provider is reimbursed for each service he or she provides. This system generates incentives to overtreat patients as a strategy to maximize reimbursement. Consider a patient who enters a hospital for a specific treatment for a specific condition. Under fee-for-service payment, the hospital will bill the insurance company for all costs incurred to provide this treatment. Each day of a hospital stay generates additional hospital revenue.

This cost-plus reimbursement system generated concerns that hospitals had an incentive to overinvest in capital equipment, such as hospital beds or CT scanners. A 1973 federal law authorized states to create certificate of need (CON) programs to address concerns about a "medical arms race." Hospitals were required to demonstrate that new facilities were needed to meet community requirements. You can see, however, a circular logic: there were no clear criteria to distinguish hospital stays that were needed to provide high-quality care from those that were simply desired due to the perverse fee-for-service payment system incentives. Statistical evidence indicated that the programs did not effectively reduce capital expenditures or contain cost, the federal law was repealed, and the state-level programs were largely abandoned.

Top-down planning efforts, such as CON programs, have largely been replaced with efforts to create incentives to induce providers and patients to make efficient healthcare decisions. As a large buyer, Medicare makes decisions about the structure and level of rates that will be paid to physicians, hospitals, and other healthcare providers. These rate decisions exert significant influence on the numbers and types of healthcare providers, healthcare decisions made by these providers, and the competitive relationships among these providers.

As it works to design an effective payment structure, Medicare faces a complex problem. Because Medicare payments constitute 20% of healthcare expenditures, the rates at which Medicare reimburses healthcare providers have far-reaching economic implications: these rates influence the mix of services provided (e.g., the relative number of primary care physicians and specialists), the number of services provided, and the structures of hospital and physician markets (National Health Expenditure Data, 2010). Federal policies also influence the supply of physicians through policies that impact medical and nursing education.

What Is the "Right" Price?

The question of how to reimburse healthcare providers is complex because:

1. The Center for Medicaid and Medicare Services (CMS) is such a large buyer that it cannot simply observe the current price: instead, the prices paid by Medicare and Medicaid exert significant impact on each segment

of the healthcare market, so that Medicare is the key "market maker." In the language of economists, Medicare has "monopsony" power. (A monopsonist is a single buyer that wields enough purchasing power to significantly impact the market. Instead of simply paying typical prices, a monopsonist has enough bargaining power to set the price.)

2. The healthcare industry is experiencing substantial competitive and technological innovation, which creates pressure for frequent price adjustments.
3. Efforts to control healthcare costs exert negative impacts on healthcare provider revenues, and some healthcare provider organizations maintain active lobbying efforts.

CMS and Congress have been struggling with the question: What is the *right* price to pay for physician services? From an economics perspective, the right price will induce enough individuals to offer physician services to see all of the patients who are willing to pay that price. (This is the equilibrium price we discussed in Chapter 1.) The question is particularly complex for physicians, because the federal government exerts significant influence on both the supply side and the demand side of the market. Federal policies, along with the American Medical Association, influence the number of students who complete medical school each year (and the number of foreign medical graduates who practice in the United States). Hence, the supply can be kept low to increase the equilibrium price. CMS payment policies also influence the number of patients who want to make appointments to see different types of providers, and the numbers of physicians willing to see Medicaid and Medicare patients. Nonetheless, Congress and CMS must answer the question: What set of prices will help CMS stretch its dollars, while still providing sufficient reimbursement to induce physicians to continue to treat Medicare patients?

Rate Design: Setting the Level of Payments

In 2003, Congress mandated that the level of Medicare payments will be adjusted to limit the rate at which expenditures increase over time. (This provision was included in the Medicare Prescription Drug, Improvement and Modernization Act.) This policy, known as the sustainable growth rate (SGR) formula, uses a blunt instrument to tackle a complex issue. Medicare expenditures for physician services reflect both the prices and the quantities of specific services, and the mix of services. The allowed growth rate was set below the rate at which utilization of services had been increasing; hence, this policy mandates that physician reimbursement rates must decline over time (unless new strategies dramatically increase health system efficiency). Since passing the law, Congress has voted repeatedly to postpone the mandated payment rate reductions. Because the law requires catch-up for any postponed reductions, the mandated cut is approximately 20% for 2013.

The implications of this blunt approach to addressing Medicare budget issues are significant. A 20% cut in physician payments for Medicare services could create access problems for Medicare recipients—if physicians respond by deciding to eschew participation in Medicare, reducing the number of Medicare patients they are willing to see, choosing to go into specialty practice areas that see fewer Medicare patients (such as plastic surgery or sports medicine), or retiring sooner than they had previously planned. A survey of 2,232 physicians (conducted in April 2012) suggests that the issue is important: the survey reports that 73% of internal medicine, family practice, and OB/GYN physicians are not accepting new Medicare patients, while 90% of cardiac physicians are accepting new Medicare patients (Jackson Health Care, 2012). In addition, Wu and Shen present evidence that Medicare payment reductions can adversely impact mortality rates for hospital patients (Wu and Shen, 2011).

The potential impact of the rate cuts on retirement decisions is also salient: American Medical Association data indicate that 40% of U.S. physicians are at least 55 years of age. Accelerated retirement by this group of individuals could significantly reduce the supply of U.S. physicians (Smart, 2011).

The magnitude of the mandated cuts also raises a third concern: Would significant cuts in Medicare reimbursement rates impact decisions of young people, who are considering investing time and money in medical education? Multivariate analyses of physician earnings indicate that—after accounting for the time and expense incurred to complete medical school—physician earnings are comparable to, or slightly less than, earnings in other professions (Rice and Unruh, 2009). Therefore, there is concern that significant rate cuts could deter bright young people from entering medical school. If we cut physician reimbursement rates, we can enjoy short-term savings, but this might also create a shortage of qualified physicians who are willing to treat Medicare patients. If this shortage occurs, seniors would experience significant wait times to obtain physician appointments.

Rate Design: Designing the Structure of Payments

When Medicare announces the reimbursement rate schedule, it sets two things: the rate level and the rate structure. (The term *rate structure* refers to the relationships among reimbursement rates for hospital services, primary care physician services, specialty physician services, radiological tests, and other types of services.) The rate level will impact the supply (and quality) of providers. The rate structure will impact specific strategies that providers use to produce healthcare services.

Medicare implements an array of policies that, together, define the payment rates for a wide array of healthcare services. These policies define the relative payments for home health services vs. nursing facility services, for physician services vs. nurse practitioner services, and for inpatient vs. outpatient services. For example, Medicare uses the resource-based relative value scale (RBRVS) system to set rates for diverse types of physician services. Medicare payment rates for physician services are computed by adding three factors (after adjusting for geographic differences in costs):

■ The estimated amount of physician labor required to perform the service
■ The practice expenses associated with providing the service
■ The malpractice liability attributed to this service

While the level of these payments impacts the overall revenue earned by physicians, the structure of these rates determines the relative profitability of specific services and specific physician specialties. For example, the relative rates paid for primary care and specialist physicians impact the relative profitability of these two types of physician practices, and this influences the proportions of medical school graduates who elect to build careers in primary care vs. specialty care (Rice and Unruh, 2009). We are reminded here of the fundamental economic principle that people respond to incentives. Effective policy design requires anticipating those responses so that the desired results will be achieved *after* groups such as medical students observe the new policies and adjust their decisions and behaviors. (Policies that successfully accomplish this task are called incentive-compatible regulations.)

The importance of the impact of the rate structure has been illustrated by cardiologists' responses to the recent Medicare decision to significantly reduce the rate for in-office echocardiograms and increase the rate for hospital-based echocardiograms. It is important to note that CMS establishes one set of rates for diagnostic radiology procedures that are performed in hospital-based outpatient facilities and a different set of rates for the same procedures performed in physician offices, even if the equipment and the tests are the same. For many procedures, CMS has been paying higher rates to hospital-based facilities than to non-hospital-based facilities. A June 2008

Government Accountability Office (GAO) report cited evidence that (1) patients treated in physician offices were significantly more likely to receive cardiology tests than patients treated in a hospital setting, (2) these tests were increasingly being performed in non-hospital-based settings, and (3) the proportions of patients receiving these tests varied dramatically across geographic areas. The GAO report concluded that the evidence supported concerns about financial incentives for physicians to overprescribe these tests in nonhospital settings. Starting in 2010, the outpatient reimbursement rates for several cardiology exams were reduced, while the hospital-based rates for the some of these tests were increased.

In response, cardiologists reevaluated whether it would be more advantageous to continue to practice as independent physician groups or sell the practice to hospitals. Early anecdotal evidence indicates that a significant proportion of cardiologist groups are selling their practices to hospitals (Cadet, 2012).

While this may or may not yield an efficient solution to the problem of unnecessary tests, it raises two new issues:

■ First, this consolidation of physician offices with hospitals may reduce the potential for competitive contracting, and this reduction in competitive vigor could lead to higher prices, particularly in small cities. For example, there were two independent cardiology physician groups in Reno, Nevada, prior to this rule change, and both groups sold their practices to the largest hospital in Reno following the rule change. To the extent that local health maintenance organizations (HMOs) were previously able to negotiate price discounts (because there were two groups), that negotiating power probably diminished. In addition, all patients incurred the higher prices associated with hospital-based tests because non-hospital-based tests are no longer available (Mullen, 2011b). This situation was subsequently reversed, following settlement of a legal case; hence, one of the physician groups has separated from the hospital and returned to private practice. However, this does not alter the central point, that CMS rate structures exert significant impacts on the organization of our healthcare markets (Hidalgo, 2012).

■ Second, when consolidation occurs in response to a governmental rule change, it raises doubts whether this is an efficient strategy—in the sense of minimizing the cost of providing the care. Prior to the change, the cardiologists apparently thought that independent practices offered enough advantages to offset the fact that the outpatient reimbursement rate was lower than the inpatient rate. As the elephant in every room, CMS triggered a dramatic change. It is not clear whether this change will yield net benefits: strengthening integration between hospital and physician services could potentially facilitate coordination of care, but it also reduces the degree of competition in the healthcare marketplace.

Efficiency Incentives: Diagnostic-Related Groups (DRGs)

The Medicare rate structure also creates incentives that impact care patterns. The first major effort to reengineer the incentive structure occurred in 1983, when Medicare implemented the diagnostic-related group (DRG) payment system for hospitals. The DRG system replaced the pre-1983 fee-for-service (FFS) system, which created incentives to keep patients in the hospital for lengthy stays. The DRG system is designed to create incentives to produce care more efficiently by focusing on the diagnoses for which patients are admitted to hospitals. For example, DRG 544 is assigned to each patient admitted to the hospital for hip replacement surgery. Medicare's payment to the hospital for each patient with DRG 544 is set by Medicare payment schedules; it is not determined by the patient's actual length of stay (or cost of care) in the hospital. This system is also known as the prospective payment system (PPS), because the reimbursement amount is estimated prospectively (prior to completion of the patient's care), based on the patient's admitting diagnosis. (We should note that this is a streamlined description of the DRG system. For a few extra details, see Box 4.1.)

Consider the impact of the change from FFS payment to DRG/PPS payment, as illustrated by Mary Smith's hypothetical hip surgery.

The pre-1983 FFS system: Suppose the FFS rate schedule specified the rates that would be paid for the surgery and for each day in the hospital. Mary Smith might have been admitted to the hospital the day before the surgery (it is convenient for the hospital to complete pre-op lab work if the patient is in the hospital), and she might have stayed for 8–10 days after the surgery—until Mary and her physician decided that Mary was ready to be discharged.

The DRG system: The DRG system introduced a dramatic change. A hospital admitting a patient under a DRG classification of hip surgery would expect to receive $12,257 on average across the United States, regardless of the length of the patient's stay (Wilson, Schneller, Montgomery, and Bozic, 2008). This created a new incentive to organize

---

BOX 4.1 ADDITIONAL FEATURES OF THE DRG SYSTEM

This is a streamlined description of the DRG system. The DRG system includes additional features, such as:

■ Categories for more complex and less complex patients (e.g., DRG 774 is vaginal delivery with complicating diagnoses, while DRG 775 is vaginal delivery without complicating diagnoses)
■ Outlier payments for unusual cases
■ Adjustments for geographic location

---

treatment efficiently, and coordinate with post-hospital care providers (such as nursing facilities or rehabilitation centers). Today, unless there is a complication, a patient undergoing hip replacement surgery can expect to have a 4- to 5-day hospital stay. Mary will be approved for discharge (regardless of her preference) once she has met the discharge criteria, which typically include stable clinical condition, ability to walk, and appropriate pain control. If she is unable to meet the discharge criteria within the 4- to 5-day time frame, a referral to a rehabilitation facility would be considered. This strategy was pioneered by Medicare, but it is no longer unique to Medicare. See Box 4.2 for a discussion of the analogous strategy employed by managed care organizations.

This shift from a cost-plus pricing system to a fixed price per episode radically altered the incentive structure faced by hospitals. Hospitals responded to the DRG system by reducing the average length of stay. Nursing homes provided early evidence of the changes in treatment patterns, when they began complaining that hospitals were discharging patients "quicker and sicker." (It is important, however, to note that concurrent development of new technology also contributed to the decrease in average length of stay shown in Figure 4.1.)

Current Issues: Two Facets of Medicare Payment Policy

Bundled Payment: Eliminate Silos

The use of separate payment systems to reimburse specific types of providers (e.g., the DRG/PPS for hospitals vs. the resource-based relative value scale (RBRVS) for physicians) creates payment silos with minimal incentives to

**BOX 4.2 MANAGED CARE ORGANIZATIONS
EMPLOY A SIMILAR STRATEGY**

Managed care organizations employ a similar strategy to eliminate the fee-for-service incentive for physicians to overtreat patients. Under a capitated (prepaid) contract between the physician and an insurance company, the physician commits to provide care for a set of patients, and the insurer pays a fixed dollar amount per person per month. We will discuss managed care issues in the next chapter; in this chapter we will maintain our focus on Medicare payment issues.

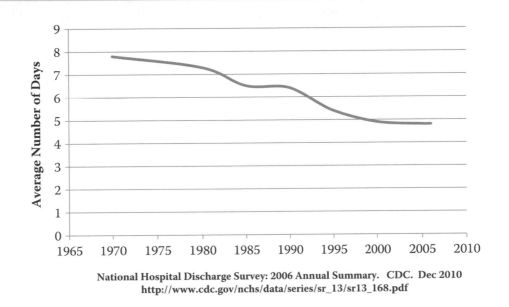

National Hospital Discharge Survey: 2006 Annual Summary. CDC. Dec 2010
http://www.cdc.gov/nchs/data/series/sr_13/sr13_168.pdf

Figure 4.1 Average length of hospital stay: surgical and nonsurgical stays. (From CDC, National Hospital Discharge Survey, 2006 Annual Summary, December 2010, http://www.cdc.gov/nchs/data/series/sr_13/sr13_168.pdf.)

coordinate care across the silos. When Medicare began using the DRG/PPS system to reimburse hospitals in 1983, it continued to use an FFS system to reimburse nursing facilities. This payment system dichotomy did not provide appropriate incentives for the two sets of facilities to coordinate care across their institutional boundaries. Consider, for example, a Medicare transfer patient. By definition, a transfer patient lives at home prior to the episode of care, is hospitalized for treatment, and then requires follow-up treatment at a nursing facility before returning home when the episode of care is complete. The DRG payment system created a financial incentive for hospitals to minimize discretionary services (such as patient teaching or physical therapy) that can be postponed until the nursing facility phase of the patient's treatment, and to discharge the patient to the nursing facility as quickly as possible.

Medicare subsequently attempted to address this problem by implementing bundled payment for transfer patients. Under bundled payment, one of these institutions (e.g., the hospital or the nursing facility) could assume financial responsibility for the entire episode of care and subcontract with the other institution. For example, a hospital could assume financial responsibility for the patient's "bundle" of care, and subcontract with a nursing facility for the second phase of the treatment. Under this system, the hospital has a financial incentive to work with nursing facilities to figure out the optimal treatment pattern and implement that pattern. Medicare is currently expanding the use of bundled payment (Miller et al., 2011).

Selective Contracting

The strategy of selective contracting offers an alternative to the approach of setting the prices Medicare will pay. Congress mandated that Medicare begin using the selecting contracting strategy for durable medical equipment (DME), beginning in 2007 (Federal Trade Commission, 2004). Instead of announcing rates that it would pay for DME, Medicare would solicit bids from DME suppliers. Companies with low bids would be selected to provide DME for Medicare recipients. This strategy would force DME suppliers to reveal the prices at which they are willing to provide DME, instead of requiring Medicare to guess at these prices (Medicare Improvement for Patients and Providers Act 154, 2008). This contracting strategy was controversial, largely due to concerns about the potential impact on small suppliers. Small business advocates were concerned that large suppliers, who might enjoy economies of scale, might underbid small DME suppliers. In addition, opponents expressed concern about the competitive bidding process, particularly in rural areas. Congress responded by delaying the phased implementation until 2011, and legislation has been proposed to terminate the program (H.R. 104–112th Congress: Fairness in Medicare Bidding Act, 2011 and Support H.R. 1041, the Fairness in Medicare Bidding Act). (Consider the overall cost implication of this concern that selective contracting might harm small business by reducing the reimbursement rate.)

Medicare can use two general strategies: Medicare could announce prices it will pay for every covered service, or Medicare could solicit competitive bids. Both systems, must address intrinsic complexities. The complexity of the DRG-type incentive approach lies in the level of necessary detail, and the complexity of the selective contracting approach lies in performance monitoring: it is essential to monitor service quality because the provider will have a strong incentive to underprovide services once the contract has been signed. Some of the strongest concerns raised by the opponents of selective contracting for DME focus on this issue.

Measuring Quality: Pay-for-Performance and Consumer Information

Implementation of the DRG payment system raised three types of concerns about the impacts on quality:

- Moving care traditionally provided in an acute care setting into a lower level, or reducing service intensity, could potentially jeopardize patient health (Rock, 1985).
- Hospitals that treated more severely ill patients (teaching and specialty hospitals) might be financially disadvantaged because they would receive the same reimbursement as hospitals treating less severely ill patients (Horn and Backofen, 1987).
- While DRGs were devised to contain the escalating cost of Medicare, there was an unintended loophole: hospital readmissions generated revenue. If a patient was discharged from the hospital and was later readmitted with, for example, a postoperative infection, the hospital received reimbursement for the second hospitalization regardless of the quality of the care that had been provided during the first hospital stay (Brown, 1995).

Medicare has been working to address these incentives to skimp on quality. The problem occurs because patients and payers cannot readily observe the technical aspects of healthcare quality. While we can easily observe the customer service aspects of healthcare quality, we generally do not have sufficient information to assess the accuracy of a physician's diagnosis and recommendation or the quality of a hospital's infection control program. This asymmetric information (individuals who produce healthcare services know more about quality than the individuals who purchase and receive the services) presents the same lemons problem that plagues the health insurance market. Competing by offering high quality is not an effective strategy when buyers cannot observe the quality differential. Instead, the pressure to compete on price leads to cost-cutting efforts, which can lead to reductions in quality.

Medicare is implementing pay-for-performance (P4P) programs for hospitals and other provider entities, to create a quality-based "race to the top." For example, hospitals are required to report data on a set of quality measures (such as the incidence of hospital-acquired infections) to a centralized database. These data are then used to compute the percentile ranking of each hospital, and these rankings are used to adjust Medicare payments to each hospital. Initially, high-scoring hospitals (in the top 10%) received a bonus equal to 2% of the Medicare payments for the relevant conditions, and hospitals in the next 10% received a 1% bonus. In contrast, hospitals in the lowest 20% were penalized 1–2% of the relevant Medicare payments (Centers for Medicare and Medicaid Services, 2005).

Thus, the pay-for-performance (P4P) system rewards providers (hospitals and individual care providers) who meet quality goals. This is essentially a merit-based system that has been implemented in the healthcare sector for nearly a decade. Werner et al. (2011) analyzed the impact of P4P on a group of 260 hospitals. These hospitals participated in a demonstration project undertaken by the Centers for Medicare and Medicaid Services in partnership with Premier, Inc. The study examined the quality measures reported by these participating hospitals, compared to a control group of 780 hospitals within the same nationwide hospital system. The findings indicated that over half of the hospitals participating in the demonstration project achieved the quality measures, compared to less than one-third of hospitals in the control group. However, after 5 years, the quality measures were undifferentiated in the two hospital groups. Factors positively affecting quality performance were high incentives, less competitive market, and being in good financial shape. These findings seem to suggest that a one-size-fits-all and a top-down pay-for-performance approach may not generate widespread and continuous quality improvements.

While P4P is generally viewed favorably by providers, concerns have been raised:

■ Providers need to purchase expensive computerized data collection systems in order to capture and report quality measures.
■ The relevance and validity of some quality measures is controversial.
■ Providers and consumers may lose autonomy and privacy.

■ Administrative costs may offset any cost savings.
■ Hospitals and providers may develop strategies to avoid providing care to high-risk patients.
■ Most complex patients have multiple care providers; hence, it is difficult to assign responsibility for poor performance. This problem is exacerbated by the fact that 50% of consumers change primary care physicians in a given year.
■ If rural and safety net hospitals are not able to meet P4P standards, their revenues will be reduced. Some commentators suggest that the financial strength of these hospitals should be tracked as P4P continues to expand its scope.

P4P strategies have also been applied to physician reimbursement. For example, the National Health Service of the United Kingdom implemented a pay-for-performance system for family physicians in 2004. Quality indicators were identified for high-volume diseases such as asthma, diabetes, and hypertension. Quality data were collected from the electronic medical records used and maintained by individual physicians. These systems used checklists and pop-up messages to prompt providers to implement the treatment guidelines. Analysis of this effort indicates that P4P incentives can generate quality improvements (Doran et al., 2006).

The best early assessment of the effectiveness of P4P for physicians in the United States was conducted in California. A collaboration of six major insurers initiated the largest and longest-running P4P program in the United States in 2004. Their program emphasized three areas of performance: clinical care processes, patient care experiences, and office-based information systems. Financial incentives are provided for achievements made in these three areas, and medical group-level performance is publically reported annually. Medical groups may redirect incentive payment directly to their physicians or use the incentive pay on other organizational priorities. McDonald and Roland (2009) found that California physicians participating in this initiative were less likely to be aware of the quality targets and less motivated by financial incentives than their British counterparts. Additionally, the California respondents indicated resentment that:

■ The quality targets differ from one insurer to another.
■ Insurers are collecting substantial new types of data to assess whether the targets are met.

Efforts are underway to expand the concept of structuring payment rates to create a quality race to the top in two directions. First, Medicare is implementing value-based purchasing (VBP). This concept focuses on tying payment rates to measured (and audited) performance on a set of well-defined quality measures. Second, we will see in Chapter 8 that the 2009 federal American Recovery and Reinvestment Act provides substantial funding for incentives to induce providers to adopt electronic medical records systems. To qualify to receive these payments, providers must report data on a substantial list of new quality measures.

Conclusion

Designing a payment system to induce an array of providers (including hospitals, physicians, and ancillary providers) to provide optimal patient care in an efficient, least-cost manner is a complex task. Because Medicare pays for a significant share of all healthcare services, the structure and level of Medicare rates impact the numbers and types of services provided, the types of integration and coordination across providers, the degree of competition in the healthcare marketplace, and the strategies providers use to address quality issues. As a result, Medicare rate policies generate substantial controversy.

In the remaining chapters of Section II, we will see other examples of innovations designed to improve efficiency and contain healthcare costs. Chapter 5 will focus on the goals and strategies of managed care organizations, and the issues triggered by the growth of managed care. We will also explore how our earlier experiences with managed care may influence the development and implementation of new primary care infrastructures such as accountable care organizations (ACOs) and medical homes. These new integrated care models require a team-based focus rather than the traditional provider-centered care delivery.

Chapter 5

Managed Care Organizations, Accountable Care Organizations, and Patient-Centered Medical Homes

Introduction

New forms of managed care organizations, including accountable care organizations (ACOs) and patient-centered medical homes (PCMHs), are expected to provide better coordination of care than our current system of individual practitioners. According to the American College of Physicians (2012), a PCMH is "a team-based model of care led by a personal physician who provides continuous and coordinated care throughout a patient's lifetime to maximize health outcomes."

ACOs differ from PCMHs in that the scope is much broader. (Elliott Fisher, director of the Center for Health Policy Research at Dartmouth Medical School, coined the term *accountable care organization* in a 2006 Medicare Payment Advisory Commission meeting.) These organizations are vertically integrated, to include PCMHs, hospitals, and other providers. The ACO is responsible for comprehensive care of a population of patients; hence, Medicare payment criteria include efficiency and quality standards. There are three widely supported core principles of ACOs:

1. Provider-led organizations with a strong base of primary care are accountable for quality and total per capita costs, across the full continuum of care for a population of patients.
2. Payments are linked to quality improvements that also reduce overall costs.
3. Reliable and progressively more sophisticated performance measurements will be used to support improvement and provide confidence that savings are achieved through improvements in care (McClellan et al., 2010).

These are extensions of some of the strategies employed by managed care organizations; hence, understanding the major controversies surrounding managed care will provide a context for anticipating issues that are likely to arise as we gain experience with ACOs and PCMHs.

Background: Managed Care Organizations

As employers faced increasing health insurance premiums in the 1980s and 1990s, they turned to managed care to help mitigate the overtreatment incentives built into the traditional fee-for-service system. The two most common types of managed care organizations are health maintenance organizations (HMOs) and preferred provider organizations (PPOs). (We will refer to managed care organizations as HMOs to simplify our discussion). The 1973 Health Maintenance Organization Act specified the legal framework for HMOs and mandated that large employers offer an HMO option.

Managed care plans are health insurance plans that provide care through contracted healthcare providers who provide services at reduced rates. The employer pays a fixed amount per month (pmpm = per member per month) for each individual enrolled in the managed care plan, and the managed care organization is responsible for providing any healthcare that the enrolled individuals utilize—as long as that healthcare is covered by the managed care contract. The managed care company is "at risk" for charges incurred by its enrollees, and it uses an array of strategies to manage that risk. These strategies focus on prevention of illnesses and injuries, care coordination, negotiation of favorable provider prices, and gatekeeper structures to ensure that patients obtain care at appropriate locations. For example, enrollees may be required to obtain a referral from a primary care physician (the "gatekeeper") before seeing a specialist, and they may be required to obtain care from a specified panel of physicians. Managed care companies contract with these providers to set reimbursement rates, performance measures, and risk-sharing provisions—to encourage care coordination and compliance with guidelines, particularly with regard to preventive care. In addition, managed care strategies include programs such as disease management and pharmacy management, because the HMO prepayment system incentivizes managed care organizations to prevent illness and promote more efficient healthcare.

Managed care organizations use these strategies to create efficiencies by coordinating and managing care, and this effort is facilitated by the fact that five conditions (heart disease, pulmonary conditions, mental disorders, cancers, and hypertension) account for a significant share of the increase in health spending that occurred during the years 1987–2000 (Thorpe et al., 2004).

Managed Care: Historical Trends

Three trends occurred concurrently in the late 1990s:

- The market share of managed care organizations increased from 27% of individuals with employment-based coverage in 1988 to 86% in 1998 (Kaiser Family Foundation, 2006).
- Healthcare cost inflation slowed, and this decrease was widely attributed to the growth of managed care (Orzag, 2007).
- Patients worried that clinical decisions were increasingly driven by financial incentives, rather than the clinical assessments of the patient's health status or potential for complications. See Box 5.1 to recall the movie versions of these concerns.

Public concerns about consumer protection sparked a wave of state and federal legislation, known as the managed care backlash. However, the backlash was not strongly supported by large-scale studies of the impact of managed care organizations on cost and quality. Instead, these studies produced mixed results. Miller and Luft (1997) reviewed the relevant peer-reviewed literature published during the years 1993–1996. They identified 15 relevant studies, and found that half concluded that HMO quality was significantly better than fee-for-service quality, while the other half reached the opposite conclusion. Miller and Luft (2002) updated the review to cover the years 1997–2001, and reached a similar conclusion: "Quality-of-care findings for HMO plans were roughly comparable to those for non-HMO plans."

> ## BOX 5.1 HOLLYWOOD REFLECTED PUBLIC CONCERNS IN A SERIES OF POPULAR MOVIES
>
> Hollywood reflected public concerns with movies such as *Damaged Care, As Good at it Gets, The Rainmaker,* and *John Q. Damaged Care,* a Showtime movie starring Laura Dern, was a fact-based drama about a medical reviewer for several HMOs, Linda Peeno, and her conflicts with the dilemma of cost versus care. In this docu-drama, she reveals the pressure she was under to deny patients care in order to save money. In *As Good as it Gets* a child receives inadequate care because of their HMO policies and the child only gets better after the character played by Jack Nicholson agrees to pay for care out of his pocket. Carol, the mother, has a famous line in which she expressed frustration with denials of care by using a series of angry expletives to describe HMO's. The physician responds, "Actually I think it's their technical name." *Rainmaker* is a movie adaptation of a book by John Grisham in which a young man with leukemia is denied a lifesaving bone morrow transplant by an insurance company, portrayed as "greedy" in the movie. *John Q,* a movie starring Oscar winner Denzel Washington, is about a father who seizes emergency room patients as hostages in order to force medical personnel to place his son's name on the heart-transplant list. (His son had just been diagnosed with an enlarged heart and had been denied a heart transplant by the HMO.) These movies typified public fears that managed care organizations restrict access to necessary care in order to make profits.

It is important to note that many medical errors are caused by overtreatment rather than undertreatment; however, public concern focused on the latter.

Managed Care: The Backlash

States responded to the consumer and provider concerns by passing hundreds of laws: for example, California passed 89 laws regulating managed care organizations during 1990–1997, and a patient bill of rights was proposed (but not passed) at the federal level (Enthoven and Singer, 1998). These laws mandated access, disclosure, and coverage for specific benefits, and they addressed patient billing, claims processing, provider contracting, and solvency regulation. These authors concluded that the backlash reflected fundamental problems faced by both consumers and providers:

- Consumers do not have a realistic understanding of the impacts of healthcare costs and insurance premiums on wages.
- Insurance rules (addressing the definition of emergency services, medical necessity, and standard vs. experimental care) are not clear.
- Physicians who contract with multiple plans face a complex set of evolving rules.
- Physicians who want to assume the managed care risk must work in large groups, to ensure the high volume needed to spread the risk and cover fixed administrative expenses.
- Pressure for increased productivity generates pressure for job cutbacks for nurses and other healthcare workers.

States passed hundreds of laws mandating that specific types of providers be included on managed care panels and specific types of treatments be covered: 1,000 coverage mandates were in place in 1999. Empirical research indicated that these mandates led to increased premiums, and these premium increases led to lower wages and decisions by some employers and employees to drop coverage. Gruber (1994) estimated that state maternity mandates implemented in Illinois, New Jersey, and New York from 1976 to 1977 depressed wages for healthcare *consumers* by 4.3%, because the full cost of these mandates was paid by working women ages 20–40: "The differences in wages of married women ages 20 to 40, for example, was 4.3% lower in Illinois, New Jersey and New York after the mandate than they were for similar women in the control states over the same period."

Using data for the period 1989–1994, Sloan and Conover (1998) concluded that individuals faced higher probabilities of being uninsured in states with larger numbers of coverage requirements. Similarly, Jensen and Morrisey (1999) concluded that mandates generate significant increases in health insurance premiums that, in turn, generate increases in the proportion of individuals who are uninsured (Jensen and Morrisey, 1999). These results point to a startling implication: eliminating benefit mandates would reduce the proportion of uninsured adults. At that time, 18% of nonelderly adults were uninsured, and Sloan and Conover's results indicated that eliminating mandates would have reduced this incidence to 14%.

The four highest-cost mandated benefits were chemical-dependency treatment, psychiatric hospital stay, psychologist visits, and routine dental services (Cubanski and Schauffler, 2002). In 1996, 41 states mandated that psychologists be included as providers, and 32 states mandated that insurers offer coverage for mental healthcare—but only 18 of the states mandated that employers purchase this coverage. In the other 14 states, insurers must offer the coverage, but employers can choose whether to purchase it. Federal legislation created additional mandates, including the 1996 Newborns' and Mothers' Health Protection Act and the 1996 Mental Health Parity Act. The federal mandates are significant, even though many states had already passed similar legislation. The federal legislation extends the mandates to self-insured employers, while state legislation does not impact self-insured employers.

Current Issues: Lessons Learned

Lesson 1. Defining Consumer Protection Is Complex

Consider, for example, the controversy over maternity care. Prior to the advent of DRGs, new mothers stayed in the hospital for an average of 4 days postdelivery. Once the DRG system was implemented, the average length of stay decreased to 24 hours for an uncomplicated vaginal delivery or 48 hours for an uncomplicated cesarean delivery. Public response was fierce: by 1996, 27 states enacted laws to force insurance companies to pay for a minimum of 48 hours of hospitalization following a delivery. Nationally, legislation (the Newborns' and Mothers' Health Protection Act) mandated insurance coverage for postpartum hospitalization for a minimum of 48 hours after an uncomplicated vaginal delivery and 96 hours for an uncomplicated cesarean section delivery (Feeg, 1996; Temkin, 1999).

One study surveyed 5,201 mothers and found that most thought a 24-hour stay was too short, even though a length of stay less than 48 hours was not statistically associated with maternal or newborn readmission. However, it is notable that a majority of these mothers said they would be willing to go home within 24 hours if additional services were covered, such as a 24-hour hotline, housekeeping services, and daycare for other children. Note that two of these three services do not address clinical issues—hence the mandate would probably have relatively low marginal health benefits.

In order to clarify this complex issue, we will examine an abstract view of this problem. Imagine that we can line up episodes of healthcare on the horizontal axis of the graph shown in Figure 5.1, with the most beneficial

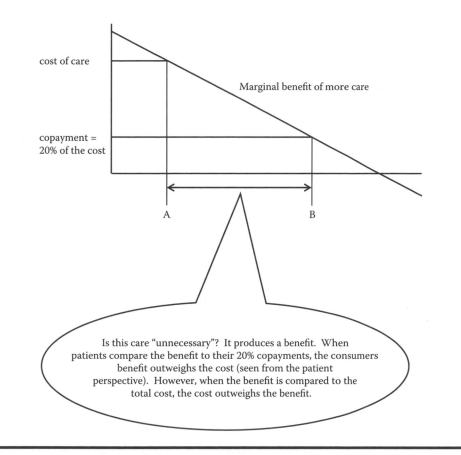

Figure 5.1   How should we define unnecessary care?

(life-saving) care on the left, and with less and less valuable care as we move to the right. The diagonal line represents this idea: it measures the marginal benefit of one more episode of care. The first unit of care (at the left edge of the graph) yields high marginal benefit, but the benefit of additional units decreases as we move to the right. For this abstract representation of the problem, we also assume that the units of care have been defined so that each unit has the same cost, which is represented by the upper horizontal line. The lower horizontal line represents 20% of the cost, which is the amount the insured individual will pay. Now we can see the conflict between the rational payer and the rational consumer:

■ The rational payer will be willing to cover care when the marginal benefit exceeds the cost, and this payer will not cover units of care for which the marginal benefit is less than the cost. Therefore, this payer will view point A as the optimal quantity of care.

■ The consumer will have a different opinion. The consumer will want to obtain all units of care for which the marginal benefit exceeds his or her copayment; hence, the consumer will think that point B represents the appropriate quantity of care. The managed care organization will view the gap between points A and B as unnecessary or inappropriate care because—from the payer's viewpoint—the benefits do not justify the cost. The managed care organization will, logically, try to prevent the patient from obtaining any care beyond point A, and the rational patient will lobby for all care up to point B.

The survey results noted above suggest that a 24-hour stay (following an uncomplicated vaginal delivery) may be represented by point A, while the longer (nice, but possibly not medically essential) stay may be represented at point B.

In addition, Chandra and Skinner (2011) provided a useful framework for conceptualizing the cost containment issue. They suggested that treatments can be categorized into three groups:

■ Treatments that are clearly cost-effective for patients who can benefit, and clearly useless for other patients (such as antiretroviral therapy for HIV)
■ Treatments that are clearly effective for some types of patients, with no clear criteria to identify which patients will benefit
■ "Gray area" treatments with uncertain clinical value (ICU days for chronically ill patient)

Cost-containment controversies focus on treatments in the second group, for which the central problem is the lack of criteria for predicting whether a specific patient will benefit from a specific treatment. Absent this scientific information, coverage decisions based on expected outcomes will seem arbitrary and unreasonable to patients who believe they might benefit from a specific treatment. Courts have agreed that it is appropriate for managed care organizations to base decisions on a population perspective (which implies some treatments—with marginal expected benefit—will *not* be covered) to forestall cost increases that could force more people to become uninsured (Rosoff, 2001).

We conclude that the real issue addressed by mandates is not consumer protection against managed care power. Instead, it is equity. Mandates make it impossible for managed care organizations to offer (and consumers/employers to choose among) different levels of policies (e.g., comprehensive/expensive vs. bare-bones/cheap). This means that employers and employees with low ability or willingness to pay can only choose between two options (high price/high coverage or no insurance). Eliminating mandates would permit an additional option—to purchase a low-price/low-coverage policy. This raises gut-wrenching social questions: Are we willing to pay enough in taxes to subsidize the high-price comprehensive option for everyone? Or, do we prefer to have a multitier system in which some purchase low-quality insurance, while others purchase high-quality insurance?

Similar issues are raised by other types of consumer protection (or provider protection) initiatives that were designed to:

- Increase malpractice liability for managed care organizations
- Restrict the flexibility of managed care organizations to deny coverage for care that is not consistent with treatment guidelines
- Require managed care organizations to contract with any provider who is willing to accept the reimbursement rate set by that organization.[1]

Managed care organizations clearly face higher costs in states that adopt these consumer protection and provider protection measures, and these additional costs will lead to higher premiums. Therefore, the key question is: How much value do these protections produce? Does the added value outweigh the premium increases?

Analysis of consumer behavior—when faced with a choice between HMO coverage and traditional fee-for-service (FFS) coverage—provides some evidence to help us think about this question. At this decision point, consumers face a tough choice: you can reduce your out-of-pocket payments (premium, copayments, deductibles) *if* you are willing to accept additional constraints on your individual healthcare decisions. Analysis of employee health plan choices indicates that consumers are willing to pay additional monthly premiums to avoid these constraints, particularly if the insured individual (or a family member) has a high-cost diagnosis (Bundorf et al., 2008).

In addition, we note that a *New York Times* article (Pear, 2005) demonstrates that the dilemma posed by this issue is not confined to managed care organizations. The article explains that a 2005 law authorizes doctors to prescribe any drug they deem "medically necessary" for their Medicare patients, even if that drug is not included on the insurer's list of preferred drugs. (This list is known as a formulary.) In addition, companies providing a drug benefit must include, on the formulary, at least two comparable drugs for every treatment category. These two provisions will constrain the companies' ability to negotiate discounts from drug makers. The first provision reduces drug makers' incentives to offer discounts, to ensure that their drugs will be included on formularies. The second provision reduces the threat that a drug might not be included in an insurer's formulary. *The New York Times* article concludes, "Without significant drug discounts, monthly premiums for the benefit could soar above the expected $35 a month." Guaranteeing that patients can access specific drugs imposes a cost: monthly premiums will increase. The critical question is: Does the treatment value of this access outweigh the cost? The answer to this question may vary across patients, diagnoses, and drugs—and analyzing these details requires balancing health issues and cost issues. As we saw, in the Chapter 3 discussion of guidelines, the answers to these questions are important—and they are also controversial.

Lesson 2. Shifting to Managed Care or ACOs Focuses on a Definition of Quality That Is New for Many Patients

Prior to the advent of managed care organizations, most consumers might have reasonably assumed that physicians had wide discretion to develop a customized treatment plan for each patient—without constraints imposed by coverage limits or provider networks. During the decade of HMO expansion, physician leaders such as David Eddy, Brent James, and Don Berwick were articulating an expanded concept of quality: that high-quality care occurs when physicians make decisions within a system of care coordination and evidence-based decision guides. Consistent with these views, the HMO concept has evolved from its initial focus on restricting care to the current emphasis on making care more systematic.

Some of the controversy about managed care is really a controversy between two definitions of *quality*. We will describe each model here, and then discuss the implications below.

The first definition of *quality* focuses on flexibility to tailor treatment plans to accommodate specific patient medical conditions and preferences. This model implies that it would be useful to pass laws to:

- Increase physician power, through anti-gag legislation and "any willing provider" legislation
- Guarantee patient access to providers and treatments through coverage mandates

■ Increase managed care malpractice liability and produce "report cards" on managed care quality
■ Mandate a consumer bill of rights

In contrast, the second definition focuses on the critical role of evidence-based decision making and systematic processes, to minimize medical errors and ensure that treatment decisions are based on current research results. This model focuses on:

■ Systematic implementation of guidelines to ensure that physicians recommend treatments that are evidence based.
■ Consumer protection efforts focused on clarifying insurance and managed care contracts.
■ Developing a strong system for reporting and analyzing data on quality. For example, the Healthcare Effectiveness Data and Information Set (HEDIS) reports performance measures for most health plans, to inform consumers about HMO quality (National Committee for Quality Assurance, 2011).

Lesson 3. Growth of Managed Care Organizations Raised Two Types of Market Power Issues

Econometric analyses indicate that managed care can reduce expenditures. The initial impact was blunted by the managed care backlash, but managed care organizations are currently producing better results. Dafny et al. (2009) present analysis of data on employer-sponsored health plans with 10 million enrollees during the years 1998–2006. These authors analyzed variations across metropolitan areas, and conclude that increased levels of managed care organizations are associated with lower healthcare expenditures for the employers as a whole. Cutler et al. (2000) use a different analytical strategy. They analyzed the treatment of heart attacks and newly diagnosed chest pain in HMOs and traditional plans. The authors argued that focusing on these conditions minimizes the selection bias issue, because most individuals cannot predict these conditions. The authors analyzed 1993–1995 claims data for a large firm that insures 200,000 employees and their dependents. For treatment of these conditions, HMO expenditures are 30–40% lower than FFS expenditures, and this difference primarily stems from lower prices. A third study analyzed hospital inpatient discharge abstracts for 932 urban counties in 22 states, to identify preventable hospitalizations due to 14 ambulatory-care-sensitive conditions (Zhan et al., 2004). These authors concluded that increased HMO market share is significantly associated with lower levels of preventable hospitalizations.

These studies suggest that managed care organizations reduce expenditures through two mechanisms: reduced provider reimbursement rates and improved organization and coordination of care. We will focus here on managed care organization's success in reducing rates paid to providers.

Reducing healthcare cost by reducing provider reimbursement sounds good, if you are a consumer, but providers see a different side of the issue. Reduced provider reimbursement rates presented a boon to consumers (because this translated into reduced premiums), but they presented a challenge to healthcare providers. To examine the physician response, we must begin by considering the underlying market structure. The fact that managed care organizations were able to use bargaining power to negotiate rate reductions implies that the physician organizations had been successfully wielding market power prior to the advent of managed care.

Managed care organizations initially achieved this result by negotiating to develop provider panels. If a physician (or other healthcare provider) agreed to the lower managed care reimbursement rate, the physician would be listed as a member of the managed care organization's provider panel, and individuals enrolled in that plan would be able to obtain care from that provider. Because managed care organizations tend to enroll large numbers of individuals, the HMO contract offers potential patient volume in exchange for the lower rate. Of course, this offer presents an implicit bargaining threat: potential loss of volume if the lower rate is not accepted. Thus, managed care organizations viewed the limited provider panel as a key strategic element—that it was essential for inducing providers to agree to accept reimbursement rate reductions.

Providers responded in two ways:

a. Physicians lobbied successfully, in many states, for any willing provider laws. These laws mandated that the managed care organizations must reimburse for treatments provided by any physicians who were willing to accept the company's rates. This blunted the company's bargaining power, and some analysts believe that these laws significantly reduced the ability of managed care organizations to impact healthcare cost escalation. One analyst examined state-level data for the years 1983–1997, and concluded that any willing provider laws led to increased per-capita healthcare expenditures (Vita, 2001). In a 2004

Federal Trade Commission and Department of Justice report on health-care competition, these agencies recommend that states examine any willing provider laws carefully, to assess whether these laws help or harm consumers and patients (U.S. Department of Justice, Federal Trade Commission, 2014).

b. Physician groups joined forces to build "countervailing market power"—as a tool to counter managed care's bargaining power. Physicians used a range of strategies to accomplish this goal: merging small practices to form a larger group practice, allying with other physicians to form an integrated practice association (IPA), or allying with a hospital to form a physician hospital organization (PHO). Analysis reported by Town and Vistnes (2001) demonstrated the potential value of provider market power (although this analysis focused on hospital reimbursement rates rather than physician rate). This paper showed that a hospital will receive a higher rate from an HMO if the HMO believes that including that hospital on its preferred provider list will help the HMO compete for employer contracts. Mergers that formed larger provider groups raised questions, because efforts to creating bargaining power (also known as market power) generally reduce competition. Any merger that focuses primarily on the creation of market power (rather than efficiency) can be challenged by the Department of Justice (DoJ), by the Federal Trade Commission (FTC), or by private parties as a violation of the antitrust laws. The DoJ issued guidance indicating that it would consider physician group mergers carefully to assess the relative importance of the two goals of increasing market power and increasing efficiency. Merging groups such as IPAs or PHOs can avoid antitrust litigation by demonstrating that the merger will increase efficiency. This requires demonstrating either financial integration (as evidenced by physician risk sharing) or clinical integration (as evidenced by investment in computer and process improvement infrastructure). Financial and clinical integration are viewed as essential first steps for achieving new efficiencies; hence, failure to take one or both of these steps is viewed as a signal that the merger (IPA or PHO) is primarily focused on enhancing market power.

Lesson 4. Managed Care Organizations Also Raised Questions about Physician Risk Taking and Solvency Regulation

Risk sharing means that physicians contracted to bear some of the risk that a group of enrollees may have higher than expected healthcare costs. In this case, the physician (or a physician group) agrees to both a reimbursement rate and a "withhold." To facilitate explanation of the withhold, assume that a managed care contract specifies a 5% withhold. Each time the provider bills the managed care organization for services rendered, the company would pay 95% of the contracted price, and withhold 5%. At the end of the year, the managed care organization would determine whether the physician group had successfully met cost control and quality targets, as specified in the contract. If the physician group met the target, the company would pay the withheld 5%; if not, the physician group would only receive a pro-rated share of that 5%. This offers opportunities—if the physician group is able to organize care and control costs. It also raises two types of concerns.

- We may be concerned about the impact of this incentive structure on patient care decisions. A 1997 federal law addressed this issue, mandating limits to physician risk sharing. No more than 25% of physician compensation can be "at risk." This was not a binding constraint at that time, since withholds were typically 10%. The law also capped cost and quality bonuses at 15%. Using data from 1994–1997, analysts concluded that the number of physicians in the group impacts the strength of the incentives on individual physician decisions: as the physician group size increases, the incentive impact weakens. Increasing the size of the physician group reduces the probability that the physician group will receive the withhold funds at the end of the year, and it also reduces the average level of quality (as measured by the reported HEDIS measures). These analysts concluded that physicians do respond to incentives, but increasing the group size diffuses the incentive—and reduces each physician's response. This result is not surprising, but it is problematic: large physician groups are essential for spreading risk, but the individual physicians in these large groups may not respond to payment incentives to increase efficiency.
- The second concern focuses on the ability of the physician group to bear the risk. Two issues were raised that are likely to reappear, as ACOs develop.

    First, regulations were implemented to limit the proportion of physician salary that could be at risk. These regulations addressed the concern that this creates a strong incentive for physicians to underprovide care. It is one thing for the managed care organization to be at risk and contract with physicians. There was concern that the incentive to underprovide would be significantly stronger if the physician were also at risk.

Second, state insurance regulations that address insurance company solvency are important. Every state has an insurance commissioner, who regulates insurance companies that do business in the state. State regulation of insurance companies typically includes requirements that insurance companies hold specified amounts of assets of specific types. These assets provide assurance that the insurance company will be able to pay claims, even if the dollar volume of claims is unusually high. These requirements, which are known as solvency requirements, address the concern that an insurance company, such as an HMO, might collect monthly premiums and then declare bankruptcy—and be unable to pay providers for completed care or provide the care for which consumers prepaid at the start of the month. As managed care organizations bargained down physician rates, physicians began to explore options for serving the managed care function themselves through the development of provider-sponsored organizations (PSOs) and IPAs.

As physician groups assumed higher levels risk (through contracting directly with employers and accepting capitated payment agreements), policy makers considered the question: Should risk-bearing physicians be required to meet the same solvency requirements that are imposed on insurance companies? Physicians argued that they did not have sufficient size or capital to meet these requirements, and the issue was resolved in their favor. However, the question of whether physician groups typically have sufficient assets (or reinsurance) to remain solvent and provide contracted care—even during a period of unusually high claims—remains. The consumer protection issue is the same, whether the risk is held by a managed care organization or a physician group. The inability to hold physicians who bear risk to the same solvency requirements that are required of insurance companies clearly raises consumer protection issues. This issue may become salient: the Advisory Board Company reported that the majority of ACOs were physician-led, in April 2013 (The Advisory Board Company, 2013).

The importance of the solvency issue posed by physician risk bearing depends on the size of physician groups. Wendel and Paterson (1996) used the Poisson distribution to illustrate the issue. The Poisson distribution is frequently used to compute the probability that a specific number of events will occur. Suppose, for example, that a provider group expects to average five high-cost episodes of care in a typical month. In addition, suppose the physician group might have difficulty providing care during an unlucky month, in which 10 of its patients have high-cost episodes of care (double the expected number). How often will this occur? The Poisson distribution allows us to calculate the answer to that question: the probability that this group has more than double the typical number of high-cost episodes of care is 0.014. What happens to this probability as the patient population increases? For a larger group that expects to have 15 high-cost episodes of care per month, the comparable level of risk would focus on the probability that the group will have more than double (30) high-cost episodes of care in a month. The probability that this will occur is only 0.0002. The difference between these numbers (0.014 and 0.0002) represents an importance reduction in the level of risk as the size of the provider group grows (because larger groups that see more patients will have higher expected numbers of high-cost episodes of care). This is the essence of the concept of risk pooling, and it means that this group's entities are less able to assume risk for the care of a specific patient population. Thus, small providers face a competitive disadvantage, which may have important implications for the concept of forming local ACOs in rural areas. Instead, it may be necessary to form larger ACOs that serve large regions of rural patients.

Lesson 5. Mental Health Parity Mandate May Constitute a Special Case

As individuals make choices between HMO and FFS plans, they wisely select plans that offer the best coverage for care that is already anticipated. If they anticipate, for example, the need for mental health treatment, they will seek out plans that offer a more generous mental health coverage benefit. Thus, a plan that offers unusually comprehensive care for a high-cost condition is likely to experience adverse selection. (Adverse selection occurs when a plan has a disproportionate number of high-cost enrollees.) Managed care organizations may therefore design coverage strategically—in an attempt to attract low-cost enrollees and discourage potential enrollees who are likely to incur high costs. Frank et al. (1998) examine the pattern of resulting coverage decisions, and conclude that this strategic behavior leads to systematic underprovision of mental health and substance abuse treatment. Mandating mental health parity is, of course, one regulatory response (Sturm and Pacula, 2012).

Managed care plans that experience higher than expected enrollment by high-cost individuals face a competitive challenge, if it's difficult for these companies to offer competitive monthly premiums (because they face higher costs than their competitors). State Medicaid agencies responded by implementing risk adjustment (RA) systems. Risk adjustment systems use healthcare encounter data from managed care plans to measure the level of risk shouldered by each plan to increase compensation to plans with higher-risk members. Analysts initially expected that private payers would also adopt this strategy, but RA is primarily used by public payers such as Medicaid. With the enactment of the new healthcare reform bill, particularly the mandate placed on insurance companies that requires them to include persons with high-cost (or potentially high-cost) preexisting conditions in the health plan, risk adjustment systems in the private-sector health insurance industry may become an important issue.

Lesson 6. Physician Rating Systems Raise Concerns

Physician rating systems are designed to:

- Help consumers choose physicians that offer evidence-based care
- Incentivize the provision of high-quality care through a reimbursement mechanism that rewards high performers and penalizes low performers

Advocates of ACOs and patient-centered medical homes assert that these delivery systems will improve both coordination of care and patient outcomes. Strategies for measuring these improvements, and reporting these measures, have been controversial. In November 2006, the Washington State Medical Association filed a lawsuit, the first of its kind, against Regence BlueShield, alleging that the physician ranking was based on inaccurate and incomplete data. Similar lawsuits followed in Connecticut, Massachusetts, and New York. In 2007, New York's attorney general developed a doctor ranking model code and garnered support from eight major health insurers in New York. This code requires insurers to:

- Identify the degree to which ratings are based on cost, and include additional factors (other than cost) in the rating scores.
- Use established national standards to measure quality, including measures endorsed by the National Quality Forum (NQF).

■ Use methods such as risk adjustment and valid sampling to permit meaningful comparisons.
■ Disclose ranking methods to consumers, and establish a consumer complaint process.
■ Disclose ranking methods to physicians, and provide an appeal process.
■ Retain a ratings examiner to audit compliance with the model code and report the audit results to the attorney general every 6 months. The audit must be conducted by a national standard setting organization, such as the National Committee on Quality Assurance (NCQA).

Similarly, Colorado enacted a law in 2008 (Cartwright-Smith and Rosenbaum, 2009) that requires that any public representation of a physician's performance (ranking, grade, or tier) must:

■ Include a quality of care component that is endorsed by National Quality Forum or a similar organization
■ Use statistically accurate and adjusted data
■ Be attributed to the right physician
■ Provide a disclaimer about the risk of error

At the national level, the Patient Charter for Physician Performance Measurement, Reporting and Tiering Programs was developed to provide guidelines for quality data reporting (Miller, Brennan, and Milstein, 2009). This program, which was supported by consumer, labor, and employer groups, articulates best practices:

■ NQF measures constitute the logical starting point, followed by measures approved by national accrediting bodies such as NCQA and the Joint Commission.
■ Provider and consumer input should be solicited on supplemental measures (if any are used).
■ The provider rating method should be transparent.
■ Data collection should be coordinated by independent third parties.

These guidelines focus on four key issues: data integrity, disclosure, fair process, and enforcement. The guidelines also delineate common ground between the consumer benefits of physician quality reporting and the provider interest in avoiding inaccurate reporting. The model code and the patient charter shift the burden of proving accuracy of data to the health plan, and highlight the importance of sound statistical methods.

Conclusion: Experiences with Managed Care Organizations Provide Significant Lessons Learned, as Providers Begin Forming ACOs and PCMHs

As we conclude this chapter, we can see that our experiences with managed care organizations provide significant lessons learned for careful consideration as we begin crafting the next ACOs and PCMHs. Consumer protection will be important to:

- Ensure that consumers know what they are paying for when purchasing health insurance, and that they get what they pay for
- Address the controversies surrounding quality measures
- Balance efficiency and market power issues among healthcare providers

In Chapter 6 we will explore the efficiency gains we can hope to achieve through wellness, prevention, and disease management programs.

Endnotes

1. The question of whether these any willing provider laws primarily protect physicians or consumers generated controversy. Managed care organizations argued that these laws blocked their ability to negotiate low provider reimbursement rates, which are essential for cost control. Providers countered that these laws lead to more inclusive physician panels that offer consumers an array of options when they are selecting a physician.

Chapter 6

Wellness, Prevention, Disease Management

Introduction

The famous saying that "an ounce of prevention is worth a pound of cure" summarizes the philosophy that underlies the creation of wellness, preventive care, and chronic disease management programs. Economists approach this idea by thinking about the inputs that are needed to produce a car—and then applying that concept of production to think about the diverse activities that produce health. The list of activities that contribute to producing health clearly includes healthcare, but it also includes individual decisions to eat healthy foods and exercise regularly, public health measures such as vaccinations and access to clean drinking water, and regulatory measures such as highway speed limits. These factors are important: public health measures account for a large share of the increase in life expectancy that occurred during the twentieth century, and as we saw in Chapter 1, comparison of U.S. and Canadian mortality rates highlight the importance of obesity and violence.

While prevention is a critical issue, we must address two challenges to achieve the goal of using prevention effectively:

- We must identify programs that are effective (and also cost-effective).
- We must develop strategies to induce appropriate patient participation.

Two recent headlines articulate the importance of solving the mystery of *how* to design prevention programs that will actually impact behavior:

- "To Double the Odds of Seeing 85: Get a Move On (When It Comes to Longevity, Regular Exercise May Be the Most Potent Weapon against Disease)" (Winslow, 2010)
- "Extra Pounds Mean Insurance Fees for Ala. Workers" (Rawls, 2008)

Most of us realize that lifestyle choices are important, but this information alone does not always spur us to action. The state of Alabama strengthened the incentive by implementing a monetary penalty for state employees with "extra pounds."

In this chapter, we use the word *prevention* broadly, to encompass a broad range of activities that are designed to prevent adverse outcomes. In addition to activities such as vaccinations that are typically viewed as prevention programs, we also consider wellness programs, preventive health-care such as prenatal care, and chronic disease management that is designed to prevent (or postpone) complications associated with chronic disease.

Background: PPACA Focuses Increased Attention on Prevention and Wellness

The Patient Protection and Affordable Care Act (PPACA) is generating renewed focus on prevention and wellness. This law creates the National Prevention, Health Promotion and Public Health Council, to develop a strategy to improve the nation's health and coordinate federal prevention, wellness, and public health activities (National Prevention, Health Promotion & Public Health Council, 2011). The council's strategic plan identifies its primary goal: to increase the number of Americans who are healthy at every stage of life. Based on evidence that prevention can reduce healthcare costs and increase productivity, the council identified a four-pronged approach to accomplish this goal:

1. Create, sustain, and recognize healthy communities
2. Ensure the availability and quality of community preventive services
3. Empower people to make healthy choices
4. Eliminate health disparities

The council established seven evidence-based priorities to reduce or prevent the leading causes of preventable deaths and major illness:

1. Tobacco-free living
2. Preventing drug and alcohol abuse
3. Healthy eating
4. Active living
5. Injury and violence-free living
6. Reproductive and sexual health
7. Mental and emotional well-being

In addition, the federal Department of Health and Human Services (HHS) provides administrative support for the U.S. Preventive Services Task Force (USPSTF). The USPSTF is an independent body that makes evidence-based recommendations, such as the mammogram screening recommendation discussed in Chapter 3.

Current Issues

To achieve the vision of increased prevention as an essential component of efforts to improve our healthcare system's access, cost, and quality, it will be necessary to address two questions.

First, it is widely recognized that accomplishing these goals will strengthen health. However, it is not clear whether they will reduce cost in the short run (or whether we should view prevention as an investment that will produce future health gains).

While many people believe that prevention always pays, existing evidence does not fully support this view (Russell, 2009). This apparent disconnect can be explained by looking at the issue from two perspectives.

- Prevention clearly pays if we *only* look at individuals who would have developed a disease or condition if they had not participated in prevention. After an individual is diagnosed with cancer, it is easy to conclude that early diagnosis and treatment would have been cheaper and produced a better outcome, compared with the more intensive treatment that may be required after a delayed diagnosis.
- However, it is generally necessary to provide numerous screening mammograms in order to identify one individual with early-stage treatable cancer (reflect back to our earlier discussion in Chapter 3, where we discussed the cost-to-benefit analysis of mammography for women between 40 and 49 years of age). Louise Russell summarized the issue

succinctly: "Evaluating the claim that prevention reduces medical spending is more complicated than it appears at first glance. Costs that look small when considered per person, or per year, start to mount up. The result is that prevention can cost more than it saves" (Russell, 2009).

Instead of simply assuming that all preventive efforts will generate fiscal savings, it may be necessary to target prevention efforts carefully to ensure that prevention dollars are well spent.

Second, some individuals are likely to enjoy substantial benefits from prevention programs, while others may not benefit at all. There is no guarantee that individuals with high potential to benefit will also have a high propensity to participate in the program. It is possible, for example, that a wellness program may seem particularly attractive to people who are already predisposed to be conscientious about engaging in recommended healthy behaviors. The wellness program will not generate a positive net benefit if the couch potatoes (who might have benefited from the wellness program's emphasis on increased exercise) remain comfortably at home, while the people who were already running marathons elect to participate in the program. To be financially viable, programs must be designed to anticipate—and manage—these self-selection issues.

A study of the impact of a subsidized prenatal care program on infant health provides an example of the importance of viewing self-selection as a program management issue. Mukhopadhyay and Wendel (2008) conclude that prenatal care produced statistically significant beneficial impacts on infant health when the mother had specific preexisting diagnoses. Unfortunately—in this sample—these mothers (whose infants are most likely to benefit from prenatal care) did *not* initiate prenatal care early in the pregnancy. This self-selection, which occurs before anyone at the clinic interacts with the pregnant women, impacts the ability of the clinic to produce good outcomes; hence, developing strategies to influence this self-selection process is an important factor that may increase the clinic's overall impact on the patient population.

This problem is not unique to prenatal care. Wendel and Dumitras (2005) reported an analogous misalignment between patients who could potentially benefit from a diabetes disease management program and patients who elected to participate in the program. The program managers envisioned that the program would generate a net financial benefit because participation would reduce the average number of visits to hospital emergency departments. However, multivariate analysis of the data indicated that patients whose pattern of care focused on physician visits (measured by a relatively high number of physician visits per prescription—and fewer emergency department visits) were more likely to participate in the program, compared with patients with a higher number of emergency department visits. This mismatch between potential benefit and self-selection patterns reduces the ability of the program to increase population health and demonstrate a positive financial benefit.

The question of *how* to manage self-selection is generating discussion—and the results will clearly impact the design and success of wellness programs. Dee Edington, in the book *Zero Trends* (2009), provides extensive and very interesting analyses of the impact of self-selection on the strategic design of employer wellness programs. Dr. Edington concluded that wellness programs should focus primarily on "keeping the healthy people healthy," while others recommend the opposite: wellness programs should target participation of the less healthy people.

After We Identify Individuals Who Are Most Likely to Benefit from Prevention Programs, Can We Design Programs to Successfully Induce Them to Participate?

The quest to understand people (why they do what they do, and choose what they choose) is pursued by psychologists, sociologists, and anthropologists. One might be surprised to learn that economists also seek to understand decisions and choices. *Behavioral economics* is the study of decision making as it relates to economic issues. The well-known book and movie *Freakonomics* provided some illustrations of this approach (Levitt and Dubner, 2005). Behavioral economists seek to understand factors that influence individual choices, and then use that information to design useful policies and programs. For example, the British government has a cabinet-level unit that is responsible for using behavioral economics to influence health behaviors such as obesity and smoking. The unit is nicknamed the Nudge Unit after the popular book *Nudge*, and it is advised by one of that book's authors (the book's other author heads an analogous unit in the U.S. government [Thaler Sunstein, 2008]). Box 6.1 summarizes three behavioral economics studies.

Behavioral and experimental economics have strong interdisciplinary ties to psychology, as researchers seek to understand individual decision processes. Behavioral economists focus on situations in which individuals

BOX 6.1 WHAT IS "BEHAVIORAL ECONOMICS"? THREE EXAMPLES

SIMON: WHY DO WE SETTLE FOR OPTIONS THAT ARE JUST "GOOD ENOUGH"?

The field of "behavioral economics" is new, but the basic ideas are well-established. Herbert Simon, a psychologist, won a Nobel Prize in 1978 for his seminal work on managerial decision making (Simon, 1957). He argued that people balance costs and benefits when they decide how much effort to invest before making a specific decision. Acquiring, organizing, synthesizing, and analyzing information is costly; hence people frequently use rules of thumb to avoid investing time and effort in a substantive decision process. We park in the same corner of the parking lot every morning, without investing time to search for a better space. Many of us choose a supermarket check-out line after a cursory inspection of the options, without detailed assessment of the amounts and types of goods in each waiting basket, and each checker's speed. Dr. Simon coined the term "satisfice" to encapsulate the idea that we simply choose an option that is "good enough," without investing time and effort to ensure that we select the "best" option.

KAHNEMAN AND TVERSKY: PEOPLE PAY MORE ATTENTION TO LOSSES, THAN TO GAINS

Daniel Kahneman, another psychologist, won a Nobel Prize in 2002 for his work with Amos Tversky that demonstrated that individual choices are impacted—in systematic ways—by the decision context. For example, individuals pay more attention to losses than gains; hence framing a choice as a loss, rather than a gain, will generate a larger response. The www.stickk.com strategy implements this idea—with surprising success (Kahneman, 2011).

AKERLOF: WHY DO WE PROCRASTINATE?

George Akerlof analyzed procrastination (Akerlof, 1991). An embarrassing example of procrastination in his own life motivated him to examine this phenomenon: he promised to mail a box to a colleague, he intended to mail the box every day for a year, his failure to mail the box was embarrassing, the box was still sitting in his office one year later. This forced him to consider the question: why did he make this decision error—repeatedly—for a year? His answer focused on the fact that this type of decision is repeated many times. Each time he considered "should I mail the box today?" he weighed the costs and benefits. If he used his time "today" to mail the box (compared to a future day—later in the week), the benefit would be small. His colleague would not really care whether the box arrived one day sooner or later. However, competing time pressures "today" were clear: if he mailed the box "today," he would not complete an immediate task. He concluded that there is a large set of similar decisions, in which individuals make decision errors because they divide time into numerous small segments. The cost of taking the desired action always outweighs the benefit—in any specific segment of time, but the accumulated decisions over a long period of time do not maximize the individual's happiness. In these situations, individuals can benefit from paternalistic schemes designed to prevent procrastination. For example, people hire personal trainers to set rigid times for exercise.

systematically make decision errors, in the sense that the decisions are not consistent with the individuals' goals. These decision errors are common: retirees wish they had saved more when they were young, smokers intend to quit but do not, and people spend money to join gyms that they do not use. Instead of processing information logically, we anchor on recent information, overemphasize low probabilities, and place undue importance on information that is frequently repeated. Behavioral economists hope to develop sufficient understanding of these decision errors to be able to help individuals make "correct" decisions by structuring incentive systems or decision frameworks.

Behavioral economists examine factors that influence choices, including information, monetary incentives, individual resources, and the decision context. For example, the British Nudge Unit is working to identify specific types, locations, and formats of nutrition labeling that would influence food choices. Will we pay attention—and use the information to increase our production of health—if alcohol content is presented on bar napkins? Or, if yellow tape visually reserves a section of the grocery cart for fresh produce? Research results reported by Elbel et al. (2009) illustrated the intrinsic difficulty of this task. The researchers collected fast-food cash register receipts and survey data in New York City and in nearby Newark, New Jersey, both before and after New York City mandated that restaurants with multiple locations (at least 15) must visibly post calorie information for their menu offerings. After analyzing the data in a multivariate difference-in-difference framework, the authors concluded that the law increased the proportion of consumers who saw calorie information, but this information did not influence consumers to reduce the number of calories purchased. Elbel et al. conclude, "In an ideal world, calorie labeling on menus and menu boards would have an immediate and direct impact on everyone's food choices. However, … greater attention to the root causes of behavior, or multifaceted interventions, or both, will be necessary if obesity is to be greatly reduced in the overall U.S. population" (Elbel et al., 2009, p. w1117).

The question of *how* to post nutrition information is clearly important: PPACA mandates that chain restaurants must include nutrition information on their menus. Healthcare adviser E.J. Emanuel (housed in the Office of Management and Budget) is working to figure out optimal strategies for posting that information in a way that will impact decisions: "Where is it likely to impact people, and what's most likely to do it?" (Dorning, 2010). Emanuel concedes that this effort is more typical of Madison Avenue instead of Pennsylvania Avenue and notes that this is a new role for government.

Another British Nudge Unit project utilizes a website created by two Yale University behavioral economists (Karlan and Ayres, www.stickk.com). This website harnesses evidence that most people pay more attention to losses than to gains. This website allows individuals to create self-financed incentives to quit smoking or lose weight, by depositing money in an account. If the individual succeeds in achieving the goal (the information is self-reported), he receives a refund of his own money. If he fails, he will forfeit the money. He can specify, at the outset, that the forfeited money would be donated to a cause that he vehemently dislikes. The researchers report that success rates for www.stickk.com users are higher than success rates in the general population, and they are particularly high for individuals who precommit that forfeited funds will be donated to a cause that the individual dislikes.

While www.stickk.com provides an example of voluntary decision framing at the individual level, behavioral economists typically aim to apply this type of strategy at the system level. The application of behavioral economics to the issue of retirement savings provides a good example. While many people intend to save for retirement, a large proportion of these individuals do not take advantage of the tax advantage offered by employer 401(k) retirement savings plans. After behavioral and experimental economists demonstrated that specifying the default option impacts decisions, a large U.S. corporation adopted a new policy for employee retirement savings accounts (Madrian and Shea, 2011). The firm switched from the traditional policy, allowing employees to opt in to the decision to open a 401(k) account, to a new system that automatically enrolled new employees in a 401(k) account, but allowed these employees to opt out. While the decision to open a 401(k) account was optional in both systems, the default option that would occur if the employee took no action switched from not having a 401(k) account to having a 401(k) account. Because inertia appears to exert significant influence on actual behavior, changing the decision framework led to substantial behavior change: 37% of employees opened 401(k) accounts under the *opt-in* system, while 86% maintained accounts under the *opt-out* system.

Economists describe this type of manipulation of the decision framework as "beneficent paternalism" to emphasize that it is designed to help individuals achieve goals that they themselves say they want to achieve. This type of policy aims to achieve—on a system level—the types of manipulations that individuals implement when they freeze their credit cards in ice (so the card cannot be used until the ice melts), refuse to keep ice cream or cookies in the house (so these foods will not be conveniently available), or put the alarm clock several feet away from the bed (so they will have to get out of bed to turn the alarm off in the morning). Despite the fine line between helping individuals achieve self-identified goals and incentivizing individuals to achieve goals defined by the employer or health insurance plan, mounting evidence that lifestyle choices exert major impacts on healthcare expenditures (O'Neill and O'Neill, 2007) is generating increasing interest.

If we design wellness and disease management programs without a clear understanding of factors that influence actual decisions, it is unlikely that the programs will be able to help/prod/induce individuals to make significant lifestyle changes. In contrast, these programs are likely to be far more successful if the programs and incentives are designed to influence real-world decisions made by real people. Designing such effective programs and incentives, however, requires in-depth understanding of real decision processes—and that conceptual framework is only partially available at this point.

It also raises a more sensitive question: Is this strategy overly manipulative? Advocates of the strategy argue that it is not, because compliance with the policy goal remains voluntary and because (ideally) the strategy is only applied to help individuals make choices that align with those individuals' goals. In the context of retirement savings, the advocates' argument is simple: There has to be a default option (*opt-in* or *opt-out*). Many seniors report—in surveys—that they wish they had saved more when they were younger. We should select the default option that helps people accomplish their goals.

Assuming that the behavioral economics results are useful, how can managed care organizations, disease management, and wellness program managers apply this information? The report of the Cabinet Office Behavioral Insights Team (2010) provides some interesting examples of applications of these ideas to tackle issues such as smoking cessation, teenage pregnancy, diet and weight management, and diabetes prevention. Some applications are relatively straightforward, such as development of an *opt-out* system for authorizing organ donation, to replace the traditional *opt-in* system. Others are more creative. For example, the report describes a collaboration between Bayer Healthcare and Nintendo DS to develop a device that awards points to diabetic children for consistent blood sugar testing. (The children can use these points on Nintendo games.) The report also describes Volkswagen's hypothesis that fun can be a strong motivator for behavior change:

> The piano stairs was one of the most popular ideas. For one day in a Stockholm metro station, Volkswagen installed motion-sensor piano keys so that musical tunes were played as people climbed the stairs. A before-and-after study showed that 66 percent more people than normal took the stairs rather than the escalator. (British Cabinet Office Behavioral Insights Team, 2010, p. 19)

To have some fun yourself, watch two videos: http://www.thefuntheory.com/ and "Turning behavioural insights into policy with Richard Thaler" at http://www.youtube.com/watch?v = f-6tNtk_H6s (Policy Exchange UK, 2011).

Conclusion

In this chapter, we examined efficiency strategies aimed at creating and maintaining a healthy populace through the use of wellness, preventative care, and disease management programs. As with other strategies we have explored in earlier chapters of Section II, these strategies offer strong potential to increase efficiency, but they also pose challenges. Effective prevention can reduce long-term healthcare costs and increase productivity of our workforce. However, prevention strategies may not be efficient in all situations and may not actually benefit those we sought to help. Can we identify effective programs? Can we identify those most likely to benefit from these programs, and once we have, can we ensure that those people will elect to participate? What types of incentives can best induce the behaviors we wish to promote? These are questions healthcare providers and policy makers must address in order to obtain the efficiencies these strategies promise. Health professionals (including psychologists, nurses, behavioral counselors, and others who manage programs and interact directly with patients) have much to offer in addressing these challenges.

In Chapter 7 we will continue to explore strategies to improve healthcare efficiencies with a look at new provider types and the changing role of patients.

Chapter 7

New Types of Providers

Introduction

In the influential book *The Innovator's Prescription: A Disruptive Solution for Health Care*, the authors mapped a strategy for reducing the cost of delivering healthcare by dramatically increasing the efficiency of the healthcare industry (Christensen et al., 2008). This strategy underlies a central component of current federal policy, which is funded through the 2009 American Recovery and Reinvestment Act (ARRA). ARRA committed substantial funds to strengthen the role of health information technology (HIT) in our healthcare system.

However, before we examine HIT initiatives in Chapter 8, we will examine the potential for generating dramatic efficiency gains by restructuring our healthcare system. Specifically, we will consider two examples of organizations that could potentially contribute to generating this type of efficiency, and we will consider the policy issues that surround these changes.

Background

The starting point for understanding this strategy is the competitive market mechanism that generates efficiency gains in other industries (Bureau of Labor Statistics, 2010).

Wal-Mart's impact on the retail industry provides a good example of this dynamic market process that produces efficiency gains, and also generates controversies. Building on the model provided by other retail chain stores,

Wal-Mart pursued a low-price/high-volume strategy. Wal-Mart's success is documented by an academic study that concludes that Wal-Mart's low prices generated a statistically significant reduction in the overall rate of U.S. inflation (Business Planning Solutions Global Insight Advisory Services Division, 2005). Wal-Mart's significant impact on the Consumer Price Index reflects both its relatively low prices, which clearly benefit consumers, and its substantial market share. However, the low prices and the substantial market share raise two types of questions:

▪ Do the low prices reflect superior efficiency or unfair tactics?
▪ When competitors respond to Wal-Mart's competitive vigor by closing their stores and businesses, how should we weigh the benefits of Wal-Mart's low prices on specific consumer goods against the negative externalities created when businesses close?

These issues are not new. Consider, for example, Wal-Mart's predecessor in both innovative retailing and national controversy: the Great Atlantic and Pacific Tea Company (A&P). A&P was founded in 1859; it grew into a successful nationwide retailer, and the United States filed an antitrust lawsuit against A&P in 1942 (accusing A&P of misusing its market power). Evidence introduced at the trial indicated that A&P focused on a strategy of offering low prices in order to sell a high volume of items. A&P harnessed economies of scale to outcompete smaller rivals (Adelman, 1959). The Austrian economist Joseph Schumpeter famously described this process as "creative destruction" (because successful new business strategies outcompete the existing businesses and drive them out of business) (Schumpeter, 1942).

You might be wondering: If A&P successfully captured market share by efficiently offering goods for sale at attractive prices, why did the U.S. government file an antitrust suit against A&P? The answer to this question reflects the ambivalence exhibited by individuals who buy groceries at Wal-Mart to enjoy the low prices, but also express concern about the impacts of Wal-Mart's vigorous competition and low prices on competitors, suppliers, and employees. The creative destruction process is two-sided, as its name suggests: it delivers progress and innovation, but the change process is disruptive, and it imposes costs on competitors and their communities.

The recent Microsoft antitrust case illustrates another issue that is likely to become important as healthcare competition intensifies: network economies. As Microsoft solidified a dominant market position for the Windows operating systems, Microsoft's success generated controversy about the question of whether this success reflected consumer preference for a superior product or unfair market tactics against competitors. Microsoft Windows standardized a previously fragmented market and made it easy for coworkers and friends to share word processing and spreadsheet files. This convenience generated network economies in the sense that the value enjoyed by one individual using Microsoft products, such as Word, increases when more of his coworkers and friends use this software. The coworkers and friends who will potentially share these Word files form a "network," and the value gained by each member of the network increases as the size of the network grows. This phenomenon, that larger networks produce value *because* they are large, is known as network economies. This generates a competitive advantage for the firm with the largest market share because it is difficult for small firms to compete with the firm that sells the large-network product.

Current Issues

In the influential book *The Innovator's Prescription*, Christensen et al. (2008) highlight two important strategies for achieving new types of efficiencies (and harnessing network economies) in technical industries such as healthcare: simplify the products and services, and streamline production processes. The authors of this book argue that this process can generate substantial efficiencies in healthcare; hence, we examine two types of providers that may offer potential efficiency gains for the healthcare system: retail clinics and specialty hospitals. These innovators offer services with attractive features, but they generate controversies similar to the issues raised by A&P, Wal-Mart, and Microsoft. The competitive success of innovative market newcomers threatens the competitive position of established entities, and generates concerns about the impacts of competitive dynamics on healthcare quality, healthcare providers, and communities. In this chapter, we will see that competitive dynamics in the healthcare industry also raise issues specific to healthcare: new types of efficiencies create opportunities to address concerns about access and the financial viability of safety net providers, but they also generate new types of concerns about consumer protection. Here, we discuss two new types of providers (retail clinics, specialty hospitals) and implications for the changing roles of patients and providers.

New Types of Providers

We will begin by looking at two relatively new types of providers: retail clinics and specialty hospitals. These innovations offer efficient strategies for delivering of healthcare services and, at the same time, raise serious concerns.

Retail Clinics

The term *retail clinics* refers to healthcare clinics that offer services in a retail setting. This innovation predates the health reform debate, ARRA, and Patient Protection and Affordable Care Act (PPACA): by mid-2008, retail clinics were offered in 1,000 sites (Target, Rite Aid, Wal-Mart, CVS Pharmacy) in 37 states (Laws and Scott, 2008). These clinics are staffed by nurse practitioners and physician assistants, who offer a specific list of services, such as school physicals, strep tests, immunizations, blood pressure screenings, and diagnosis and treatment for routine, uncomplicated illnesses. The retail clinic concept focuses on providing cost-effective primary care services for patients, with referrals to higher levels of care as needed. Patients are seen on a drop-in basis, the clinics are typically open the same hours as the retail pharmacy (including evening and weekend hours), prices are posted for specific services, and some stores offer restaurant-style beepers to permit patients to shop in the store while waiting for care. These clinics were initially established in urban areas (Rudavsky et al., 2009).

Although the initial growth rate has subsequently slowed, retail clinics have become an established component of our healthcare system. Figure 7.1 shows that the number of these clinics grew rapidly from 2006 to 2009, and it has grown more slowly since then. To read more about Wal-Mart's plans to increase its market share within the retail clinic and traditional physician office settings, see http://www.npr.org/blogs/health/2011/11/09/142156478/wal-mart-plans-ambitious-expansion-into-medical-care?sc=fb&cc=fp.

The market success of retail clinics raises four types of issues:

1. These clinics offer basic services with prices below the level typically charged for physician office care. These prices facilitate access to these services for uninsured and underinsured patients, and they may indirectly create competitive pressure for physicians to respond with careful consideration of their pricing policies—as they experience increased competition. Similarly, consumer response to the clinics suggests that

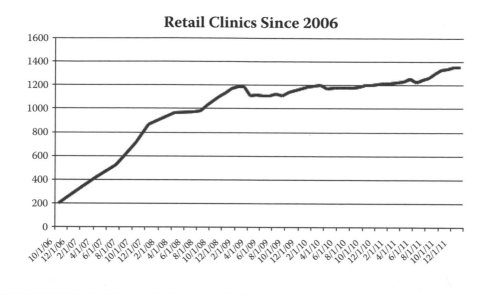

Figure 7.1   Retail clinics since 2006. (From http://www.merchantmedicine.com/home.cfm.)

many patients (insured and uninsured) value the extended hours, drop-in care, and colocated pharmacies. Now that retail clinics have generated this evidence on consumer preferences, some physicians are exploring options for providing comparable convenience in their practices. (The American Association of Family Practitioners articulates concerns about retail clinics (AAFP, 2009).)

2. The clinics highlight the importance of state licensure laws that define the scope of practice of nurse practitioners and detail the "physician supervision" requirements. States that require physician supervision may specify the amount of time that a supervising physician must be on-site, while other states require retrospective chart reviews to ensure that appropriate care has been delivered (Christian and Dower, 2008). These differences in the definition of *physician supervision* impact clinic operating costs and potential service offerings in each state. The authors of *The Innovator's Prescription* offer a valuable perspective on this issue. They begin by noting that technology development in other industries followed a pattern:

■ When new technology emerges, such as the mainframe computer technology that developed in the 1950s and 1960s, highly skilled professionals are needed to harness the power of this technology to solve customer problems.

■ As the technology matured, it became possible to deliver more user-friendly hardware and software. The skill level required to use computers was reduced—until the products were widely used by consumers (on our desktops, laptops, tablets, and cell phones) with minimal assistance from computer professionals.

The authors argue that this type of technical progress is occurring in healthcare: scientific progress is shifting *some* types of healthcare from the realm that requires highly skilled intuition to the realm in which new types of lab tests make diagnosis routine and treatment guidelines are well specified. For these types of healthcare (such as diagnosis and treatment of strep throat), nurse practitioners working in retail clinics can administer the test and then implement treatment recommendations. However, licensure regulations that limit nurse practitioner scope of practice in many states have been inhibiting the process of permitting individuals with lower levels of training to provide care that is within their skill set. (This situation may be changing, as states revise scope of practice regulations.)

3. The availability of clinic care—for a narrow set of services—also raises the specter of increasing fragmentation of care at a time when we are seeing increasing emphasis on efforts to integrate and organize and coordinate care. However, the emerging health information technology offers the potential to resolve this issue. Consider, for example, prenatal care. Mukhopadhyay et al. (2008) indicate that there may be substantial numbers of pregnant women with low levels of prenatal care, and studies indicate that barriers to obtaining prenatal care include pragmatic considerations such as transportation, inability to take time off work, and difficulty in scheduling child care (Poland et al., 1987; GAO, 1987; Brown, 1988; Goldenberg et al., 1992; Perez-Woods, 1990). New types of care providers could provide convenient access to care (that ameliorates some of these barriers) and coordinate with the physician who supervises prenatal care via electronic medical records and health information exchange.

This raises the question: Could retail clinics potentially offer a strategy to increase routine and follow-up care *if* they used health information technology to transmit this information to the patient's primary healthcare provider? A study conducted by RAND researchers (Weinick et al., 2010) found that the majority of retail clinics utilize electronic medical records, but they do not currently have the ability to communicate medical information to practitioners outside their facility. Thus, the challenge to coordinate care across segments of the healthcare system remains. (We explored this issue in Chapter 5.)

Using this logic, the PPACA provided $200 million to develop school-based health clinics from 2010 to 2013. In FY 2011, the U.S. Department of Health and Human Services (HHS) funded 278 school-based clinics (HHS, 2011) that will implement a slightly different slant on this concept of offering basic care at convenient locations and using health information technology to address the coordination issue. These clinics will be staffed by nurse practitioners. To be eligible for grant funding, the school-based clinics must have an electronic medical record system, the capability to transmit records to community providers, and connection to a 24/7 referral network. The clinic nurse practitioners will provide basic services such as health screenings, primary care, activities related to health promotion and disease prevention, including identification of mental health issues, and appropriate referrals for higher-level care (HHS, 2011).

4. Retail clinics have sparked legislative opposition in some states. For example, the state of Illinois considered a bill that would have blocked the operation of retail clinics by outlawing the provision of healthcare in a building that also houses the sale of cigarettes (one cannot create health and destroy health in the same building!). The Federal Trade Commission responded by issuing a letter indicating that this type of regulation would be viewed as anticompetitive, because it would block the process of creative destruction that generates efficiency gains, consumer price reductions, competitive pressure on suppliers and competitors, and service quality innovation (Federal Trade Commission, 2008).

Single Specialty Hospitals

As the name implies, single specialty hospitals (SSHs) focus on one specific type of treatment or procedure. In 2003, a report by the Government Accountability Office noted that 100 SSHs were in operation, with an additional 26 under development. Most of these hospitals were clustered in seven states that house 26% of the U.S. population: Arizona, California, Texas, Oklahoma, South Dakota, Louisiana, and Kansas. The authors of *The Innovator's Prescription* highlighted specialty hospitals as a competitive innovation with strong potential to help make our healthcare system more efficient (Christensen et al., 2008). Their logic focuses on process efficiency. Whereas a general hospital organizes flexible work processes, to provide customized treatment for any type of patient who might arrive at the hospital, a specialty hospital organizes a small number of streamlined work processes to treat specific types of cases. This permits specialty hospitals to be more efficient for treating those specific types of cases than equally well-managed general hospitals.

Despite this potential efficiency advantage offered by specialty hospitals, the Centers for Medicare and Medicaid Services (CMS) imposed an 18-month moratorium on billing by new specialty hospitals in 2003–2004. The moratorium was extended, and then allowed to expire. However, PPACA implemented new constraints, that are expected to effectively block development of new single specialty hospitals. These actions reflect concern about two issues.

- First, policy makers are concerned about the fact that many specialty hospitals are owned and operated by the physicians who diagnose patient conditions and refer patients to their own hospitals for treatment. This type of self-referral generates the same types of concerns as those generated when an auto mechanic provides diagnosis and repair as a bundled service.
- Second, policy makers have expressed concern about the impact of specialty hospitals on the financial viability of general hospitals (Federal Trade Commission, 2008, p. 17). Our current system expects for-profit and nonprofit general acute care hospitals to provide uncompensated care to uninsured and underinsured patients, and to generate the revenue needed to support this activity by earning profit (or positive net revenue) on other types of care. SSHs exert competitive pressure on general hospitals because they compete for *insured* patients who require specific types of care (primarily orthopedic or oncology care). SSHs do not typically offer emergency department services, they are typically owned by for-profit organizations, and they do not typically offer high levels of uncompensated care. Empirical evidence on the provision of uncompensated care indicates that hospitals reduce provision of uncompensated care when they are faced with increased competitive pressure (Banks et al., 1997). (However, it is important to remember that not-for-profit hospitals enjoy a significant competitive benefit when they compete against for-profit hospitals: the not-for-profit hospitals do not pay federal taxes. To maintain their not-for-profit status, they must demonstrate that they provide community benefit (such as uncompensated care).)

Barro et al. (2006) examined Medicare claims for cardiac patients in 1993, 1996, and 1999, and concluded:

> We find support for both sides of this debate. Markets experiencing entry by a cardiac specialty hospital have lower spending for cardiac care without significantly worse clinical outcomes. In markets with a specialty hospital, however, specialty hospitals tend to attract healthier patients and provide higher levels of intensive procedures than general hospitals. (Barro et al., 2006)

The policy question is whether we should respond to this dilemma by:

1. Limiting the expansion of the specialty hospital industry (to protect the profits of general hospitals—so they can continue to offer uncompensated care), or
2. Developing a more transparent system for funding uncompensated care, so that general hospitals can compete on a more level playing field

Five issues will be considered as policy makers address this dilemma:

1. Our current system for financing care for uninsured patients requires insured patients to pay high enough rates to generate sufficient revenue to cover the cost of providing care to uninsured patients. This cross-subsidy mechanism for financing uncompensated care is attractive to politicians because it is not transparent. It does not require a visible tax increase to finance the care for uninsured patients, but it imposes a hidden tax on insured patients, whose rates must be sufficient to cover these hospital expenditures. Economists refer to the cross-subsidy mechanism of financing social programs as "taxation by regulation" because the uncompensated care regulations impose a virtual tax on people who buy insurance (Posner, 1971).
2. If the authors of *The Innovator's Prescription* are correct to predict that specialty hospitals will produce specific types of care more efficiently (and effectively) than general hospitals, then blocking this new type of competition will increase *total* healthcare expenditures because it will prevent the substitution of a lower-cost option for a higher-cost option. Allowing this new type of innovation, however, will require transitioning from the cross-subsidy strategy for financing uncompensated care to a more transparent strategy based on tax revenue. While no one likes

to think about raising taxes, economics logic suggests that the tax strategy may reduce our total expenditure. A transparent tax-based approach is also likely to permit the development of a more fair distribution of the burden of financing care for the uninsured. (Opponents of SSHs argue that blocking SSHs reduces the *average cost* of patients treated in general hospitals because low-risk patients are not permitted to elect treatment at the SSH. However, forcing the low-risk patients to obtain treatment in a relatively high-cost facility is not a cost-effective strategy. In fact, this strategy increases *total cost*, which is a much more relevant variable.)

3. This dilemma is not new. The United States has a long history of using cross-subsidy systems to finance socially beneficial goods and services—and facing the dilemma posed by new types of competition, as noted in Box 1.4.

4. U.S. policy makers can block development of new specialty hospitals, but they cannot block the development of an international industry that will provide this service. The fact that specialty hospitals are not spread across all 50 states, in proportion to population, suggests that state laws may also block market entry by these new providers. While these laws and regulations reflect concerns about self-referral and the impact on the uncompensated care cross-subsidy system, it is important to note international competition developing. A recent article in the *Wall Street Journal* described large cardiac and eye specialty hospitals in India that provide accredited care at prices significantly lower than typical U.S. hospital prices. This article reports that the average price charged for coronary artery bypass graft surgery was $20,000 to $42,000 for Medicare patients treated in U.S. hospitals, and $2,000 for patients treated at the Narayana Hrudayalaya Hospital in India. Some of the cost savings achieved by this hospital reflect volume: two large hospitals in the U.S. (Cleveland Clinic and Massachusetts General Hospital) performed 1,367 and 536 of these procedures, respectively, while the number performed at the Narayan Hrudayalaya Hospital in the same year (2008) was 3,174 (Anand, 2009).

The entrepreneur who owns these hospitals has announced plans to partner with a U.S. healthcare firm to build large specialty hospitals in the Cayman Islands and seek accreditation from the international arm of the organization that accredits U.S. hospitals (Ascension Health, 2012). If you are wondering "What is important about the Cayman Islands?" note that the Cayman Islands Department of Tourism website highlights the convenience of this location for Americans who live east of the Mississippi River: air travel time from the Cayman Islands to Miami is an hour, and it is 3 hours to New York City and 3.5 hours to Chicago (Cayman Islands Department of Tourism, 2013).

(This phenomenon of individuals traveling outside their local areas to obtain high-quality or low-price medical care is known as medical tourism.)

5. The federal agencies responsible for antitrust enforcement recommend that the cross-subsidy system for financing uncompensated care should be replaced with a transparent financing mechanism.

> Governments should reexamine the role of subsidies in health care markets in light of their inefficiencies and potential to distort competition. Health care markets have numerous cross-subsidies and indirect subsidies. Competitive markets compete away the higher prices and supra-competitive profits necessary to sustain such subsidies. Such competition holds both the promise of consumer benefits and the threat of undermining an implicit policy of subsidizing certain consumers and types of care. Competition cannot provide resources to those who lack them; it does not work well when certain facilities are expected to use higher profits in certain areas to cross-subsidize uncompensated care. In general, it is more efficient to provide subsidies directly to those who should receive them, rather than to obscure cross subsidies and indirect subsidies in transactions that are not transparent. Governments should consider whether current subsidies best serve their citizens' health care needs. (Federal Trade Commission, 2008, p. 23)

Nonetheless, under current policy, CMS will not provide Medicare reimbursement for care provided in new (or expanded) specialty hospitals.

New Roles for Patients

This strategy of harnessing competitive market forces clearly offers strong upside potential, but it also raises concerns about the impacts on individuals with low health literacy, low income, or high-cost health conditions. The strident political debate about health reform reflects, in part, differing assessments of the relative magnitudes of the positive and negative impacts of this strategy. Increased competitive vigor will highlight the importance of consumer behavior, provider quality data, licensure issues, coordination of care across multiple providers, and competition from out-of-area providers.

As you consider the possibility of healthcare providers posting and advertising prices, it may be instructive to note that the question of how advertising impacts consumers has been addressed in other professional services. For example, Benham (1972) concluded that the price of eyeglasses is lower in states that permit direct-to-consumer advertising for eyeglasses, compared with states that prohibit such advertising, because advertising helps new types of competitors enter established markets.

We will see in Chapter 8 that some components of the health information technology initiative are intended to produce new types of provider-level quality data. The ongoing debate about the impact of direct-to-consumer advertising of prescription drugs illustrates the two sides regarding the appropriate roles of consumers, providers, and competition in the healthcare industry. While many people bemoan these advertisements, it is important to note three things:

1. FDA regulations mandate that the ads include substantial disclosure and warning information.
2. Consumer Reports has developed the Best Buy Drugs program to provide information about prescription drugs to support consumer decision making. This information combines scientific information about drug effectiveness and side effects (from the Drug Effectiveness Review Project and from other reviews) with additional information about dosing convenience and prices. The project aims to increase consumer access to the results of scientific studies and to price information. While some people decry direct-to-consumer advertisement of prescription drugs, this project reflects the opposite view: it aims to inform consumers, to support meaningful interactions with healthcare providers (Findlay, 2006).
3. Patients are increasingly utilizing online sources of information such as Mayo Clinic and WebMD to research health conditions, diagnoses, and treatments. A recent study conducted by the Pew Research Center's Internet and American Life Project and the California HealthCare Foundation (CHCF) found that 80% of Internet users seek health information online.

This cacophony of information raises concern that this information will lead to inaccurate self-diagnosis and consequent demand for inappropriate treatment. If, however, healthcare researchers succeed in developing logical decision paths and treatment guidelines for conditions that have become relatively routine (as defined in *The Innovator's Prescription*), Internet sources of information could potentially provide useful tools to help patients navigate the healthcare system, manage chronic conditions, and comply with treatment recommendations. Health literacy is a serious issue that highlights the importance of consumer protection for vulnerable individuals. However, the subset of individuals who actively compare price and quality information generate an external benefit for everyone else by creating the competitive discipline that gives providers an incentive to compete for high quality ratings to attract consumers/patients.

Competitive market forces will also receive a boost from the new development of health savings accounts (HSAs). Individuals and employers can deposit tax-exempt money in these accounts, and individuals can use these funds to pay for medical care (Internal Revenue Service (IRS) regulations define the maximum annual deposits and the list of approved uses). To be eligible to open an HSA, the individual must also have catastrophic insurance (which Milton Friedman recommended as the only kind of health insurance that specifically focuses on the risk-management function of insurance). This combination of tax-advantaged funds to pay for non-catastrophic care in conjunction with catastrophic insurance provides two types of subsidy for purchasing medical care:

1. Employers can contribute to the account.
2. HSA deposits are exempt from federal income tax.

At the same time, the HSA strategy focuses on strengthening individual incentives to use non-healthcare strategies to produce health, to use the healthcare system efficiently, and to shop carefully for cost-effective healthcare providers.

HSAs, which were first approved in 2004 and expanded under PPACA, extends the older Section 125 plans in two ways:

■ Section 125 plans permitted individuals to deposit funds in a tax-exempt account and then use those funds to pay for a wider array of medical expenses that were not covered by health insurance. Funds from HSAs can also be used to pay for specific types of care provided by chiropractors, Christian science practitioners, dental hygienists and dentists, optometrists, osteopaths, nurses, physicians, psychiatrists,

and psychologists. In addition, HSA funds can be used to purchase healthcare in the international medical tourism market. (For a full list of medical expenses approved by the IRS, see IRS Publication 502.)
■ While unused Section 125 funds expired at the end of each year, unused HSA funds will roll over into the next year; hence, the HSAs can be used to save money during healthy years for use during higher-cost years. This is important, because individuals tend to experience high year-to-year variability in healthcare expenditures.

The two federal agencies that enforce antitrust law and help shape competition policy (the Department of Justice and the Federal Trade Commission) issued a report in 2004 that cited evidence that vigorous competition among providers generates lower prices (U.S. Department of Justice and Federal Trade Commission, 2004). Based on this evidence, the report recommends that states should carefully consider strengthening competition by taking steps to:

■ Replace the cross-subsidy mechanism for financing uncompensated care with a more transparent system
■ Reduce regulations that block the development of new types of healthcare providers

National and state policy debates regarding appropriate scopes of practice for all types of healthcare providers revolve around the question: What type of provider can and should perform each type of healthcare service? From a cost-effectiveness standpoint, it makes sense to utilize the least expensive healthcare provider to perform services. However, the appropriate balance between cost-effectiveness and the provision of safe, appropriate care is heavily debated. For example, consider the struggle between physician organizations and nursing organizations, as they try to resolve the issues surrounding licensure and practice requirements for advanced practice nurses. While the cost-effectiveness of using advanced practice nurses is generally accepted, there is much debate about the types of services they should be licensed to provide and how much physician oversight is appropriate. Efforts made by nurse practitioner professional organizations to change regulations that constrain the practice of advanced practice nurses have been met with heavy opposition by the physician professional organizations.

Currently, licensure and practice regulations for nurse practitioners vary widely from state to state; with physician supervision required in California, while independent practice for nurse practitioners permitted in Colorado. According to the American Academy of Nurse Practitioners (2011):

- 19 states require collaborative practice,
- 18 states permit autonomous practice,
- 13 states require physician supervision/delegation, or
- impose other requirements such as physician collaboration only when prescribing medications.

Three factors compel the consideration of more fully utilizing advanced practice nurses (nurse practitioners (NPs), certified nurse midwives (CNMs), certified registered nurse anesthetists (CRNAs), and clinical nurse specialists (CNSs)) and physician assistants (PAs) more than we have in the past:

1. Current and projected primary care physician shortages, particularly in poor and rural areas
2. PPACA provisions that expand healthcare coverage and increase the number of people who may seek care
3. Rising costs for healthcare

Cost savings could be realized:

- Medicare reimbursement rates for PAs, NPs, and CNSs are 85% of the physician fee schedule, while rates for CNMs are 65% of the physician fee schedule.
- NPs could provide care to those patients with less complex conditions, thus freeing the availability for physician visits for those with more complex needs.
- To remain competitive with other healthcare delivery innovations (retail clinics), physician practices can integrate physician assistants and nurse practitioners into their practices to reduce wait times for appointments and offer more services during nontraditional office hours.

As we conclude this discussion of new types of providers and new roles for patients, it is important to note that these types of innovations can potentially lead to radical changes in the healthcare system.

Markets for healthcare services have traditionally been confined to local areas—partly due to preferred provider lists and state-level regulation of insurance—but these innovations may change this. Health savings accounts may create more price-conscious patients who are willing to invest time to locate and utilize high-quality and cost-effective providers. For nonemergency care, some of these patients will be increasingly willing to travel outside their local areas to obtain care.

Retail clinics offer efficiency gains such as consumer price reductions, competitive pressure on suppliers and competitors, and service quality innovations. However, they also raise questions about the impact of competition on traditional care providers (physician offices/clinics) and on the determination of who is qualified to provide care that has traditionally been under the domain of physicians. They also raise the issue of an increased fragmentation in the healthcare delivery system.

Specialty hospitals promise high-quality, low-cost treatment for disease/body system-specific ailments but call into question the viability of the cross-subsidy system for financing uncompensated care. Efforts to block the proliferation of specialty hospitals will not negate the impact from international medical tourism.

The wide availability of medical information on the Internet and public reporting of quality measures has the potential for producing consumer behavior changes. The role of patients in demanding particular diagnostics, medications, or treatments raises some of the same issues we explored when examining the managed care backlash. However, the most serious concerns may focus on the potential—and yet unknown—impact these innovations may have on individuals with low health literacy, low income, or high-cost health conditions.

Before we close this chapter, we will leave you with one final thought. If you are concerned that it may be risky to encourage new types of healthcare providers, consider the potential impact of the growth of medical tourism. You might be skeptical: traveling to a foreign country for medical care or surgery raises a series of questions:

■ Will the hospital be accredited?
■ How will I travel home after the surgery?
■ How will I pay for the surgery in the foreign country—and follow-up care in the United States? What if something goes wrong—will I be able to sue for malpractice?

However, these issues are being addressed:

- The Joint Commission International (JCI), a U.S.-based accrediting organization, accredits hospitals in more than 50 countries.
- Medical tourism facilitators can earn certification through the Medical Tourism Association.
- Blue Cross and Blue Shield of South Carolina announced in 2008 that it is organizing an infrastructure to support travel by its members to obtain healthcare in foreign countries (Einhorn, 2008).
- Your employer can purchase liability insurance to cover possible liability resulting from the implementation of an overseas medical care benefit option from Compass Benefits Group, your medical tourism facilitator can purchase facilitator liability insurance, and you can purchase patient medical malpractice insurance from AOS Assurance Company Limited.

Chapter 8

HIT = EMR + HIE

Introduction

Building a strong health information technology (HIT) infrastructure is a major component of the current federal strategy for increasing quality and reducing cost. HIT consists of two components:

- Electronic medical record (EMR) systems are used by providers to replace the current paper record systems.
- Health information exchange (HIE) that permits providers to exchange electronic information—even if it is generated by different proprietary EMR systems. (Systems that can exchange information through the HIE are said to be interoperable.)

The telephone system provides a good analogy. We purchase and use a variety of phones, including landline telephones and cell phones, from a variety of manufacturers and retailers. A telephone exchange permits us to call each other, regardless of the type of phone we are using.

Several types of evidence suggest that HIT can generate simultaneous cost and quality improvements. The Veterans Administration (VA) healthcare system has long experience with electronic medical records that are shared among all VA providers. Empirical evidence indicates that this system has effectively generated efficiencies (Yaisawarnga and Burgess, 2006). In addition, recent analyses of health maintenance organization (HMO) quality report that managed care organizations have successfully generated specific types of quality improvements, such as preventing avoidable hospital stays (Zhan et al., 2004).

This idea is not new: In 2004, President Bush advocated widespread adoption of interoperable electronic health records by 2014. However, the 2008 Congressional Budget Office (CBO) report indicated that only 5% of physicians were using EMR systems at that time. Several barriers hindered physician adoption of EMR systems (Congressional Budget Office, 2008b).

1. The value of EMR to individual physicians hinges on the availability of infrastructure to enable exchange of EMR information with other providers who treat the same set of patients. The interconnection between the value of the EMR software and the availability of exchange capability creates a chicken-and-egg problem: physicians do not purchase EMR software prior to the availability of exchange infrastructure, and investors do not build the exchange infrastructure because local physicians do not have EMR information to exchange.

2. This problem is compounded by continuing lack of clearly specified technical standards: surveys indicate that physicians hesitate to invest until they can be sure that they are purchasing systems that will be compatible with future standards.

3. While there is broad agreement about the potential efficiency value of exchanging a core set of information from patient medical records, there is no agreement on the precise information that should be included in that exchanged core.

4. Patient confidentiality issues (and provider confidentiality issues) have not been resolved. It is not clear whether—or how—patients might designate the precise set of information that may be exchanged, and the precise set of approved recipients for the information.

5. Nationwide communication across delivery systems is needed to achieve the full value of EMR (consider the possibility of a retiree who travels between two homes). However, private sector efforts have focused on exchanging health information among units within individual healthcare organizations. For example:
   - A hospital might purchase EMR software and offer software licenses, data warehousing, and IT support to physicians who admit patients to that hospital.
   - An HMO might offer a similar arrangement to physicians that participate in its panel of preferred providers.

These groups of providers may successfully leverage health information to strengthen patient care and coordination for care that is provided within the group. Successfully organizing the coordination process (that is needed to obtain value from the HIT infrastructure) may be easier to accomplish within a small group of providers who have purchased a common system, compared with the task of achieving efficiencies among a larger and more diverse group. Indeed, these organizations may be creating "neighborhood" HIEs, rather than "statewide" HIEs.

Background: Simultaneous Public- and Private-Sector Initiatives

Progress toward building a strong HIT infrastructure is occurring is two separate, but overlapping, realms. Private healthcare providers, particularly large hospitals, large physician groups, and integrated provider organizations, have been implementing EMR systems and exploring strategies for using the new information as a tool to strengthen patient care and generate efficiencies for many years. The federal effort is more recent: the 2009 American Recovery and Reinvestment Act (ARRA) committed almost $50 billion to jumpstart more rapid construction of this "information highway."

Federal Initiatives

Healthcare providers have been using information technology to organize, coordinate, and streamline care for decades. Most claims are submitted in an electronic format, diagnostic test results are frequently transmitted to providers electronically, and some prescription information is sent electronically. Based on the Medicare diagnostic-related group (DRG) payment system, providers use a standard and well-established system of codes for hospital admissions (DRG codes), diagnoses (ICD9 codes), and procedures (CPT codes). These electronic claims processing systems generate large databases that support substantial analyses of patterns of care and the efficacy of an array of healthcare interventions (e.g., prevention, disease management, wellness, and prenatal care programs).

However, EMR systems will be significantly more useful than these electronic systems that were designed to generate bills and process claims. Surveys indicated that the proportion of hospitals and physicians who were implementing EMR systems prior to 2009 was low. Further, it was not possible to exchange medical record information among diverse "brands" of EMR systems—partly due to lack of standardized definitions and formats.

The 2009 American Recovery and Reinvestment Act addressed the twin problems of low adoption rates and lack of intersystem communication by committing funds to incentivize and facilitate widespread adoption of EMR and HIE. The effort is overseen by a federal agency, the Office of the National Coordinator (ONC), within the federal Department of Health and Human Services. Most of the funds are allocated to provide subsidies to induce physicians and hospitals to purchase and implement EMR software, and to induce states to develop HIE infrastructure to permit the providers to exchange electronic information.

This two-pronged strategy is designed to address the fundamental problem—that many providers have not purchased EMR systems because there is no mechanism to exchange electronic health information with other providers, while investors have not developed HIE capability because many providers do not have any electronic information to exchange. (This problem is not unique to the healthcare industry. It has been widely recognized in a variety of settings—and governments have attempted to design subsidies to jump-start industries in several of these situations. Unfortunately, a review of empirical analyses of the outcomes of these attempts concludes: "Few of the empirical analyses find that (this strategy) has been particularly effective" (Pack and Saggi, 2006).)

To receive the subsidies, physicians and hospitals must purchase and implement EMR systems, and demonstrate meaningful use (MU). Among the criteria for demonstrating MU, physicians must treat a sufficient proportion of Medicaid or Medicare patients, exchange electronic health information with other entities, and report on a substantial number of new quality measures. Physicians express three types of concerns:

■ The subsidy will not cover the entire cost to purchase, install, and maintain the new systems.
■ Under current law, Medicare is scheduled to reduce physician reimbursement rates by nearly 20% in 2013, unless Congress votes to postpone this rate cut. (This is a perennial problem, due to the Sustained Growth Rates (SGR) formula: Congress voted five times, in 2010, to postpone similar cuts.) The magnitude of the short-term subsidy pales in the context of this potential long-term reimbursement rate reduction.

■ Physicians realize that the mandated reports on the new quality measures could potentially develop into a system with which the Centers for
Medicare and Medicaid Services (CMS) could monitor guideline adher-
ence and penalize physicians who do not conform to specific guidelines
(Adler-Milstein et al., 2009).

Committing significant funds to subsidize EMR adoption and statewide
HIE was a risky federal gamble: physicians might not respond to the
incentives to adopt EMR systems, state HIE strategies might prove unsuc-
cessful (the failure rate of early area-wide HIEs has been disappointing),
and it is not clear how the evolving mix of area-wide HIE initiatives and
organization-specific initiatives will interact. We might wonder: Why did
Congress take this risk, instead of waiting for these technologies to dif-
fuse through the healthcare industry via market forces? The natural diffusion process would have been substantially slower, but less visible—and
therefore less risky. To understand the strategic vision embedded in ARRA
2009, it is useful to examine the impacts of analogous technology in other
industries. While we will not be specifically talking about healthcare in the
next few paragraphs, please be patient: examination of dynamic competitive
processes in other industries will provide a useful perspective for thinking
about issues and controversies that are likely to shape health policy discussions related to HIT over the next several years.

In the first half of the 1800s most Americans were either self-employed or
employed in small firms with fewer than 50 employees (Chandler, 1977). In
the middle of the century, rapid railroad construction knit together diverse
regions of the country, and drastically altered the economic landscape.
Prior to the railroad construction boom, transportation of raw materials and
finished goods was slow and uncertain. Therefore, most businesses focused
on purchasing inputs and selling outputs in their immediate geographic
neighborhood. Each butcher shop in Philadelphia, for example, competed
with only a small number of nearby butcher shops. Swift's meatpacking
plant in Chicago and the refrigerated rail car brought a dramatic change.
Swift's new meatpacking and transportation process produced significant
efficiencies, and substantially lower retail prices. Suddenly, small butcher
shops in Philadelphia found themselves competing with new types of competitors, and these competitors offered low prices, which were lower than
the cost of production. The railroad infrastructure, that connected markets,
generated a new type of vigorous competition. It was the best of times

and the worst of times: consumers enjoyed new low prices, but producers faced new low prices they couldn't match. In *The Lexus and the Olive Tree*, Friedman (1999) tells a similar story about the role of Internet connections in generating new types of global commerce. New global competition sparked the same two effects: consumers enjoyed the benefits of new price competition, while producers had to cope with a host of new types of competitors—and new price pressures.

This implies that the critical question we should ask at this point is: Will the new HIT information highway generate an analogous explosion of innovation and efficiency improvements? The evidence is mixed. A 2008 CBO report surveyed evidence on the likely impacts of a federal HIT initiative (CBO, 2008b). This report concludes that there were no credible estimates of the overall impact of an HIT initiative. (The report reviews two studies that were widely cited in support of the ARRA subsidies, and concludes that these studies were not designed and conducted to answer this overarching question.) One reason it is so difficult to estimate the likely impacts of HIT is that HIT is expected to produce two types of impacts:

■ Some impacts such as eliminating the medical transcription process (because providers will enter information directly into the EMR system), are relatively straightforward. Cost savings generated by these impacts probably can be estimated.

■ Other impacts are far more difficult to envision. If HIT will facilitate and support new types of providers—building on the retail clinic and school-based clinic innovations—then the cost savings may be far more substantial. However, these innovations have not yet come into view. In addition, these innovations may not reach their potential unless CMS also revises its payment methodology (some state Medicaid agencies do not reimburse retail clinics, for example), and state and federal agencies revise other regulatory requirements to accommodate the innovations. Given that all innovation generates initial opposition (changes always harm or inconvenience someone), it is difficult to forecast the regulatory evolution that will be needed to support the innovation process.

Private Sector Initiatives

Private sector initiatives are long-standing and well funded. In recent years, large information and computer firms and large healthcare providers such as Cleveland Clinic and Kaiser Permanente have been working to use

EMR software systems to increase the potential for electronic data to support health system efficiency improvements. EMR-generated databases are substantially more rich than claims-generated databases. Claims data can indicate that a patient had a diagnostic test; EMR data will also provide information about the outcome of the test.

A widely cited RAND study predicted that expanded use of health information technology will generate several types of improvements (Girosi, 2005):

- Coordination across multiple providers.
- Reduction of duplicate tests.
- Increased reliance on guideline-driven medical decisions. (After a physician enters information about patient diagnoses into EMR software, EMR systems can provide relevant guideline information, and then monitor and report the proportion of physician decisions that are consistent with guideline recommendations.)
- New types of quality reporting, and research on process effectiveness.

Large organizations have invested significant resources in exploring the analytical and business process innovations that will be needed to reap the potential benefits of HIT. For example, Kaiser Permanente and Intermountain Healthcare provided early leadership. The Cleveland Clinic partnered with IBM to leverage this technology to deliver efficient and effective care. Several organizations, including the Mayo Clinic, Cleveland Clinic, Baylor Health Care System, UCLA Health System, and Dartmouth Institute for Health Policy and Clinical Practice, formed the High Value Health Care Collaborative (HVHCC). Members of this collaborative provide de-identified EMR data to the collaborative, to build a database that is large enough to support innovative analytics. IBM (Millenson, 2006) summarized the competitive challenge that engages these organizations: "Our ultimate challenge is [to figure out] how to use IT as an enabling tool to supplement the art of medicine."

This concept—that analysis of large EMR data sets can support comparative effectiveness research—to identify treatment strategies that work on patients with specific characteristics (these characteristics could include genetic traits) challenges our traditional concept of medical research. The Federal Drug Administration is considering options for modifying our drug approval regulatory process to adjust to these changes. The Personalized Medicine Coalition focuses on providing analysis and leadership to address these public policy and regulatory issues.)

Concerns

Proponents of widespread implementation of EMR, statewide and nation-wide HIE, and analytical use of the resulting data sets for quality reporting and innovative comparative effectiveness research focus on the potential benefits of this new technology. However, they are describing fundamental changes in the ways:

- Physicians will practice medicine
- HMOs, ACOs, and insurance companies monitor compliance with treatment guidelines and reimburse providers
- Patients use information to:
  - Compare and select healthcare providers and insurers
  - Track preventive care, the results of health screenings, and healthcare treatments, and
- Compare, track, and manage chronic health conditions

We should not be surprised, therefore, that these changes are also raising some concerns. We will focus here on concerns about provider and patient privacy.

Provider Privacy

EMR and HIE systems will generate information that could potentially be used to analyze provider decisions. In order to be eligible for the EMR subsidies (outlined in ARRA), providers must demonstrate meaningful use (MU), which requires reporting a substantial amount of new information. ARRA specifies that the MU reporting requirements will be phased in; hence, providers do know yet the full scope of the required data elements. While the data generated by electronic billing made it possible, in the past, to track by provider the number of patients who received cholesterol tests (for example), the new EMR data will also make it possible to track whether the test results indicate that a specific provider's patients were achieving cholesterol goals.

The authorized uses for this type of information are not defined; hence, it is not clear whether provider privacy will be protected appropriately. A 2004 article in the *Journal of Health Economics* outlined the concern: Will the new information be used to support new types of mandatory medical error reporting systems, and will this reported information generate new types of malpractice liability?

Physicians also articulate related concerns about data accuracy and integrity (because an individual patient's record will include data entered by an array of providers, diagnostic labs, and pharmacies). It is not clear yet how the new statewide HIE organizations will set up data challenge and data correction processes.

Patient Privacy

Patients articulate potential benefits (Accenture, 2012) of personal health records that store the patient's entire medical record in one location. (In contrast, many adults have portions of their medical histories strewn across provider organizations—and across cities, states, and (possibly) countries.) Google offered free accounts (Google Health), in which individuals could store, organize, and share their health data. The individual could also request alerts (e.g., it's time to renew a vaccination) or warnings (e.g., two prescriptions are incompatible). Google's business model was straightforward: as people accessed their health record accounts, they might do health-related queries, generating information that could be sold to advertisers. Google Health integrated with an array of reputable healthcare organizations, including the University of Pittsburgh Medical Center, Cleveland Clinic, MinuteClinics (retail clinics inside CVS stores), the Harvard-affiliated Beth Israel Deaconess Medical Center, Blue Cross Blue Shield of Massachusetts, Medicare fee-for-service users in Utah and Arizona, Quest Diagnostics, and Surescripts (the nation's largest electronic prescribing network). However, Google Health's initiative did not succeed, and it has been terminated. Young people who are tech-savvy used the service, but adoption did not spread among the larger population. Observers speculate that the fundamental problem was individual concerns about the privacy of the health information. While HIPAA Section II specifies detailed requirements for the privacy of health records maintained by healthcare providers, it does not specify requirements for the privacy of health records maintained outside this environment. It may be necessary for the federal regulatory infrastructure to catch up with HIT innovations, to play an enabling role.

Conclusion

Will EMR and HIE produce this type of dramatic efficiency gains in the healthcare industry? If so, will we see a dichotomy of consumer benefits and producer anguish (comparable to the dichotomy observed when railroads knit distinct U.S. markets into a national market, Wal-Mart achieved cost reductions through dramatic supply chain innovations, and the Internet created new types of international markets)? This is the central HIT question, and it is also a central question for healthcare payers, providers, and patients. In *The Innovator's Prescription*, Christensen et al. (2008) describe the ongoing process of substantive innovation and industry restructuring that is occurring in the healthcare industry. HIT could provide essential infrastructure to support integration of new diverse types of care providers, such as school-based clinics and retail clinics. Coupled with telemedicine, HIT could provide essential infrastructure to enable rural providers to increase the quality of care offered in sparsely populated areas. These technologies could potentially—and radically—alter the geographic distribution of healthcare providers. Telemedicine and HIT could permit large national providers to compete successfully to provide patient care across the United States. At the same time, it is important to note that other components of federal policy are constraining competition from telemedicine and teleradiology: Medicare, however, does not pay for services (such as interpretation of an x-ray) performed outside the United States (Van Moore et al., n.d.), even though some firms are achieving cost savings by using international teleradiology resources.

It is too early to predict the final impact of the diffusion of HIT; however, it is clear that federal efforts to ensure widespread adoption of this technology represent an attempt to spark a transformation of the U.S. healthcare system. In order to fulfill the promise of efficiency gains, these systems will need to support new types of quality reporting and research on process effectiveness. It is also clear that changes will also be needed in the payment systems and regulatory systems that shape the environment in which patients receive healthcare. Cutler (2010) analyzed factors that impede innovation in the healthcare industry and concluded that two features of our current system create significant inertia:

■ Medicare and Medicaid payment systems tend to focus on the volume of care inputs, rather than the value of treatment outputs.
■ It is difficult to modify these payment systems because we currently do not have good information about the quality of care.

Advocates of the federal HIT initiative argue that the new information that will be generated by EMR and HIE can create the meaningful measures of care quality that are needed to develop better strategies for Medicare and Medicaid payment systems.

The new HIT is also welcomed by advocates of strategies that would strengthen the role of individuals in selecting providers and insurers that deliver high-quality and cost-effective care. Empirical evidence indicates that consumers do not pay close attention to the quality measures reported on health plan report cards when they select plans. When consumers do pay attention, healthcare quality professionals are disappointed to see that consumers are primarily influenced by information about patient satisfaction scores (rather than measures of care quality, such as mammogram screening rates) (Dafny and Dranove, 2005). In addition, consumers cannot effectively compare healthcare treatment prices due to the current lack of readily available price information. If analysts devise methods to use the new HIT data to develop robust quality reporting measures, these measures could potentially support user-friendly information to help individuals engage in meaningful comparisons of quality and price across providers. Much work will be needed, however, to develop a strategy for presenting meaningful and user-friendly information to support consumer decisions.

Conclusion to Section II

In this section we looked at several efficiency strategies and we explored the promises and challenges related to these innovations. In Chapter 4 we explored strategies to align incentives through payment system redesign. We conclude that current Medicare rate structures create inefficient silos, that some proposed cost-cutting efforts may create unintended consequences related to provider competition, and that any strategies to address the rate-setting issues must include a quality component. In Chapter 5, we looked at lessons learned from the era of managed care in hopes of anticipating and possibly avoiding similar issues with the advent of ACOs and medical homes. Consumer protection is a complex issue, definitions of quality will need to be redesigned, and market power, solvency issues, adverse selection, and public reporting of provider quality measures must be addressed. Chapter 6 revealed that wellness programs, preventive care, and disease management will only achieve their promised results if we can identify appropriate, cost-effective programs and find ways to incentivize participation by the individuals who could most benefit from them. Chapter 7 explored new types of providers: retail clinics and specialty hospitals, and the new role of the consumer in this "disruptive innovation" environment. We noted that these innovations present opportunities to gain new types of efficiencies, and they also present issues related to competition, access, and financial viability of safety net providers. Finally, in Chapter 8, we discussed the potential for health information technology to organize, coordinate, and streamline care. However, issues related to federal funding to incentivize HIT adoption, barriers related to inadequate infrastructure, and new patient privacy challenges need to be addressed in order to fully realize the positive impact of this strategy.

After Section I demonstrated that we must increase efficiency within the healthcare system, Section II provided an overview of a diverse array of public sector and private sector strategies designed to achieve this goal. Change is occurring; we should expect:

- More competition
- More consumer financial responsibility
- More efforts to design incentive structures to spark and support innovation

Identified issues that must be addressed to fully actualize these efficiencies include:

- Competition is not compatible with cross-subsidy systems (a direct general will be needed to finance tax subsidies for low-income and high-cost individuals).
- More consumer direction may imply more inequality, particularly for those individuals with low health literacy.
- The CMS incentive structure issue is complex because it is difficult for the government to play this role because of the strong role of private sector innovation.
- Government regulation will have to change to allow the innovations that could deliver on the promises for a better healthcare system.

Conclusion

As we experience substantial changes in the way we access and finance healthcare in the coming years, your familiarity with economic issues and trends will help you navigate these changes in ways that best serve you and your patients. Armed with this perspective, you will be able to assess practice opportunities and threats, identify viable strategies for adapting to the changes, participate in the policy debates, and identify sound policy options. Over the course of this book, we identified the pressures for change within our healthcare system efficiency strategies lessons learned from earlier attempts and new pressures generated by new initiatives.

In Section I we identified issues surrounding access, cost, and quality and we explored potential solution options within an economic framework.

- In Chapter 1 our focus was on the issue of the uninsured, who they were and why those with access to health insurance don't always take up the insurance offer. We then went on the explore solution options such as prohibiting health insurance restrictive practices, employer mandates, expanded public programs, and offering tax credits to purchase health insurance.
- In Chapter 2 we looked at issues related to the cost of healthcare and concluded that the main driver of escalating healthcare costs is technology. Three possible solutions to check the increasing cost for healthcare included reducing research and development, accepting reduced consumption of goods that are not healthcare-related, or entertaining some rationing scheme.
- Chapter 3, the final chapter in Section I, presented a discussion on issues related to quality. We explored data that suggest that other countries achieve better health outcomes for less money, looked at the impact medical errors have on quality of care, and discovered regional

variations in quality and utilization. We then reviewed current solutions to the quality issues, which included Total Quality Management (TQM), clinical pathways, and clinical guidelines.

In Section I, we reach the conclusion that these three issues can't be resolved without increasing the efficiencies within our healthcare system.

In Section II we focused our discussion on those potential efficiencies, and the potential benefits and challenges of each. We base this exploration on current proposals as well as previous attempts to innovate our healthcare system from a lessons learned perspective.

We conclude our presentation of these economic issues with the following:

- The problems within our healthcare system are long-standing and complex.
- All healthcare providers must understand the issues and be actively engaged in finding and implementing the solutions.
- Lessons learned from other industries and past efforts to fix our healthcare system must be applied to new innovations and policy proposals, in order to achieve the benefits we seek.

As you face the challenges that lie ahead, you can rely on what you have learned from the content of this book to assist you in evaluating and negotiating through the ever-changing healthcare landscape. The changes will not be smooth; they will generate controversy. As new controversies arise, evidence-based assessments of the debates and policy proposals will help you navigate the changes.

References

AAFP. 2009. Recent retail clinic studies may misinform patients. American Academy of Family Physicians (September 3).

Abraham, J.M., and Feldman, R. 2010. What will happen if employers drop health insurance? A simulation of employees' willingness to purchase insurance in the individual market. *National Tax Journal* 63:191–214.

Accenture. 2012. *Reconciling the great healthcare consumer paradox: Are consumers willing to change to get what they want?*

Adelman, M.A. 1959. *A&P: A study in price-cost behavior and public policy.* Cambridge, MA: Harvard University Press.

Adler, N.E., Boyce, T., Chesney, M.A., et al. 1994. Socioeconomic status and health. *American Psychological Association* 49:15–24.

Adler, N.E., and Coriell, M. 1997. Socioeconomic status and women's health. In *Health care for women: Psychological, social, and behavioral influences*, ed. S.J. Gallant, G.P. Keita, and R. Royak-Schaler. Washington, DC: American Psychological Association, pp. 11–23.

Adler-Milstein, J., Bates, D.W., and Jha, A.K. 2009. U.S. regional health information organizations: Progress and challenges. *Health Affairs* 28(2):483–492.

Aizer, A. 2007. Public health insurance, program take-up, and child health. *Review of Economics and Statistics* 89:400–415.

Aizer, A., and Grogger, J. 2003. *Parental Medicaid expansions and health insurance coverage.* NBER Working Paper 9907.

Akerlof, G.A. 1970. The market for 'lemons': Quality uncertainty and the market mechanism. *Quarterly Journal of Economics* 84(3):488–500.

Akerlof, G.A. 1991. Procrastination and obedience. *American Economic Review* 81(2):1–19.

American Academy of Nurse Practitioners. 2011. State practice environment. http://www.aanp.org/legislation-regulation/state-practice-environment (accessed October 16, 2011).

American College of Physicians. 2012. What is the patient-centered medical home? http://www.acponline.org/running_practice/pcmh/understanding/what.htm.

American Health Association. 2009. American Society of Echocardiography coding and reimbursement newsletter. American Society of Echocardiography (December). http://www.asecho.org/files/public/advocacy/codingnews2010.pdf.

Anand, G. 2009. The Henry Ford of heart surgery: In India, a factory model for hospitals is cutting costs and yielding profits. *Wall Street Journal* (November 25). http://online.wsj.com/article/SB125875892887958111.html.

Anderson, A. Sears's bankruptcy and auto repair AG settlements. http://www.law.columbia.edu/center_program/ag?exclusive=filemgr.download&file_id=92512&rtcontentdisposition (accessed December 16, 2011).

Arrow, K.J. 1963. Uncertainty and the welfare economics of medical care. *American Economic Review* 53(5).

Ascension Health. 2012. Narayana Hrudayalaya Hospitals teams with Ascension Health Alliance to build health city at Grand Cayman (April 10). http://www.ascensionhealth.org/index.php?option=com_content&view=article&id=339:narayana-hrudayalaya-hospitals-teams-with-ascension-health-alliance-to-build-health-city-at-grand-cayman&Itemid=182.

Baicker, K., and Levy, H. 2007. *Employer health insurance mandates and the risk of unemployment*. NBER Working Paper 13528.

Bamberger, R., and Yacobucci, B.D. 2007. *Automobile and light truck fuel economy: The CAFE standards*. RL33413 (January 19). http://www.fpc.state.gov/documents/organization/82504.pdf.

Banks, D.A., Patterson, M., and Wendel, J. 1997. Uncompensated hospital care: Charitable mission or profitable business decision? *Health Economics* 133–143.

Bansak, C., and Raphael, S. 2006. The effects of state policy design features on take-up and crowd-out rates for the State Children's Health Insurance Program. *Journal of Policy Analysis and Management* 26:149–175.

Barro, J.R., Huckman, R.S., and Kessler, D.P. 2006. The effects of cardiac specialty hospitals on the cost and quality of medical care. *Journal of Health Economics* 25:702.

Benham, L. 1972. The effect of advertising on the price of eyeglasses. *Journal of Law and Economics* 15(2):337–352.

Berg, W. 2010. Benefits of Screening Mammography. JAMA 303(2): 168–169.

Blumberg, L., Buettgens, M., Feder, J., and Holahan, J. 2011. Why employers will continue to provide health insurance: The impact of the affordable care act. Urban Institute. *www.urban.org/.../412428-The-Impact-of-the-Affordable-Care-Act*.

Bourdon, K.H., Rae, D.S., Narrow, W.E., Manderschield, R.W., and Regier, D.A. 1994. National prevalence and treatment of mental and addictive disorders. In *Mental health: United States*, ed. R.W. Manderschield and A. Sonnenschein. Washington, DC: Center for Mental Health Services.

Brown, J.G. 1995. Memorandum from the Department of Health and Human Services, Inspector General. http://oig.hhs.gov/oas/reports/region1/19800504.pdf.

Brown, S.S., editor. *Prenatal Care: Reaching Mothers, Reaching Infants*. Washington, DC: National Academy Press, 1988.

Buchmueller, T., Cooper, P., Simon, K., and Vistnes, J. 2005. The effect of SCHIP expansions on health insurance decisions by employers. *Inquiry* 42:218–231.

Bundorf, M.K., Levin, J.D., and Mahoney, N. 2008. *Pricing and welfare in health plan choice*. National Bureau of Economic Research Working Paper 14153. http://www.nber.org/papers/w14153.

Bureau of Labor Statistics. 2010. *Preliminary multifactor productivity trends*. http://www.bls.gov/news.release/pdf/prod3.pdf.

Business Planning Solutions Global Insight Advisory Services Division. 2005. *The economic impact of Wal-Mart*. Washington, DC: U.S. Government Printing Office. http://www.ihsglobalinsight.com/publicDownload/genericContent/11–03–05_walmart.pdf.

Cabinet Office Behavioural Insights Team. 2010. Applying behavioural insight to health. http://ww.cabinetoffice.gov.uk/sites/default/files/resources/403936_BehaviouralInsight_acc.pdf.

Cadet, J. 2012. ACCA: The changing face of physician-hospital integration. Cardiovascular Business. Mar 23, 2012. http://www.cardiovascularbusiness.com/topics/healthcare-economics/acca-changing-face-physician-hospital-

Calabresi, G., Bobbitt, P. 1978. Tragic Choices (Fels Lectures on Public Policy Analysis). W.W. Norton and Co. 256 pages.

Cartwright-Smith, L., Rosenbaum, S. "Fair Process in Physician Performance Rating Systems: Overview and Analysis of Colorado's Physician Designation Disclosure Act." BNA Health Care Policy Report, Issue No. 30. Vol. 17 BNA, Jul 27, 2009.

Cayman Islands Department of Tourism. 2013. Cayman Islands. http://www.caymanislands.ky/planatrip.aspx.

Centers for Medicare and Medicaid Services. 2005. *Rewarding superior quality care: The premier hospital quality incentive demonstration* (March). http://www.cms.gov/Medicare/Quality-Initiatives-Patient-Assessment-Instruments/HospitalQualityInits/downloads/HospitalPremierFactSheet.pdf.

Centers for Medicare and Medicaid Services, the Boards of Trustees Federal Hospital Insurance and Federal Supplementary Medical Insurance Trust Funds. 2010. *The 2010 annual report of the boards of trustees of the federal hospital insurance and federal supplementary medical insurance trust funds*. http://www.cms.gov/Research-Statistics-Data-and-Systems/Statistics-Trends-and-Reports/ReportsTrustFunds/downloads//tr2010.pdf.

Chandler, A.D. 1977. *The visible hand: The managerial revolution in American business* (4th ed.). Cambridge, MA: Harvard University Press.

Chandra, A., and Skinner, J. 2011. Technology growth and expenditure growth in health care. National Bureau of Economic Research Working Paper Series (April). http://www.nber.org/papers/w16953.

Chen, K. 2002. Railroad to settle EEOC litigation over genetic test. *Wall Street Journal* (May 9).

Christensen, C., Flier, J., and Vijayaraghavan, V. 2013. Christensen, Flier, and Vijayaraghavan: The coming failure of 'accountable care'. *Wall Street Journal* (February 18). http://online.wsj.com/article/SB100014241278873248805045782 96902005944398.html?KEYWORDS=clayton+Christensen.

Christensen, C.M., Grossman, J.H., and Hwang, J. 2008. *The innovator's prescription: A disruptive solution for health care* (1st ed.). New York: McGraw-Hill.

Christian, S., and Dower, J.D. 2008. *Scope of practice laws in health care: Rethinking the role of nurse practitioners*. Issue Brief. California HealthCare Foundation. http://www.chcf.org/~/media/MEDIA%20LIBRARY%20Files/PDF/S/PDF%20ScopeOfPracticeLawsNursePractitionersIB.pdf.

Claxton, G., and Damico, A. 2011. *Snapshots: Employer health insurance costs and worker compensation*. Kaiser Family Foundation http://kff.org/health-costs/issue-brief/snapshots-employer-health-insurance-costs-and-worker-compensation/.

Committee on Quality of Health Care in America and Institute of Medicine. 2001. *Crossing the quality chasm: A new health system for the 21st century*. Washington, DC: National Academy Press, Institute of Medicine.

U.S. Congress. Congressional Budget Office. 2002. A 125-Year Picture of the Federal Government's Share of the Economy, 1950 to 2075. Long-Range Fiscal Policy Brief No. 1 (June 14, revised July 3). p 4. http://www.cbo.gov/showdoc.cfm?index=3521

Congressional Budget Outlook. n.d. Key Assumptions in Projecting Potential GDP—February 2013 Baseline. http://www.cbo.gov/publication/43910. Accessed June 21, 2013.

Congressional Budget Outlook. 2012. The 2012 Long-Term Budget Outlook. June 2012

Congressional Budget Office. Budget Projections. http://www.cbo.gov/publication/44195

Congressional Budget Office. 2004. *Fuel economy standards versus a gasoline tax*. Economic and Budget Issue Brief (March 9). http://www.ftc.gov/bcp/workshops/energymarkets/background/austin.pdf.

Congressional Budget Office. 2008a. *Key issues in analyzing major health insurance proposals*. Publication 3102 (December). http://www.cbo.gov/sites/default/files/cbofiles/ftpdocs/99xx/doc9924/12-18-keyissues.pdf.

Congressional Budget Office. 2008b. Evidence of the costs and benefits of health information technology (May).

Congressional Budget Office. n.d. *The long-term outlook for health care spending*. http://www.cbo.gov/sites/default/files/cbofiles/ftpdocs/87xx/doc8758/11–13-lt-health.pdf.

Cubanski, J., and Schauffler, H.H. 2002. Mandated health insurance benefits: Tradeoffs among benefits, coverage, and costs? California Health Policy. http://www.kff.org/insurance/loader.cfm?url=/commonspot/security/getfile.cfm&PageID=13995.

Cutler, D. 2010. *Where are the health care entrepreneurs? The failure of organizational innovation in health care*. NBER Working Paper 16030 (May).

Cutler, D., and McClellan, M. 2001. Is technological change in medicine worth it? When costs and benefits are weighed together, technological advances have proved to be worth far more than their costs. *Health Affairs* 20:11–29.

Cutler, D., McClellan, M., and Newhouse, J. 2000. How does managed care do it? *RAND Journal of Economics* 31(3):526–548.

Dafny, L., and Dranove, D. 2005. *Do report cards tell consumers anything they don't already know? The case of Medicare HMOs.* NBER Working Paper 11420 (June).

Dafny, L., Duggan, M., and Ramanarayanan, S. 2009. *Paying a premium on your premium? Consolidation in the U.S. health insurance industry.* National Bureau of Economic Research Working Paper Series.

Darby, M., and Karni, E. 1973. Free competition and the optimal amount of fraud. *Journal of Law and Economics* 16(1).

Dartmouth Institute for Health Policy and Clinical Practice. 2012. All surgical discharges per 1,000 Medicare enrollees by race. In *The Dartmouth Atlas of health care.* http://www.dartmouthatlas.org/data/map.aspx?ind=60 (accessed June 17, 2012).

Davidoff, A., Kenney, G., and Dubay, L. 2005. Effects of the State Children's Health Insurance Program expansions on children with chronic health conditions. *Pediatrics* 116:e34–e42.

Deming, W.E. 1993. *The new economics for industry, government and education.* Cambridge: Massachusetts Institute of Technology Center for Advanced Engineering Study.

DeAngelis, C., Fontanarosa, P. 2010. US Preventive Services Task Force and Breast Cancer Screening. JAMA 303(2): 172–173.

De Navos-Walt, C., Proctor, B., Smith, J. 2012 Income, Poverty, and Health Insurance Coverage in the United States: 2011. United States Census Bureau. Current Population Reports.

Doran, T., Fullwood, C., Gravelle, H., et al. 2006. Pay-for-performance programs in family practices in the United Kingdom. *New England Journal of Medicine* 355(4).

Dorning, M. 2010. Obama adopts behavioral economics. *Bloomberg Businessweek* (June 24). http://www.businessweek.com/magazine/content/10_27/b4185019573214.htm.

Dorsey, E., Thompson, J.P., Reminick, J.I., et al. 2010. Funding of us biomedical research, 2003–2008. *Journal of the American Medical Association* 303(2): 137–143.

Doyle, J.J., Jr., Ewer, S.M., and Wagner, T.H. 2008. *Returns to physician human capital: Analyzing patients randomized to physician teams.* NBER Working Paper 14174 (July).

Dushi, I., and Honig, M. 2005. *Offers or take-up: Explaining minorities' lower health insurance coverage.* Economic Research Initiative on the Uninsured Working Paper 40. http://www.umich.edu/~eriu/pdf/wp40.pdf.

Eddy, D.M., Hasselblad, V., McGivney, W., and Hendee, W. 1988. The value of mammography screening in women under age 50 years. *Journal of the American Medical Association* 259:1512–1519.

Edington, D. 2009. *Zero trends: Health as a serious economic strategy.* Ann Arbor, MI: Health Management Research Center.

The Editors. 2009. Auto workers: Rescue them or not? *New York Times* (March 9). http://roomfordebate.blogs.nytimes.com/2009/03/09/auto-workers-rescue-them-or-not/.

Einhorn, B. 2008. Medical travel is going to be part of the solution. *Bloomberg Business Week: Global Economics* (March 17).

Elbel, B., Kersh, R., Brescoll, V.L., and Dixon, L.B. 2009. Calorie labeling and food choices: A first look at the effects on low-income people in New York City. *Health Affairs*, w1110–w1112. doi: 10.1377/hlthaff.28.6.w1110. http://content. healthaffairs.org/content/28/6/w1110.abstract#cited-by.

Emanuel, E.J., and Fuchs, V.R. 2009. Who really pays for health care? The myth of "shared responsibility." *Journal of the American Medical Association* 299:1057–1059.

Enthoven, A.C., and Singer, S.J. 1998. The managed care backlash and the task force in California. *Health Affairs* 17(4), 95–110.

Every, N.R., Hochman, J., Becker, R., Kopecky, S., and Cannon, C.P. 2000. critical pathways: A review. *Circulation* 101:461–465.

Federal Register. January 26, 2012. Annual Update of the HHS Poverty Guidelines. V.77, N.17. P. 4034–4035

Federal Trade Commission. 2008. Letter to Elaine Nekritz (May 29).

Feeg, V.D. 1996. The bittersweet maternal health policy victory. *Pediatric Nursing* 22(5):366–445.

Feinstein, C.D. 1990. Deciding whether to test student athletes for drug use. *Interfaces* 20:80–87.

Findlay, S.D. 2006. Bringing the DERP to consumers: 'Consumer reports best buy drugs.' *Health Affairs* 25(4):w283–w286. doi: 10.1377. http://www.consumerreports.org/health/best-buy-drugs/index.htm.

Fisher, E.S., and Bell, J.E. 2010. *Dartmouth Atlas project finds substantial variation in joint replacement surgery*. Dartmouth Institute for Health Policy and Clinical Practice.

Fisher, E.S., Bynum, J.P., and Skinner, J.S. 2009. Slowing the growth of health care costs—Lessons from regional variation. *New England Journal of Medicine* 360:849–852.

Fisher, E.S., Wennberg, D.E., Stukel, T.A., Gottlieb, D.J., and Lucas, F.L. 2003. The implications of regional variations in Medicare spending. Part 1. The content, quality, and accessibility of care. *Annals of Internal Medicine* 138:273–287.

Fisher, J.E., and O'Donohue, W. 2006. *Practitioner's guide to evidence-based psychotherapy*. New York: Springer.

Frank, R.G., Glazer, J., and McGuire, T.G. 1998. *Measuring adverse selection in managed health care*. National Bureau of Economic Research Working Paper 6825.

Friedman, M. 2001. How to cure health care. *Hoover Digest* 3.

Friedman, T.L. 1999. *The Lexus and the olive tree*. Garden City, NY: Anchor Books.

Fronstin, P. 2010. *Sources of health insurance and characteristics of the uninsured: Analysis of the March 2010 current population survey*. ERBI Issue Brief 347. Retrieved from Employee Benefit Research Institute. http://www.ebri.org/publications/ib/index.cfm?fa=ibDisp&content_id=4643 (accessed April 1, 2013).

Garber, A., and Skinner, J. 2008. *Is American health care uniquely inefficient?* NBER Working Paper 14257 (August).

Gechert, S. 2009. *Supplementary private health insurance in selected countries: Lessons for EU governments?* CESIFO Venice Summer Institute.

Girosi, F., Meili, R., Scoville, R. 2005. Extrapolating evidence of health information technology savings and costs. RAND. www.rand.org

Glazer, A., and Rothenberg, L.S. 2001. *Why government succeeds and why it fails.* Cambridge, MA: Harvard University Press.

Goldenberg, R.L., Patterson, E.T., and Freese, M.P. 1992. Maternal demographic, situational and psychosocial factors and their relationship to enrollment in prenatal care: A review of the literature. *Women Health* 19:133–151.

Grady, D. 2009. Premature births are fueling higher rates of infant mortality in U.S. *New York Times* (November 3). http://www.nytimes.com/2009/11/04/health/04infant.html.

Gravalle, H., and Siciliani, L. 2009. Third degree waiting time discrimination: Optimal allocation of a public sector healthcare treatment under rationing by waiting. *Health Economics* 18:977–986.

Grove, A. 2005 Efficiency in the health care industries: A view from the outside. *JAMA* 294:490–492.

Gruber, J. 1994. The incidence of mandated maternity benefits. *American Economic Review.* http://www.jstor.org/stable/2118071.

Hall, R.E. 2003. The unbearable forward burden: Health, education, and retirement (Mimeo). Stanford University.

Hall, R.E., and Jones, C.I. 2007. The value of life and the rise in health spending. *Quarterly Journal of Economics* 122:39–72.

Hastie, T., Tibshirani, R., and Friedman, J. 2009. *The elements of statistical learning: Data mining, inference, and prediction* (2nd ed.). New York: Springer.

Health Insurance Portability and Accountability Act of 1996. 42 USC § 1320d-9 2010.

Heckman, J.J. 2012. The developmental origins of health. *Health Economics* 21:24–29.

Herring, B. 2005. The effect of the availability of charity care to the uninsured on the demand for private health insurance. *Journal of Health Economics* 24:225–252.

Herszenhorn, D.M. 2009. Senate blocks use of new mammogram guidelines. *New York Times* (December 3). http://prescriptions.blogs.nytimes.com/2009/12/03/gop-amendments-aim-at-new-cancer-guidelines/.

Hidalgo, J. 2012. FTC approves settlement where Renown releases cardiologists from non-compete contract. Reno Gazette Journal. 12/5/2012. p 1. Reno, NV.

Holahan, J., and Chen, V. 2011. *Changes in health insurance coverage in the great recession, 2007–2010.* Urban Institute. http://www.kff.org/uninsured/upload/8264.pdf.

Horn, S., and Backofen, J. 1987. Ethical issues in the use of a prospective payment system: The issue of a severity of illness adjustment. *Journal of Medicine and Philosophy* 12(2):145–153.

H.R. 1041—112th Congress: Fairness in Medicare Bidding Act. 2011. http://www.govtrack.us/congress/bills/112/hr1041.

Illinois HB 5372. 2008.

Jackson Health Care. 2012. *A tough time for physicians: 2012*. Medical Practice and Attitude Report. http://www.jacksonhealthcare.com/media-room/surveys/physician-practice-trends-survey-2012.aspx (accessed December 11, 2012).

JCAHO Patient Safety. 2012. Summary—Part III. https://www.premierinc.com/safety/topics/patient_safety/index_3.jsp#Sentinel (accessed June 17, 2012).

Jensen, G.A., and Morrisey, M.A. 1999. Employer-sponsored health insurance and mandated benefit laws. *Milbank Quarterly* 77:425–459.

Jewell, K., and McGiffert, L. 2009. *To err is human—To delay is deadly*. Austin, TX: Consumers Union.

Joint Commission on Accreditation of Healthcare Organizations. 1993. "The Measurement Mandate: On the Road to Performance Improvement in Health Care".

Jones, C.I. 2005. Federal Reserve Bank San Francisco economic letter: More life vs. more goods, explaining rising health expenditures. San Francisco Federal Reserve Bank.

Kahneman, D. 2011. *Thinking fast and slow*. New York: Farrar, Straus and Giroux, p. 499.

Kaiser Family Foundation. 2004. Uninsured workers in America. http://www.kff.org/uninsured/loader.cfm?url=/commonspot/security/getfile.cfm&PageID.

Kaiser Family Foundation. 2006. Trends in health insurance enrollment. Section 2 (March 15). http://www.kff.org/insurance/7031/ti2004-list.cfm?RenderForPrint=1=44470.

Kaiser Family Foundation. 2011a. Individual market guaranteed issue (not applicable to HIPAA eligible individuals). http://www.statehealthfacts.org/comparetable.jsp?ind=353&cat=7.

Kaiser Family Foundation. 2011b. Nevada: Distribution of state general fund expenditures (in millions), SFY2010. http://www.statehealthfacts.org/profileind.jsp?ind=33&cat=1&rgn=30.

Kaiser Permanente. 2009. Low blood sugar events increase dementia risk in elderly patients with type 2 diabetes, Kaiser Permanente study finds. Kaiser Permanente (April 14). http://xnet.kp.org/newscenter/pressreleases/nat/2009/041409diabetesdementia.html.

Khrushchev, N. 2011. http://www.great-quotes.com/quote/215785 (accessed May 30, 2012).

Kohn, L.T., Corrigan, J.M., and Donaldson, M.S. 2000. *To err is human: Building a safer health system*. Committee on Quality of Health Care in America, Institute of Medicine.

Kramer, M.S., Barros, F.C., Demissie, K., Liu, S., Keily, J., and Joseph, K.S. 2005. Does reducing infant mortality depend on preventing low birth weight? An analysis of temporal trends in the Americas. *Paediatric and Perinatal Epidemiology* 19:447–448.

Ku, L., and Waidmann, T. 2003. *How race/ethnicity, immigration status, and language affect health insurance coverage, access to care and quality of care among the low-income population*. Urban Institute.

Landau, E. 2010. 'Landmark' cancer vaccine gets FDA approval. CNN Health. http://articles.cnn.com/2010-04-27/health/provenge.prostate.cancer. fda_1_provenge-prostate-cancer-attack-cancer-cells?_s=PM:HEALTH.

Laws, M., and Scott, M.K. 2008. The emergence of retail-based clinics in the United States: Early observations. *Health Affairs* 27.

Lemaire, J. 2005. The cost of firearm deaths in the United States: Reduced life expectancies and increased insurance costs. *Journal of Risk and Insurance* 72:359–374.

Levitt, S.D., and Dubner, S.J. 2005. *Freakonomics: A rogue economist explores the hidden side of everything*. New York: William Morrow.

Lichtenberg, F. 2003. The benefits to society of new drugs: A survey of the econometric evidence. *Proceedings, Federal Reserve Bank of Dallas* (September), 43–59.

Lichtenberg, F. 2009. *The quality of medical care, behavioral risk factors, and longevity growth*. NBER Working Paper 15068 (June).

Madrian, B.C., and Shea, D.F. 2001. The power of suggestion: Inertia in 401(k) participation and savings behavior. *Quarterly Journal of Economics* 116(4):1149–1187.

Mathews, A.W. 2013. To save, workers take on health-cost risk. *Wall Street Journal* (March 18), B1.

McClellan, M., McKethan, A.N., Lewis, J.L., Roski, J., and Fisher, E.S. 2010. A national strategy to put accountable care into practice. *Health Affairs* 29:982–990. doi: 10.1377/hlthaff.2010.0194.

McDonald, R., and Roland, M. 2009. Pay for performance in primary care in England and California: Comparison of unintended consequences. *Annuals of Family Medicine* 7(2):121–127.

McGlynn, E.A., Asch, S.M., Adams, J., et al. (2003). The quality of health care delivered to adults in the United States. *New England Journal of Medicine* 348(26): 2635–2645.

MCI WorldCom. 1999. History. http://www.fundinguniverse.com/company-histories/mci-worldcom-inc-history/ (accessed June 5, 2012).

McWilliams, J.M., Meara, E., Zaslavsky, A.M., and Ayanian, J.Z. 2007. Use of health services by previously uninsured Medicare beneficiaries. *New England Journal of Medicine* 357:143–153.

Meara, E., Rosenthal, M.B., Sinaiko, A.D., and Baicker, K. 2007. State and federal approaches to health reform: What works for the working poor? *Forum for Health Economics and Policy* 10, article 5.

Medicare Improvements for Patients and Providers Act 154. 2008.

Millenson ML. 2006. The Promise of Personalized Medicine: A Conversation with Michael Svinte. *Health Affairs* 25(2), w54-w60.

Miller, D., Gust, C., Dimick, J., Birkmeyer, N., Skinner, J., and Birkmeyer, J. 2011. Large variations in Medicare payments for surgery highlight savings potential from bundled payment programs. *Health Affairs*. doi: 10.1377/hlthaff.2011.0783. http://www.http://content.healthaffairs.org/content/30/11/2107.

Miller, R.H., and Luft, H.S. 1997. Does managed care lead to better or worse quality of care? *Health Affairs* 16(5):7–25.

Miller, R.H., and Luft, H.S. 2002. HMO plan performance update: An analysis of the literature, 1997–2001. *Health Affairs* 21(4):63–86.

Miller, T., Brennan, T., Milstein, A. 2009. How can we make more progress in measuring physicians' performance to improve the value of care? Health Affairs, 28, n 5 (2009): 1429–1437.

Mukhopadhyay, S., and Wendel, J. 2008. Are prenatal care resources distributed efficiently across high-risk and low-risk mothers? *International Journal of Health Care Finance and Economics* 8(3):163–179.

Mukhopadhyay, S., Wendel, J., Lee, W., and Yang, W. 2008. Analyzing the impact of prenatal care on infant health: Do we have useful input and output measures? *Economics Bulletin* 9(21):1–14.

Mullen, F.X., Jr. 2011a. FTC, state investigate Renown Health for possible antitrust violations. *Reno Gazette Journal* (November 29). http://pqasb.pqarchiver.com/rgj/access/2522061551.html?FMT=ABS&date=Nov+29%2C+2011.

Mullen, F.X., Jr. 2011b. Patients love their doctors, hate rising costs. *Reno Gazette Journal* (November 29). http://pqasb.pqarchiver.com/rgj/access/2522061381.html?FMT=ABS&date=Nov+29%2C+2011.

Murphy, A. 2010. Mammography screening for breast cancer: a view from 2 worlds. JAMA 303(2): 166–167.

Murray, C.L., Kulkarni, S.C., Michaud, C., et al. 2006. Eight Americas: Investigating mortality disparities across races, counties, and race-counties in the United States. *PLoS Med* 3:260. doi: 10.1371/journal.pmed.0030260.

Nardin, R., Himmelstein, D., and Woolhandler, S. 2009. *Massachusetts' plan: A failed model for health care reform.* Physicians for a National Health Program. http://www.pnhp.org/mass_report/mass_report_Final.pdf.

National Center for Environmental Economics. 2013. http://yosemite.epa.gov/ee/epa/eed.nsf/pages/MortalityRiskValuation.html#whatisvsl (accessed March 31, 2013).

National Center for Health Statistics. 2012. *Health, United States, 2011.* With special feature on socioeconomic status and health. Hyattsville, MD.

National Committee for Quality Assurance. 2013. HEDIS Measures. http://www.ncqa.org/HEDISQualityMeasurement/HEDISMeasures.aspx

National Health Expenditure Data. 2010. Centers for Medicare and Medicaid Services. http://www.cms.gov/Research-Statistics-Data-and-Systems/Statistics-Trends-and-Reports/NationalHealthExpendData/index.html.

National Institute for Health and Clinical Excellence. 2011. Measuring effectiveness and cost-effectiveness: The QALY. http://www.nice.org.uk/newsroom/features/measuringeffectivenessandcosteffectivenesstheqaly.jsp.

National Prevention Council. 2011. *National prevention strategy.* Washington, DC: U.S. Department of Health and Human Services, Office of the Surgeon General (June). http://www.healthcare.gov/prevention/nphpphc/strategy/report.pdf

National Prevention, Health Promotion and Public Health Council. 2011. The national prevention strategy: America's plan for better health and wellness. http://www. healthcare.gov/news/factsheets/2011/06/prevention06162011a.html.

Newhouse, J., and Sinaiko, A. 2007. Can multi-payer financing achieve single-payer spending levels? *Forum for Health Economics and Policy* 10(1), article 2.

Newman, T.B., Johnston, B.D., and Grossman, D.C. 2003. Effects and costs of requiring child-restraint systems for young children traveling on commercial airplanes. *Archives of Pediatric and Adolescent Medicine* 157:969–974.

Norbeck, T., Thompson, W., Muney, A., Allan, D., Baratta, P., and Barasch, R. 2013. Cost, efficiency and accountable care organizations. *Wall Street Journal* (February 26). http://online.wsj.com/article/SB10001424127887323884304578326424211839236.html.

Nordhaus, W.D. 2003. The health of nations: The contribution of improved health to living standards. In K. Murphy and R. Topel (eds.), *Measuring the gains from medical research: An economic approach.* Chicago: Chicago University Press.

O'Donohue, W., and Cucciare, M. 2005. The role of psychological factors in medical presentations. *Journal of Clinical Psychology in Medical Settings* 12(1):13–24.

Okeke, E.N., Hirth, R.A., and Grazier, K. 2010. Workers on the margin: Who drops health coverage when prices rise? *Inquiry* 47:33–47.

Okunade, A.A., and Murthy, V.N. 2002. Technology as a 'major driver' of health care costs: A cointegration analysis of the Newhouse conjecture. *Journal of Health Economics* 21:147–159.

O'Neill, J.E., and O'Neill, D.M. 2007. *Health status, health care and inequality: Canada vs. the U.S.* NBER Working Paper 13429. Forum for Health Economics and Policy. v 10, issue 1. article 3 (Frontiers in Health Policy Research).

Orzag, P. 2007. The Long-Term Outlook for Health Care Spending: sources of growth in projected federal spending on Medicare and Medicaid. Congressional Budget Office. November 2007.

Pack, H., and Saggi, K. 2006. Is there a case for industrial policy? A critical survey. *World Bank Research Observer* 21(2):267–297.

Patient Protection and Affordable Care Act, Public Law 111-148, § 2702, 124 Stat. 119, 318–319. 2010.

Pauly, M.V. 2001. Making sense of a complex system: Empirical studies of employment-based health insurance. *International Journal of Health Care Finance and Economics*, 1, 333–339.

Pear, R. 2005. Medicare officials insisting on wider choices in drug benefits. *New York Times* (June 15). http://www.nytimes.com/2005/06/15/health/15drug.html?_r=1&pagewanted=print.

Perez-Woods, R.C. 1990. Barriers to the use of prenatal care: Critical analysis of the literature 1966–1987. *Journal of Perinatology* 10:420–434.

Poland, M.L., Ager, J.W., and Olson, J.M. 1987. Barriers to receiving adequate prenatal care. *American Journal of Obstetrics and Gynecology* 157:297–393.

Policy Exchange UK. 2011. Turning behavioural insights into policy with Richard Thaler (June 11). http://www.youtube.com/watch?v=f-6tNtk_H6s.

Polsky, D., Stein, R., Nicholson, S., and Bundorf, M.K. 2005. Employer health insurance offerings and employee enrollment decisions. *Health Services Research* 40:1259–1278.

Rawls, P. 2008. Extra pounds mean insurance fees. *Reno Gazette Journal* (August 22).

Regier, D.A., Narrow, W.E., Rae, D.S., Manderscheid, R.W., Locke, B.Z., and Goodwin, F.K. 1993. The *de facto* US mental and addictive disorders service system: Epidemiologic catchment area prospective 1-year prevalence rates of disorders and services. *Archives of General Psychiatry* 50:85–94.

Rice, T., and Unruh, L. 2009. *The economics of health reconsidered* (3rd ed.). Chicago: Health Administration Press, p. 268.

Risha, B. 2012. Actually, I think that's their technical name. Hark. http://www.hark.com/clips/gryvzwdlzz-actually-i-think-thats-their-technical-name.

Robinson, J.C. 2001. Theory and practice in the design of physician payment incentives. *Milbank Quarterly* 79(2):149–177.

Rock, R.C. 1985. Assuring quality of care under DRG-based prospective payment. *Medical Decision Making* 5(1):531–534.

Rosoff, A.J. 2001. Evidence-based medicine and the law: The courts confront clinical practice guidelines. *Agency for Research Healthcare and Quality* 26(2).

Rudavsky, R., Pollack, C.E., and Mehrotra, A. 2009. The geographic distribution, ownership, prices, and scope of practice at retail clinics. *Annals of Internal Medicine* 151(5).

Russell, L.B. 1994. *Educated guesses: Making policy about medical screening tests.* Berkeley: University of California Press.

Russell, L.B. 2007. *Prevention's potential for slowing the growth of medical spending.* Washington, DC: National Coalition on Health Care. http://www.ihhcpar.rutgers.edu/downloads/RussellNCHC2007.pdf.

San Francisco Federal Reserve Bank. 2003. Federal reserve bank San Francisco economic letter: The fiscal problem of the 21st century.

Scanlon, W. 1998. Health Insurance Standards: New Federal Law Creates Challenges for Consumers, Insurers, Regulators. 1998. US. General Accounting Office. GAO/HEHS-98–67. p 30.

Schumpeter, J.A. 1942. *Capitalism, socialism, and democracy* (3rd ed.). New York: Harper Perennial.

Simon, H.A. 1957. *Models of man: Social and rational; mathematical essays on rational human behavior in society setting.* New York: John Wiley & Sons.

Singh, G.K., and Siahpush, M. 2006. Widening socioeconomic inequalities in U.S. life expectancy, 1980–2000. *International Journal of Epidemiology* 35:969–979.

Sloan, F.A., and Conover, C.J. 1998. Effects of state reforms on health insurance coverage of adults. *Inquiry* 35(3):280–293.

Smart, D. 2011. *Physician characteristics and distribution in the US* (1st ed.). American Medical Association Press. http://wdn.ipublishcentral.net/impelsys549/viewinside/1762471537873.

Sommers, B. 2006. Insuring children or insuring families: Do parental and sibling coverage lead to improved retention of children in Medicaid and CHIP? *Journal of Health Economics* 25:154–1169.

Song, Y., Skinner, J., Fisher, E., Wennberg, J., Bynum, J., and Sutherland, J. 2010. *Considering moving? Where you go determines whether you will be told you're sick*. Dartmouth Institute for Health Policy and Clinical Practice.

Sowell, T. 1993. *Is reality optional? And other essays*. Stanford, CA: Hoover Institution Press.

Sowell, T. 1995. *The vision of the anointed*. New York: Basic Books.

Stanton, M.W., and Rutherford, M. 2006. *The high concentration of U.S. health care expenditures*. Agency for Healthcare Research and Quality. http://www.ahrq. gov/research/ria19/expendria.pdf.

Sturm, R., and Pacula, R. 2012. State mental health parity laws: Cause or consequence of differences in use? *Health Affairs* 18(5).

Support H.R. 1041, the Fairness in Medicare Bidding Act. n.d. Congressman Glen "GT" Thompson. http://thompson.house.gov/sites/thompson.house.gov/ files/1%20PAGER%20%20Support%20HR%201041%20FAIRNESS%20IN%20 MEDICARE%20BIDDING%20ACT%20(FIMBA).pdf.

Temkin, E. 1999. Driving through: Postpartum care during World War II. *American Journal of Public Health* 89(4):587–595.

Tengs, T. 1996. An evaluation of Oregon's Medicaid rationing algorithms. *Health Economics* 5:171–181.

Thaler, R.H., and Sunstein, C.R. 2008. *Nudge: Improving decisions about health, wealth, and happiness*. New Haven, CT: Yale University Press.

The Daily Briefing. 2013. ACO-roundup. Most ACOs are led by physicians, not hospitals. Advisory Board Company. www.advisory.com/DailyBriefing/2013/04/18/ ACO-roundup-mostACOs-are-led-by-physicians-not-hospitals

Thorpe, K.E., Florence, C.S., and Joski, P. 2004. Which medical conditions account for the rise in health care spending? *Health Affairs* W4:437–445.

Thurm, S. 2013. Will Companies Stop Offering Health Insurance Because of the Affordable Care Act?. Wall Street Journal (U.S. edition), June 17, 2013, p. R5

Timmins, N. 2010. Letter from Britain: Across the pond, giant new waves of health reform. *Health Affairs* 29(12):2138–2141.

Town, R., Vistnes, G. 2001. Hospital competition in HMO networks. Journal of Health Economics 20(2001)7330753.

Tuerck, D.G., Bachman, P., and Head, M. 2011. *The high price of Massachusetts health care reform*. Beacon Hill Institute. http://www.beaconhill.org/ BHIStudies/HCR-2011/BHIMassHealthCareReform2011–0627.pdf.

U.S. Bureau of the Census. n.d. Quickfacts. http://quickfacts.census.gov/qfd/ states/00000.html (accessed March 16, 2013).

U.S. Department of Health and Human Services. 2011. News release: HHS announces new investment in school-based health centers. Washington, DC (July 14). http://www.hhs.gov/news/press/2011pres/07/20110714a.html

U.S. Department of Health and Human Services, Agency for Healthcare Research and Quality. 2011. Medical expenditure panel survey. http://meps.ahrq.gov/mepsweb/about_meps/survey_back.jsp.

U.S. Department of Health and Human Services, Centers for Disease Control and Prevention, National Center for Chronic Disease Prevention and Health Promotion. 2003. *The power of prevention: Reducing the health and economic burden of chronic disease*. http://www.welcoa.org/freeresources/pdf/power_of_prevention.pdf.

U.S. Department of Health and Human Services, National Center for Health Statistics, Centers for Disease Control and Prevention. 2009. *Health insurance coverage trends, 1959–2007: Estimates from the national health interview survey*. National Health Statistics Report 17.

U.S. Department of Justice, Federal Trade Commission. 2004. *Improving health care: A dose of competition* (July). http://www.ftc.gov/reports/healthcare/040723healthcarerpt.pdf.

U.S. Department of Labor, Employee Benefits Security Administration. 2010. Patient Protection and Affordable Care Act. http://www.dol.gov/ebsa/healthreform/.

U.S. Government Accountability Office. 1987. Prenatal care: Medicaid recipients and uninsured women obtain insufficient care. HRD-87–127.

U.S. Government Accountability Office. 2003. *Specialty hospitals: Geographic locations, services provided and financial performance*. GAO-04-167. http://www.gao.gov/new. items/d04167.pdf.

U.S. Government Accountability Office. 2008. Medicare Part B imaging services: Rapid spending growth and shift to physician offices indicate need for CMS to consider additional management practices (June). http://www.gao.gov/assets/280/276735.pdf.

U.S. Government Accountability Office. Testimony before the Committee on the Budget, U.S. Senate.

U.S. Preventive Services Task Force. 2009. Screening for breast cancer: U.S. Preventive Services Task Force recommendation statement. *Annals of Internal Medicine* 151(10).

Van Moore, A., Allen, B., Campbell, S.C., et al. n.d. *Report of the ACR Task Force on International Teleradiology*. American College of Radiology. http://www.acr.org/Membership/Legal-Business-Practices/Telemedicine-Teleradiology/Report-of-the-ACR-Task-Force-on-International-Teleradiology.

Vistnes, J., and Monheit, A.C. 2011. The health insurance status of low-wage workers: The role of workplace composition and marital status. *Medical Care Research and Review* 68:607– 623.

Vita, M.G. 2001. Regulatory restrictions on selective contracting: An empirical analysis of "any-willing-provider" regulations. *Journal of Health Economics* 20:955–966.

Wachenheim, L., and Leida, H. 2012. *The impact of guaranteed issue and community rating reforms on states' individual insurance markets*. America's Health Insurance Plans. http://www.ahipcoverage.com/wp-content/uploads/2012/03/Updated-Milliman-Report.pdf.

Waidmann, T., Garrett, B., and Hadley, J. 2004. *Explaining differences in employer sponsored insurance coverage by race, ethnicity and immigrant status*. Urban Institute. http://www.umich.edu/~eriu/pdf/wp42.pdf.

Waldron, H. 2007. *Trends in mortality differentials and life expectancy for male social security–covered workers, by average relative earnings*. Social Security Administration. ORES Working Paper 108 (October). http://www.ssa.gov/policy/docs/workingpapers/wp108.html (accessed August 2012).

Walker, D.M. 2007. Long-term budget outlook: Saving our future requires tough choices today. U.S. Government Accountability Office (January).

Weinick, R.M., Pollack, C.E., Fisher, M.P., Gillen, E.M., and Mehrotra, A. 2010. *Policy implications of the use of retail clinics*. Santa Monica, CA: RAND Corp. http://www.rand.org/pubs/technical_reports/2010/RAND_TR810.pdf.

Wendel, J., and Dumitras, D. 2005. Treatment effects model for assessing disease management: Measuring outcomes and strengthening program management. *Disease Management* 8(3):155–168.

Wendel, J., and Paterson, M. 1996. Managing risk in a changing health care system. *Journal of Health Care Finance* 22(3):15–22.

Werner, R., Kolstad, J., Stuart, E., and Polsky, D. 2011. Pay-for-performance: The effect of pay-for-performance in hospitals: Lessons for quality improvement. *Health Affairs* 30(4).

Whalen, J. 2005. Britain stirs outcry by weighing benefits of drugs versus price. *Wall Street Journal* (November 22), A1.

Wilson NA, Schneller ES, Montgomery K and Bozic KJ. 2008. Hip And Knee Implants: Current Trends And Policy Considerations. *Health Affairs* 27(6), 1587–1598.

Winslow, R. 2010. To double the odds of seeing 85: Get a move on (when it comes to longevity, regular exercise may be the most potent weapon against disease). *Wall Street Journal* (March 9). http://online.wsj.com/article/SB10001424052748703954904575109673558885594.html (accessed March 20, 2013).

Wisconsin Policy Research Institute. 2006. *The history of health care costs and health insurance*. www.wpri.org/Reports/Volume19/Vol19no10.pdf.

Woloshin, S., and Schwartz, L.M. 2010. The benefits and harms of mammography screening: Understanding the trade-offs. *Journal of the American Medical Association* 303:164–165. doi: 10.1001/jama.2009.2007.

Woolf, S. 2010. The 2009 Breast Cancer Screening Recommendations of the US Preventive Services Task Force. JAMA 303(2): 162–163.

Wu, V.Y., and Shen, Y.-C. 2011. *The long-term impact of Medicare payment reductions on patient outcomes*. NBER Working Paper 16859 (March).

Yaisawarnga, S., and Burgess, J.F. 2006. Performance-based budgeting in the public sector: An illustration from the VA health care system. *Health Economics*
15:295–310. http://www.interscience.wiley.com.

Zhan, C., Miller, R.M., Wong, H., and Meyer, S.G. 2004. The effects of HMO pen-
etration on preventable hospitalizations. *Health Services Research* 39:345–361.

Zivin, J., and Pfaff, A. 2004. To err on humans is not benign: Incentives for
adoption of medical error-reporting systems. *Journal of Health Economics*
23:935–949.

Index

Page references in **bold** refer to tables.